Queer 13

Also by Clifford Chase

The Hurry-Up Song: A Memoir of Losing My Brother

Queer 13

*Lesbian and Gay Writers
Recall Seventh Grade*

**Edited by
Clifford Chase**

ROB WEISBACH BOOKS

WILLIAM MORROW AND COMPANY, INC.   NEW YORK

Published by Rob Weisbach Books
An Imprint of William Morrow and Company, Inc.
1350 Avenue of the Americas, New York, N.Y. 10019

The Library of Congress has cataloged a previous edition of this title.

Library of Congress Cataloging-in-Publication Data
Queer 13 : lesbian and gay writers recall seventh grade / edited by
  Clifford Chase.—1st ed.
     p. cm.
   ISBN 0-688-15811-0 (hardcover)
   1. Gay students—United States—Biography. 2. Lesbian students—
United States—Biography. 3. Seventh grade (Education)—United
States. 4. Gay men's writings, American. 5. Lesbians' writings,
American. I. Chase, Clifford.
LC2575.Q84 1998
372.1826'64'092'2—dc21
   [B]   98-17147
                                                          CIP

Paperback ISBN 0-688-17161-3
Printed in the United States of America

First Paperback Edition 1999

1 2 3 4 5 6 7 8 9 10

BOOK DESIGN BY LOVEDOG STUDIO

www.robweisbachbooks.com

For John

For John

Contents

Foreword   xi
  Dale Peck

Introduction   xiii
  Clifford Chase

MACOS   1
  Michael Albo

How We Get That Way   5
  Mariana Romo-Carmona

Three from Thirteen   13
  Robert Glück

The Number Line   21
  Regina Gillis

The Beginning of My Worthlessness   39
  Justin Chin

Train   49
  Gabrielle Glancy

Outtakes   55
  Clifford Chase

Notes on Camp   69
Robert Marshall

Mud Pies and Medusa   79
Marcus Mabry

Becky's Pagination   89
Rebecca Zinovic

1976   103
Doug Jones

A Close Escape   117
David Bergman

Waiting for Blastoff   135
Bia Lowe

Fashions of 1971   143
Wayne Koestenbaum

Still Life with Boys   151
Lisa Cohen

Lost in Translation   157
Michael Lowenthal

Awake   173
Jim Gladstone

Nancy Booth, Wherever You Are   179
Rebecca Brown

The Change of Life   191
Ralph Sassone

Cool for You   211
Eileen Myles

''The White Album''   **217**
Joe Westmoreland

Underwater   **227**
Paul Russell

First Passion   **237**
Etel Adnan

The Wind in the Louvers   **247**
Andrew Holleran

Thirteen   **257**
Jacqueline Woodson

Contributors   **263**

Foreword

Queer 13 reminds us that adolescence was the last time nothing could go wrong, thirteen, the one moment when uncertainty held only promise. Of course we didn't know that then: Puberty's monstrous deformations were terrifying, revolting even. Now we understand that fear was just the explainable edge of excitement; that revulsion, whatever else it did, also made our mouths water. The world was our oyster—but what are oysters save grit-filled, briny molluscs scraped off the ocean floor and served up raw.

Desire was still a single urge then, undifferentiated at its core but beginning to ribbon apart at its edges; like an octopus, it reached out in so many directions that it came to seem like several different desires. Though we came up with a thousand different answers, we continued to ask the same question, over and over: *What do I want?* But we dismissed each answer we came up with—*I want a sandwich, I want to write a story, I want to kiss LaMoine Weibe*—because the one thing we thought we knew was that we didn't have a name for what we wanted. Indeed, we suspected that it might not even have a name.

It's this vagueness that makes a criminal out of every adolescent. Every child knows what's good: it's only bad things that hide in the dark, ashamed to show themselves. And so, when our own desires led us out of well-lighted streets into shadowed alleyways, we attempted to shuck other attributes of childhood's simplicity, our innocence, our naïveté, and the haircuts that went with them. What we didn't realize was that these things would leave *us* behind, but not until they were good and ready.

Now, years after the fact, we see homosexuality as the bottle into which all those undifferentiated impulses have been poured. It feels so simple now—lust's urge, love's complacency—no more complicated, at any rate, than it is for our heterosexual peers. It can be hard to remember a time when queerness meant more than physical or emotional happiness or even the ongoing political struggle to pursue that happiness. But this collection reminds us that queer once meant the world: Queer was the desire to live in another time, queer was the dream of traveling to another planet, queer was the need to *do* something. Now queer is an evening shared with *Ellen* (reruns, but it's better than no show at all) and that's just fine. The dreams of adolescence are to the dreams of adulthood what the Hanging Gardens of Babylon are to Central Park: one is paradise re-created on earth, the other, a more mundane miracle but a miracle nonetheless, is what we live with every day.

Age replaces exuberance with wisdom, confusion with clarity, Oxy 10 with the Aveda product best suited to your skin type. Though most of us wouldn't trade our wrinkles for our zits, it's worth a look back at what we now realize was the transition between childhood's idyll and adult awareness. During that rough-and-tumble interlude nothing meant what it had meant when we were kids, and, though we couldn't articulate it, we intuited that things were only going to keep changing. For those few years, every touch was imbued with extra feeling, every action was a pebble dropped into an ocean sending out ever-widening circles of effect. We were afraid of everything yet willing to try anything once. Nothing satisfied us, but nothing bored us either, except denial. When we look back on it, all we can safely say is that love—that life—offered us too many choices, and it's only now, with the wisdom of age, that we realize none of them were wrong.

—Dale Peck

Introduction

Seventh grade: For me, the words evoke the seventh trumpet of Judgment Day, or maybe the seven plagues of Egypt. Not to mention a few deadly sins. And yet that awful, pivotal time is also one of the seven wonders of my world.

"Trickles of hair appear in my pits, face, crotch; reedy voice, zits. What *is* dignity?" asks Robert Glück in his memoir, "Three from Thirteen." In "The Number Line," Regina Gillis sums up the age this way: "Seventh grade meant scrutiny on every conceivable level—hair, clothes, skin, jewelry—followed by some sort of public humiliation." Like Glück and Gillis, all of the writers in this collection relived some of their most sublimely humiliating moments and risked their dignity in order to capture the tenor and meaning of that period.

There's sweet sixteen, and then there's queer thirteen. Passing from childhood to adolescence is a gauntlet of discovery and shame for everyone, but that obstacle course is even weirder for gay and lesbian kids. Just as you might be realizing who you are, you're also realizing that perhaps there's nothing worse to be than queer. "What are you—a lesbian?" Jacqueline Woodson's mother yells at her in "Thirteen," and the girl meekly answers no. "Femme," a classmate of Wayne Koesten-baum's calls his LOVE shirt in "Fashions of 1971," and the shirt goes in the drawer. "Hey, you little fairy," a tough kid taunts Michael Albo in "MACOS," and Albo can only ask, helplessly, "Why are you doing this to me?"

While most seventh-graders, even the misfits, are busy "coming out" sexually—*Playboy* for boys, teen-star posters for girls, kissing parties for both—those of us with more unusual urges are learning in a thousand intricate ways how to deceive ourselves and others. Desire intensifies just as it must go into hiding; if sexuality begins now in earnest, so does the closet. "One night I took a friend to the flat roof outside my bedroom window," writes Lisa Cohen in "Still Life with Boys." "The sky was dark and full of stars; her hair was brilliant black and wild; the roof was soft black tar. My mother's room was underneath. I spread out some old towels; she lay down. I sat up paralyzed: feverish with the closeness of her mouth and hair and laugh, and too afraid to move."

Again and again, the writers in this collection describe a time of over-whelming emotions combined with searing loneliness. But just as often, these essays can be surprisingly funny—as the queer child tries to under-stand the rules and boundaries of a suddenly sexual world. Recalls Rob-ert Marshall in "Notes on Camp": "I slept with my arms beneath my blanket. The angel face in the next cot asked, 'What are you doing, jerking off?' Then I slept with my arms on top of the blankets. I wasn't sure if this was what I should do—did it mean I was admitting he had been right? And I also thought that possibly I was *supposed* to be jerking off."

For most gay and lesbian kids, even today, there's simply no one to confide in about their sexuality. "My body seemed at once a lure, a hindrance, a half-awake, expanding thing," writes Gabrielle Glancy in "Train." The available sources of information—from the encyclopedia to school-yard stories—tend to offer sketchy or wildly skewed portraits of gay and transgendered people. As a queer thirteen-year-old, you're on your own. It's your first taste of self-invention.

But that's the inspiring part: Against all odds, you find a way to be yourself. In fact, you can't help it. In "How We Get That Way," Mariana Romo-Carmona describes finding refuge from her loneliness while ad-miring a dogwood; she points it out to a girl from school: "The small tree with the pink blossoms. It is so lovely, I am in love with this tree!" In "The Wind in the Louvers," Andrew Holleran tells how he got out of kissing a girl in spin-the-bottle: "I made a point to trip over the furniture, bang my shin, and completely dissipate the erotic atmosphere by a string of Jerry Lewis–like pratfalls."

When I myself began writing about junior high, a few years back, I soon found I couldn't stop with the brief memoir I'd originally planned, and for several months there seemed no end to the unfolding of memories both hilarious and disturbing (of which I offer a few in my essay "Outtakes"). I became something of a connoisseur of embarrassment and began talking to other queer writers about the period, wondering if it was as rich and resonant for them. The stories they told were fascinating and complex, and this is how the idea for an anthology came about.

The settings in this collection range from Maryland in the eighties (Michael Lowenthal's "Lost in Translation") to Beirut in the thirties (Etel Adnan's "First Passion"). Most of the memoirs take place in the seventh grade, but the time frame varies from sixth to ninth grade—depending on when each writer underwent that key transitional moment of revelation, shame, or denial that I was looking for. One piece, "1976" by Doug Jones, isn't a recollection at all, but excerpts from his actual journal written in seventh grade.

Why recall such a painful time? Until I took courage and began to write about it, junior high was a period I preferred to forget. More than one author I approached said, "I've blotted it out." Distancing myself from that shamefaced, luckless thirteen-year-old was one important, practical step in coming out. For a long time I found it too painful to remember being called a femme and a fag day after day, or to recall my lonely, circuitous strategies for self-preservation—trying to live down my femmy reputation, lying to myself about the boys I desired, hoping to turn myself straight. But over the years—the years since my own coming out, and maybe the cultural years since Stonewall—those mortifying scenes appear to have lost their power to overwhelm. That seventh-grader seems not just an embarrassing self I'd like to forget, but also a wily subversive, an intrepid traveler. What might I learn from him now?

—Clifford Chase

Queer 13

MACOS

Michael Albo

dedicated to the memory of Tom Brickhouse

In sixth grade, students in the Springfield, Virginia, school system were required to take the four-section science/health requirement, "Man: A Course of Study," unhumorously nicknamed MACOS on all the stickers, folders, filmstrips, textbooks, and worksheets. In MACOS, we studied four creatures: the salmon, the herring gull, the baboon, and the Eskimo, one each quarter. We learned about their traits, instincts, and habitat, but now I remember only one thing about each organism: the salmon swims upstream to spawn and then dies; the herring gull regurgitates its food to feed its young; baboons exist in close-knit packs and have no single mother after birth; Eskimo families live tightly together in their igloos. We were supposed to see there was a consistent, common thread among all living things: that we are born, we reproduce, we die.

I had somehow conned my mother into doing my final projects for me for the first two sections. Trying to be firm with me, she would occasionally suggest I start thinking about my MACOS final project a month in advance. I would always procrastinate until she'd angrily whip something up, with me looking on, trying to be innocently repentant, as if I were learning a vast amount about fish or birds by observing her.

She cooked salmon cakes for the first section, and I brought them to school on a gigantic shallow tray covered in tinfoil. For the second section she made a herring-gull pillow stuffed with cotton balls, with Magic Marker eyes and feathers. "I am not giving you any help on your baboon assignment, do you hear me?" she snapped, roughly handing me the stuffed gull.

My MACOS teacher, Mrs. Moore, didn't like me. I think it was because I was quiet, frightened, dutiful, and unpopular. There were many teachers who, like Mrs. Moore, loved only the popular kids. Behind the sham of rewarding good quiz grades and completed homework, Mrs. Moore secretly encouraged the popularity hierarchy, which in sixth grade was delicately taking shape like a larva. Mrs. Moore's face shone bright when Kristi Cook, a pretty, blond, well-dressed girl being groomed for future homecoming courts and cheerleading squads, asked a question. And if the sporty, soccer-playing Chris Graham burped loudly in class, she would admonish him with a tiny detectable grin. Mrs. Moore wore wrap dresses that exposed her pale, minnow-thin collarbones. We called her Moore the Whore because cleavage meant you were loose. Ian Gordon, the burnout, also got special treatment from our MACOS teacher, even though he was more delinquent-popular than a member of a cliquish inner circle. He had unbrushed teeth, greasy, long, bowl-cut hair, far-apart slitty eyes, and wore a Judas Priest baseball shirt every day. With his dark peach-fuzz mustache and a body odor vaguely reminiscent of Campbell's soup, he seemed to exude the oil of early puberty. He slept in school, skipped class, walked the halls cruelly, making comments about anyone who was unpopular. "Pick 'em up, you little fag," he said to me once in the hall, kicking the books out of my hands.

Ian Gordon sat next to me for the baboon section of MACOS. He brushed into class minutes after the bell, a waft of smoke, beer, and leather Camaro interior following him. I was afraid to look at him. Mrs. Moore was showing a film from the Mutual of Omaha's *Wild Kingdom* "Classroom Series" in which Marlon Perkins and his sidekick, Jim, trailed a pack of baboons. They observed the baboons as they hunted an injured antelope and whooped across the yellow, flat, African landscape. In an unfortunate example of the cruel jungle, the youngest baboon was killed in a sudden chase and attack by cheetahs. As the baboon let out its last breath, Mrs. Moore gasped and turned away from the screen.

I sat stiff and primed, but Ian Gordon didn't bother me in class. He did tease Kristi Cook constantly, until finally she raised her hand and asked to be moved. Ian said, "Why shouldn't she sit next to me, she's carrying my child!"

"Shut up that's a lie!" Kristi cried. Mrs. Moore released a nervy laugh, telling Ian to go out in the hall. A few days later, or a week or so, I can't remember, he was not in class anymore. From then on, my friends and I called Kristi "Mother of the Baboons" behind her back.

I had lied to my mom and told her I'd finished my baboon final project, but the hard reality was undeniable: I had once again waited until the night before. At eleven o'clock that night (late for sixth grade), I remembered Mrs. Moore's soft spot for the baby baboon. I decided to write a poem about its sad death. I can only remember the last two lines: "And so the littlest baboon/Sadly waved good-bye." To my shock, Mrs. Moore's eyes teared up when she read it the next day.

That year Linda Ronstadt released her album *Living in the U.S.A.*, with her on the cover in a red satin jacket, tight blue satin shorts, and big rubber-wheeled roller skates. I loved roller-skating, and this album cover affirmed what I deeply knew: that someday, somewhere, when I got to be older, I would be a part of a supportive, joyous roller-disco crowd. At lunch, I ate quickly and went to the tennis court, which had a smooth, debris-free skating surface that made you feel professional and somehow more mature when you skated on it. I would roll around and around the edge of the court all through lunchtime.

It was almost spring; buds were becoming blooms, the custodians were repainting the blacktop, and in MACOS we started the Eskimo section. We were shown filmstrips of Idee Magmak and his wife, Kinyook, depicting how they lived hand-to-mouth, ate whale parts, relied on the capricious tundra for survival.

On a warm day, I was skating during lunch on the tennis court and a rock flew by me. I stopped and looked around but didn't see anything. A minute later another rock whizzed right by my eye. I looked up again and saw Ian Gordon walking toward me. He threw another rock, this one hitting my arm. Next to him was a girl my age whom I had never seen before. She had winged brown hair, thick eyeliner, and she wore torn jeans and a Rolling Stones baseball shirt. Her stomach was unnaturally fat—perfectly, centrally round. She was pregnant. She looked at me with an absent expression, and I immediately thought she was "on something," even though I had no real concept of drugs. I began to quickly take off my skates and put on my shoes so I could run. Ian Gordon glowered at me with his shoulders pushed back, in a parody of a bully. He blocked the opening to the tennis court. "Hey, you little fairy." Sick with fear, I reacted the way I always did in these situations, as if I were possessed by some sort of British ambassador. "Why are you doing this to me?" I said shakily, with this weird sense of propriety.

"Fuck off!" Ian Gordon said. "Fuck you! I'm gonna fuck you up."

"Just leave me alone," I said.

"No. I'm gonna fuck you over," he said. "Do you know what it's like to be fucked?"

I looked at the girl, thinking that she knew because she had been fucked, and also thinking she would help me because she was a girl and not as naturally malicious. But she stepped up next to him with this bitter, foul expression on her face. She lifted a hand, pointed at herself, and said with a theatrical, *Afterschool Special* vibrato in her voice, "It hurts. It really hurts."

Even then, businesslike with fear, I couldn't believe how staged this seemed. I was so drawn to Ian and his wife, and I looked at them with concern. I thought I could help them or still befriend them, or train them like animals to like me by somehow sending the right signal. And later on, in junior high, when the burnouts were at the peak of their power, and I heard about Drew Groves getting it on with two girls out by the baseball field, or Alisa DuShaw getting an abortion, or Tammy Brownside swallowing Andrew Schwertzer's come, or even later on in high school, when the burnouts *did* burn out, I knew I had missed my chance at communicating with them. On the tennis court, the teachers came out and yelled at Ian Gordon to get off the school grounds, and someone gently pulled me back in through the blue school doors. I just remembered to remember them—because they were important, because I felt fear, because they made me meek.

How We Get That Way

Mariana Romo-Carmona

On some suburban street in central Connecticut, there must be a pink dogwood tree that is fully grown by now and opens every spring in beautiful blossoms of an inexpressibly, superbly pink, pink. I know this because in the spring of 1967 I walked to school every day and passed that tree. It had been a long, very snowy winter, and the little tree saved my soul when it bloomed.

At the very early hour of seven-thirty, I passed that tree on the way to Alfred Plant Junior High School. I usually walked alone because I was the new South American girl at school and I didn't have many friends. In fact, I didn't have any. The neatly trimmed lawns with sprouting crocuses and daffodils became familiar. The faux-Tudor façades and the brick-and-white-clapboard houses with wraparound wooden porches and flower boxes all became part of what I learned to understand was suburban in that pretentious neighborhood. My own home was the middle-floor apartment of a three-story wooden house on the main road, painted gray like its duplicate neighbors. I came to know that this is where the working class and the immigrant class lived, not in the smaller streets with the manicured gardens and nasturtiums by the hedge. Having no one to talk with about these things, I did plenty of solitary musing.

Besides, after seven months my English was still somewhat flat and rudimentary. I couldn't explain the finer points of the opinions I was forming. At least the weather was improving and I was feeling a little less depressed.

My tree helped. It became my tree. It was about five feet, not much taller than I was then, and its dark brown branches bent in such poetic fashion—palms upturned, small hands dancing—that I would sometimes sigh when I saw it. The blossoms opened and blushed so exquisitely that I would stop and gaze at the delicate arrangement with half-closed lids until I had drunk in all the tree's beauty. My heart felt soothed after I glimpsed my tree, and I would march on to school where I would be the foreign girl again and nothing more for the rest of the day.

Once, though, one of the more tolerant girls in my class happened to be leaving her yellow and rust Victorianish house when I passed by, and she didn't make an excuse, such as having to get to homeroom early, so she walked to school with me. Her name was Andrea; she had curly brown hair and glasses. She could almost look like me, except she didn't; she was clearly American, and she kept to her tall, slightly goofy stride and nerdy New England patter. When we passed my tree, in a rush of budding adolescence and South American romanticism, I decided to confide in her.

"Look," I said, gesturing poetically. "There is the tree I love."

"Excuse me?"

"Oh, are you all right?" I asked, concerned that she may have hurt herself, or burped, and asked to be excused.

"No, I mean, what tree?" She shoved her hornrimmed glasses back up on the bridge of her nose.

"The small tree with the pink blossoms. It is so lovely, I am in love with this tree!"

"Oh." Andrea looked around, to make sure we had not been seen together. We hadn't, so she quizzed me again. "What do you mean you are *in love* with the tree?"

"I love this tree because its beauty . . . upsets my heart so!" I explained, transported.

"Well, you can like a tree, that I can understand," she said, as she resumed her pace up the street. "But you can't be in love with it, that's all!"

I don't think Andrea talked to me much after that day. She was in practically all my classes, but whenever I saw her she adopted a kind yet pained expression and excused herself, as though she were a missionary and I an exuberant savage who might cause a scene with my unruly passions.

I got used to this way for things to be, for the rest of my high school years and into college. There was no way that I wasn't going to be a little bit odd, wherever I was, and I realized years later that being an immigrant, usually the only Latina in any situation, was only part of the reason. I am sure that the episode with the pink dogwood expressed feelings that had already been stirring in my heart.

Before we emigrated to the United States, my parents had gone to the north of Chile in search of better jobs. We left Santiago with its old streets and comfortable familiarity and moved to Calama, a small oasis town in the middle of the Atacama Desert. Everything was new there, the houses, the schools, the theater, and even the buses, which were clean and speedy without the spewing of smelly diesel fuel we had to put up with in the capital. The sky in Calama was always blue; it never rained, and some of its relative well-being seemed to have spilled over from the only nearby town, the copper-mining Chuquicamata.

In Calama I was enrolled in the all-girls' school, sex-segregated schools being the norm in Chile. This happened to be a Catholic one, run by Spanish nuns of the Dominican Order. There was a public coed high school, but when my very progressive parents had to choose between a secular education and one where I would be safe from adolescent boys, there was no question. And I certainly didn't mind.

The code of behavior was the same as in girls' schools everywhere, I imagine. That is how I had grown up, with women teachers, and surrounded by girls. So my new school provided me with something familiar, the same comfort experienced by all Chilean girls, as had my mother and her sisters before me. I wonder now how much of this is lost with the introduction of coed schools.

But the important development at this new school was that we were all entering the years of existential angst, of longing for the unfathomable reaches of love. We were programmed to make our parents' lives miserable. At least at school we had each other. We were very democratically in love with each other and sexual orientation had little to do with this. Even though our devotion was unshakeable, we were growing up in the 1960s and most of us did imagine ourselves as Hollywood starlets who would one day date one of the Beatles, preferably Paul.

I remember the day of my initiation. It was recess, and I'd gone to stand by two girls sitting together on the sunniest part of the steps by the playground. This was the desert, but winter mornings were cool. Fatima was a beautiful girl with long black hair and dark eyes shaded by luxurious eyelashes. I don't think there was one of us who didn't long to be her best friend. Next to her on the steps was María Eugenia, who was the favorite of the nuns for being an orphan, or at least half an orphan because only her father was dead, and because she stayed in the school on weekends, including holidays. As for me, I had nothing to recommend me; I was an ordinary Chilean girl.

Fatima and María Eugenia were playing at hiding María Eugenia's gold chain in the folds of her shirt collar against her skin. Fatima had to find it with her fingers before her friend raised her shoulders and hid her neck in the collar of her uniform's white shirt and navy blue sweater. Fatima's fingers couldn't reach far enough. They invited me to join them. María Eugenia winked at me with playful brown eyes, her lips in a teenage smirk all defiance and beckoning.

I sat with them on the steps, all three of us in navy blue pleated skirts, our legs gathered underneath sporting cinnamon-colored knee socks and, of course, brown leather shoes with a spit shine. We played the game and soon gathered a crowd around us, the desert sky shining blue above. There was a lot of shoving and laughing, and within five minutes it seemed I had known those uniformed girls all my life. María Eugenia pulled up her chain and told me to try and get it. It was a stupid game, I know, but how delicious.

It didn't take long. I guess Fatima was tired of the game, so she let me try, draping her arm around me, instructing me on how to grab the chain before María Eugenia shrugged and it slipped away. I placed my hands on María Eugenia's shoulders and waited for her to let go of the chain. She was clearly enjoying the attention. "Ready?" she asked me, and dropped the chain down her neck and into the folds of her shirt. I dipped my fingers without shame around her collarbone and got hold of it. Her neck was warm.

Naturally, María Eugenia claimed I didn't have hold of the chain, and Fatima and I maintained I had won fair and square, the three of us falling all over each other, tickling and slipping fingers around our necks. The rest of the girls joined us in their own roughhousing and loving embraces, until the nuns came to break it up and call us back into class. But María Eugenia and I had bonded for life.

Nothing like this easy and inclusive intimacy awaited me at Alfred Plant, and I'm sure I didn't help matters by arriving late in the school year— and being South American. I could have been tall, blond, and French, but I had to be difficult.

Andrea wasn't the only girl who was afraid of getting too close to me. There was also Cherry, who played field hockey and thought she might have seen in my short Chilean legs the promise of a good guard on the team. But later in the locker room she also saw that I didn't shave my legs, and she was horrified. That was the end of my career in sports. Meanwhile, at home, nothing would make my mother change her mind about letting me near a razor or a depilatory cream, because she had a theory that this business of leg shaving was strictly an American subterfuge designed to get boys. No amount of my tears was going to make her understand I just wanted to be friends with Cherry.

If Cherry was the first to ditch me, the rest of the girls didn't wait long. The junior high experience was fiercely heterosexual. Everyone was dating or going steady with someone of the opposite sex, except for the absolute nerds, and nobody bothered with them. I scanned the possibilities open to me, and the panorama was bleak—those boys were just plain ugly. Besides, dating before one's eighteenth birthday was unheard of in my family, and even then it would be with a chaperone. In our new country, there were no Latina role models to show me how to be a teenage girl. My only identification with stars and public figures was with American blacks, who I understood were closer to Latinos, but even they were hardly ever on TV to explain how the dating game was played.

So I watched *Star Trek* for Nichelle Nichols, and *I Spy* for Bill Cosby, bought records by the Supremes and Dionne Warwick, and held on to my crush on Paul. Inside though, I hadn't changed. Gym class was torture, and I was the only girl who still wore Cross Your Heart double-A's and didn't shave her legs.

I had never been confronted with a custom as bizarre as communal showers. It happened my first week at Alfred Plant, on a Thursday afternoon, the first day of our phys-ed class. By this time I could speak exactly ten words of English, and that included "thank you" and "how do you do." After making us climb ropes that blistered my palms and jump on a pommel horse that only tall girls could gracefully mount, the imposing Mrs. Eames sent us all to the showers.

There was a new word, *showers,* and soon I learned another one: *embarrassed.* Because this is what all the girls whispered in the locker room when they saw me retreat and put my school clothes back on in a hurry. Meanwhile, all the shameless Americans stripped naked and jumped into the wide open shower, draping minuscule towels around their breasts when they came out. All my years of female bonding had not prepared me for this, and from that day until the end of the school year, I made sure never to break a sweat in gym class because there was no way I was going to take a shower in that place.

Over the summer it seemed as though life became more understandable, though I am still not entirely sure why. Part of it, I know, was due to being able to communicate. In my journal I began to write more enthusiastically about living in this new country, and my sentences were gradually shifting from Spanish to English, but I was still lost somewhere between teenage angst and plain loneliness. Understanding more of the language around me brought me closer to the youth culture; I could hum some of the tunes I heard and my head floated in psychedelic sound, and when I discovered the ethic and the value of baby-sitting for our neighbors, my mother was finally persuaded to let me buy a pair of flared-leg jeans.

By the time fall rolled around once more, our small family had witnessed the turning of the seasons in New England and moved away from the suburbs to a little semirural town in eastern Connecticut, where the schools had no showers, the houses had no fences, and the yards ended at a brook surrounded by blackberry bushes. Half the neighborhood was

African-American or Polish, and there was even a Puerto Rican family down the street. Memories are hazy now, but I remember feeling wistfully happy, brave enough to abandon my memories of Chile, looking forward to the new school, where perhaps I wouldn't be so odd anymore.

And for a while, perhaps I wasn't. In this school there were blue-eyed kids who came to homeroom smelling like a barn because they had been up at dawn milking cows with their fathers. These boys got beaten up by the football team before they got on the bus at the end of the day. The English teacher got pelted with spitballs as soon as he walked into the classroom because his hair was too long. I liked him right away. And there were two pregnant girls in my gym class—one of them by the geometry teacher, who was said to be a faggot because he wore different-colored socks and penny loafers. I wasn't sure what a faggot was—to tell the truth, I had no idea—but I took this information in with equanimity.

By the second day of school just about everyone had asked me where I was from and to say something in my language. The kids who hadn't asked me were obviously not ever going to speak to me, so I figured it was better to have people talking to me than to be ignored. I played the game. Some people thought my father was a diplomat, others that we were fleeing political persecution. One girl asked if my mother was a singer, and another if I was an orphan. It didn't matter, it was what they wanted to hear, so I said yes and embroidered the facts when I could. School wasn't going to be so bad. And besides, finally, I found a friend.

Jackie, twice as tall as me, with bright red hair and brown eyes, lived on a farm, and since she was a girl she didn't have to milk the cows, but her cousin Jimmy did. By the second week of school he already had a shiner.

That week also signaled the advent of Queer Thursday, a New England custom known to all the locals except me, which dictated that the entire student body should not wear green that day, unless they wanted to shout to the world that they were gay. I was wearing a lovely green pleated jumper my mother had made for me, with a fetching blue-and-green plaid shirt that had a little navy blue ribbon tie around the neck. I loved the little tie.

It didn't take long for the whispers—she's queer, she's queer!—to register. I wasn't sure what it meant, but I figured it had to do with me. There were some other unhappy souls caught wearing green that day, including Jimmy, who was wearing green overalls. Jackie despaired of what to do with the two of us but, to her credit, still consented to sit with us in the cafeteria at lunch. I played with my little tie. Looking around, I remember being aware that even though I could say most things in English, I still thought in Spanish.

Everyone was talking; the cafeteria was a strange, rowdy place. There were the two pregnant girls, having lunch with the football team. Most of the black kids were sitting at one table, girls on one side, boys on the other. The English teacher was eating sloppy joes with a fork and had his nose stuck in a book. The principal was trying to fix his toupee. The farmer boys had double plates of food on their trays; the pretty girls laughed derisively as they passed by. At our table, Jackie was telling me I wasn't really queer, it's just that I was a foreigner and all.

And in Spanish I thought, no, this is true; I am queer. This is me.

Three from Thirteen

Robert Glück

1. The Greeks Came First

Jacking off into the toilet, into the slit between pushed-together beds, into paper-towel tubes (*Ugh*, my little sister shouts, *what's this stuff?*), in the shower, while standing in the crotch of a tree, while standing on my head. What belongs to me except the next orgasm? Even shame is not mine. I can't afford to fantasize or to connect mind and body. Strip poker with Mike Cogan: Since we're naked, we might as well masturbate. *Don't look,* he keeps whining. His orgasm is like him, a pipsqueak.

Lessons at the Art Shack, an artist-supply store in Sherman Oaks, taught by Dagmar, the local Flemish master's vivacious daughter. I paint a courtier playing a lute as though I were already safely dead and great. Rembrandt shadows surround and define the musician; he wears tights and sort of floats above a relentless one-point–perspective checkered floor. My smock is too short to hide my random boner, but Dagmar is European about it. Her father, the old master, strolls among us; he takes my brush and palette and lays a few bright swatches on my canvas, alarming until I gain distance by squinting and see that my mud puddle has been given a shape.

My bar mitzvah portion is Sodom and Gomorrah—I side with God. My older brother whispers to my mom, "Bob walks like a *girl*, even the little bump." I read *Great Expectations* while monitoring the halls at Parkman Junior High—a job to camouflage my disgrace at having no one to eat lunch with. The Pierce twins terrorize me—dark, athletic, amoral, *noir de soleil*. The threat of violence and grueling sarcasm. When they see me working at my easel in my backyard (sad clown? kitty in a brandy snifter?), one says, "So that's what Glück does"—he doesn't even care if I hear. I'm glad when he's killed in Vietnam. Later, a mutual friend says they were jealous of me.

After a typical family fight at dinner, my mother complains, "We have no dignity." It's almost a moral flash point, a completely unusual grievance that comes from a place outside. My family has nothing to say to that. I try to contain it with sarcasm, but I only smirk—*dignity?* Trickles of hair appear in my pits, face, crotch; reedy voice, zits. What *is* dignity? I get a boner while baby-sitting the Feldmans' boy. We're wrestling, and he knows a boner is something to shout about. I resent what's happening to me—it seems undignified. How dare nature meddle with my body? I never *agreed* to that.

Feldman shows my father the pistol he will kill us with if we try to force our way into his bomb shelter when Armageddon comes. My dad tells Feldman he intends to pull our Plymouth station wagon over the entrance, trapping Feldman's family below. My family thinks this is hilarious—it's our sense of humor in a nutshell. Feldman tags after my dad for weeks. *You wouldn't really do that. Would you do that?*

"All children seem, to me, either kept or abandoned," writes Matthew Stadler. A kept child is "a decorative wing of the family that can be used to store what will not fit elsewhere . . . innocence, for example, or joy." An abandoned child? My father is snoring. My mother leans against the family-room doorway. *Go to bed,* she says without conviction. I'm allowed to miss school, stay up late, whatever, as long as I keep my grades up. Actually, I invent this rule to fool myself into thinking the adults are watching. I could stay up for the late late show if I were a mass murderer. Eventually my parents adopt my good-grade rule without ever needing to enforce it. I have no effect on anyone.

"I Only Have Eyes for You," the hero croons to the ingenue in their jazzy Broadway show. I don't know their names yet. She's a hoofer leaning into her routine with one arm cocked. His lilting voice generates the wonder: For some reason it's delicious to glorify this horse of a starlet. The lovers rush from a busy street down to the subway on a miraculously expanding stage—they break the rules of space and time by just ignoring them.

As he continues to sing, her face replaces the subway ads, a face that multiplies in every dimension, but mechanically, a Deco assembly line, a little clunky, a little scary. Dick Powell's obsession doesn't heap overwhelming finality onto all places and times. Instead, Ruby Keeler is endlessly reversible, elastic without tension. Is that love, if you are made of film? Bad temper from the real world simmers beneath her performance and her Kewpie-doll expression.

Bangs and hat crowd Ruby's face, the only female face in the movie with actual eyebrows, a sign of sincerity. It just keeps smiling woodenly. Love is an optical illusion: Ruby rises through her own iris and steps into a mirror as the reflection of her self, the woman who lifts the mirror as its reverse side reflects the young lovers, Ruby and Dick, in their subway car. The end of the line. It's night; it's beginning to rain. Dick carries Ruby across the tracks of the huge empty train yard as though he's a gentleman and the whole world has become a mud puddle, strange desolation.

I'm amazed, as though I've discovered buried treasure, but this old film is so despised that the TV station keeps the projector running during the long commercial breaks—Stanley Stanley Stanley Chevrolet/ Two blocks off of the Santa Ana Freeway—so when the movie returns the plot has advanced beyond understanding. I don't care, so long as the musical numbers are left whole. Their glamour and failed effects belong to me in a way I don't understand. Even the TV doesn't want them. The screen goes white, just static and blur. I'm alone on the floor as though propelled backward by a slingshot. It means the film broke and the projectionist is asleep. There's nothing to do but turn it off. No "Star-Spangled Banner," no broadcasting message. It's 4:00 A.M. in L.A. What next?

Behind my tract there's a little hill; on it stands a tree, last gasp of wood in Woodland Hills. I haul myself up and out. My idea is—what?—

an idea from books: Viewing my neighborhood from above will give me perspective, as though looking down through the years. It's still dark when I reach the top, and I'm afraid of the tree—what if a snake or rat or an insect lives in it? The air is too weak to carry a scent. For some reason the ground is lit, a sparse layer of dry weeds and grasses.

I stand above my tract. In the clear darkness, the sky seems manageable. Below, streetlights illuminate ranch-style houses, mirror images that are raucously artificial. I assume the humans in these identical dwellings are robbed of dignity, that dignity means living beautifully. Under these roofs, families are sunk in mute desolation and each family member labors under the curse of unrelenting failure. Weakened by sleep, they invent a useless hodgepodge of dreams. I'm the only one awake, too excited below the sky and above the earth. Morning, yet to begin, is already old and jangled from my weariness.

Fatigue is disheveled isolation. I don't know how to be part of the world. When darkness disappears and light has not yet come, pale gray turns to mist white. A bird makes frail peeps. If I had the knowledge, I'd recognize that rare bird and know it never flew through Woodland Hills before. It's an exhausted thought because what would I know if I knew that? In Will and Ariel Durant's history, I read that the Greeks came first, then the Romans. That's consoling somehow. Is the march of civilization heading my way? Will I be allowed to join the parade? Its splendor seems undermined by fatigue and wasted effort.

I want someone to love me. I already love whoever it is. Somehow the first light makes my grief explicit—*so much endlessness stored up and in store*. The sunless light casts no shadows, yet it reveals my dense flesh to itself and shrinks my emotions by making them seem organized. My face, struck by the light, feels caked and rigid. I sit down on the hard ground and cry a little. I fish my aged cock out of my jeans as though I can *mark* the scene with pleasure so later I can find it and reread it for understanding. Once imagined, it is my responsibility to jack off in front of it all. The air feels funny on my cock, which usually squirms like a larva in the darkness; it's more sensitive than I am to the prickle of a slight breeze. There is nothing to arouse me except myself. My tract looks so boring, its emptiness so lacks potential, that I can almost believe in reality, since here is appearance spreading out at my feet. It only takes a minute. My crotch rings like an alarm clock, some pump mechanism kicks in, and after short flights my sperm falls on the gray dirt. I feel edgy and shallow, emptied out by the day ahead, and twinges of residual pleasure make me twitch.

The white is replaced by pastels. I have not prevented the sunrise—a red smudge on the horizon—or the flat mineral-blue.

2. Do Be. Don't Be.

My Hollywood cousin says watch out for queers in theater toilets; if they bother me, I should punch them in the shoulder and they'll go away. I'm impressed by my cousin's sophistication. I'm a country mouse and he is letting me feel the difference between Hollywood savoir faire and the barbarism of the West Valley. And sure enough, the next time I go to the movies in Hollywood, a queer speaks to me. I don't remember the movie; I do remember the bathroom but so what? It was empty even though we were in it. The little man in a checked sports jacket stands too close to me at the urinal. Is he subnormal? Doesn't he understand social distance? He has an accent—British? Cockney? Maybe he's wearing a bowler? "Excuse me?"

"*Xxxx'x* x xxxx *xxxx* xxx xxxx xxxxx."

"What?"

"*That's* a nice *cock* you have there." He's offering his, a prim pink boutonniere; I can see why he likes mine better. A nice cock? Is it separate from my body, which is not nice? Separate, like my beautiful eyes? He's will-less as a dust bunny, and when I tap him on the shoulder, he drifts away.

Later, in a smelly gas-station toilet, I realize the wad of toilet paper left on top of the dispenser is filled with someone's sperm. Some pervert left it there, I tell myself wonderingly. To be found, I add. And recognized. As what? An offering, an assertion? I don't forget to be grossed out. I smell it—sure enough, sperm. Consciousness the predicament, orgasm the escape. I look around for the masturbator as though I'm dreaming, as though I can hear his *I'm coming* noises. Obviously no one else could fit inside the tiny stinking cinder-block cell. I try to remember the face of a man slouching outside the door, and the face of a man who gave me the key.

As though waking up, I consider the writing on the walls: garish fat cocks spurt buckets of sperm into hairy cunts as though to reassert the straight and narrow. In the corner, there's a simple double line in pencil, an hourglass silhouette of breasts, waist, and hips that men used to carve in the air to indicate a sexy broad, and I feel a pang of nostalgia for a decent inner life. Outside: relentless sun, the "flow" of the gas station, and my family interacting in the car. It's impossible to make a dent in that world or be recognized by it, yet the whole endlessly collapses under the weight of its own hokum. It's impossible to separate the anguish of having a mother, father, siblings, mind, and body from the failure of my particular family, mind, and body. I pick up the sperm wad by a dry corner as though it were mine to keep or throw away and drop it into the toilet. I watch it drift, then flush it down. I still live with my family, and though I can't imagine a place for myself in the world, I hope the world can imagine it for me.

3. Mexico

A black-and-white photo—I have it here: *Tijuana 1959 Mexico* blazoned above our heads on a muslin backdrop of palms and banners and hillsides, and my family positioned in front on a wagon, each of us under a sombrero—PONCHO, TIJUANA, KISS ME, and OH BOY embroidered on the crowns—and a serape for my dad (laughter—he looks, he *really* looks Mexican), and bongo drums for my big brother and a pith helmet for my little brother, who sits on a mule painted like a zebra, which supposedly draws the cart. We sit in the frustrating sunlight. We are an American family; each of us looks like a section of American family. Pop and hot mariachi music and fast Spanish from tinny loudspeakers conflict in the street. Donald Duck taught me that Mexico is a joke to be exploited, with a slovenly language and jumping beans for traditions. I feel vulnerable in the face of these high curbs, pitted roads, bleached colors, squat buildings, constant hustle, wind and dust.

We separate for shopping. I roam through the intricate booths, admire the gods carved in alabaster, hand-turned chess sets with mother-of-pearl inlay, rich things I can have cheap. There are also striptease decks displaying middle-aged women, and stilettos, switchblades, bullhorns, cherry bombs. I saved and now I can acquire, the spirit of acquisition making my heart beat, my saliva flow, and my eyes bright. We told each other informationally that bargaining is expected and encouraged. Although usually at a high pitch of trembling niceness, as a customer I can haggle and sweat and worry a shopkeeper until he puts in his own money to help me buy the object so he can get rid of me.

I browse along, relishing the high blue malls, and turn into a store that is like the other stores. I narrow my eyes for the exact treasure. I look at the chess sets, the red low-fire pottery, the Aztec bookends. I look in a case of hammered-silver rings. The shop attendant steps into place. I look at him. He's very slender. He is older, but he reminds me of Bernie Barbash from the third grade, whose ears and fingers were translucent and whose face always hovered in the outskirts of the cry position. "You like me to open the case?" I shake my head no. I think, *I bet he sleeps on a cot, I bet he's poor.* I feel as though I spent my life sitting on a birthday cake. He opens the case and I move my hand over the rings. He strokes the top of my hand and says, "A ring for your boyfriend? You have a boyfriend?" He smiles directly into my eyes. I don't have the language to respond in any way; I move in order to disappear, but he comes around the counter and as I look back at him, both of us stepping over pottery jars, he brushes my thigh with his hand and says, "You be my boyfriend?" Does he want my money? I don't exactly stay, but I don't leave either. I just move around, followed, until, not knowing how to say good-bye to all this, I slip away.

I've been touched by a pervert in a border town, I say over and over, I lose track. The colors of the piñatas, the degraded cheapness everywhere reiterates, *I was touched by a pervert in Mexico. Touched by a pervert. A pervert touched me in a border town.*

I meet my family at the Cantina Tres Panchos. Soda from the bottle: Even so, on the surface of the pop there floats a pubic hair that carries every disease in the world. The long drive back. My dad looks for his lighter. "Somebody musta went south with it." Laughter—we *were* south. I'm preoccupied by a ringing telephone in my crotch that won't stop. I sense news of a misfortune so complete that its scope is beyond me. "When You Were Sweet Sixteen," "Elsie Schultzenheim," "I'm Looking Over a Four-Leaf Clover," "Old Black Joe," "Coming 'Round the Mountain," "Night and Day," "Hava Nagilah," "Dixie," "America the Beautiful." They talk about my grandmother's will. Who will get the good diamond earrings, the bad diamond earrings. Aunt Helen will be provided for, the pearls, the lot in California City. My sister says, "I'm going to poke you with this ruler if you don't answer me and carry on a decent conversation."

When we arrive home, I drift into the pastel bathroom and masturbate. I fear the authority it gives to the experience, locating as it does a human response. I sit there utterly drained, caught in the vise of my loathsome excitement, hating Mexico and hating the U.S.A.

Tell me, given the options, where would your anger take you—where has it taken you?

The Number Line

Regina Gillis

My mother pushed open the door, came into my room without knocking, and said, "Get up. Get dressed. We have to get gas." It was five-thirty in the morning.

"Now?" I asked.

"Just shut up, wiseass, and get in the car. I found someone who has gas." Her eyes were wild with panic.

The Arab Oil Embargo had ended the year before, but not in my mother's mind. This was one of her more lucid moments, between chemotherapy, painkillers, bouts of nausea and vomiting. My sisters and I got in the car on a mythical quest for gasoline, too groggy to argue.

My mother put the keys in the ignition, sighed, and bowed her head into the steering wheel. The car smelled like egg-farts. We weren't moving.

"Well, let's go," I said, annoyed with this delusion and my part in it.

"Never mind, kids. I don't know what I was thinking. Get back in the house."

We got out. A few weeks earlier she woke us up to say we weren't going to school, that there was going to be a war, and that we were spending the day in church praying for world peace. We got as far as the church parking lot, when my mother had a similar lapse back into reality, circled the empty lot, and went home. I had always thought these episodes were the result of the drugs, or the sheer terror of waking up every day with cancer, but lately I was beginning to wonder.

We went back inside and got ready for school. I was in seventh grade and had recently discovered showers. Long, hot ones, where I felt clean and good, where I could reenact all the things I said and did wrong at school the day before, and where I could strategize to undo it all. Every morning was the same: I would stay in the shower for ten or twenty minutes, until my father flushed the downstairs toilet and yelled from the bottom of the stairs, "Get out. This isn't a hotel." I would emerge with my skin all hot and glowing.

I would spend another twenty or thirty minutes getting ready. Seventh grade meant scrutiny on every conceivable level—hair, clothes, skin, jewelry—followed by some sort of public humiliation. And today I would have to get in front of my French class and have a "quiz" conversation in French with Ms. Tryon, the teacher. The possibility of displaying my proficiency in the language was overshadowed by the likelihood of something permanently embarrassing happening instead.

I remember the first day of French class. In walked Ms. Tryon. She had long, brown, wavy hair, the kind of look women had when they were trying to let their shags grow out; she wore a cardigan sweater vest, bell-bottoms, and Dr. Scholl's with socks. Her face was long and tired-looking, like she had spent the night arguing with her boyfriend or husband. Her brown eyes were large and dolorous, like the Hush Puppies dog or Jesus.

Now, as Ms. Tryon quizzed me in front of the class, I began to fall into the black holes of her eyes. We exchanged French in my new, limited lexicon. She seemed genuinely interested in my answers, as if this mock dialogue were original and thought-provoking.

I got an A. After I answered all her questions, I remained at the front of the room, unable to move.

"*Excellente. Très bon.*" I just stood there. "*Asseyez-vous.*"

I was staring at Ms. Tryon's sad face, her outgrown shag, and noticed for the first time that she had very large pores. They were mesmerizing.

"What?"

"Sit down," she said. I had made her break into English.

"Oh, yeah, right." I went back to my seat. I waited for something to happen—for someone in the class to notice how I was temporarily paralyzed, caught up in the complexity of Ms. Tryon's face. As much as I wanted to see if she was still sad after talking to me, I let my bangs fall and stared long into my notebook.

Our junior high was shaped like the Pentagon—three hallways connected to an auditorium and cafeteria on one side. Getting to class meant either going clockwise or counterclockwise in the building that encircled a courtyard to which no one, not even the teachers, had access. Every day I would pass the same kids making the same *wooj-wooj* sounds with their new corduroys in front of the same lockers between the same classes. Everyone had bad skin, even the teachers. The courtyard in the middle looked fake, like a diorama or a failed terrarium. The sharks in the aquarium swim counterclockwise, I remembered, and have huge calluses on their snouts from bumping the thick glass, probably from the sheer boredom of swimming in circles. We're like the sharks, swimming around that damn courtyard. But instead of calluses, we get zits. Acne is caused by boredom, I decided.

When I got home I made Blueberry Toast 'Ems.

"What is that god-awful smell?" my mother yelled from the top of the stairs.

"Toast 'Ems," I yelled back. "You want some?"

"God, no. Go outside and eat those. The smell is making me nauseous."

Every day there was a new smell that was making her nauseous. At first it was only really strong odors—Pledge, Pine-Sol, nail polish. But lately it was everything, especially food. I had made Toast 'Ems the day before without any complaint. I went out the back door and wolfed them down. I was going to be late to my baby-sitting job. My mother was still yelling at me from the top of the stairs.

"Gina. GINA!" I hated that name—too girly—so much so that I let my sister Monica call me Greg (she thought I looked like one) and even signed my Christmas and birthday cards to her and my parents with "Love, Greg."

"What, Ma?"

"Can you call Dr. Roth?" I went upstairs. "I feel lousy. I'm really sick."

But she was always feeling really sick. Sometimes it was the chemotherapy, sometimes it was the other drugs she was taking, and sometimes it was a high fever or intense healing pain. One of us would have to call an ambulance, leave a note on the kitchen table, and get her to the hospital. Usually me, because I was home from school first.

"But Ma, Dr. Roth is a dentist." I suggested calling the oncologist.

"No. Call Dr. Roth. He knows about me. He knows what to do." I couldn't tell if this was another one of her delusions or if she had actually spoken with him recently and he really did know what was going on.

Her room was really hot—like a nursing home—and I was beginning to feel feverish. "Ma, it's hot in here."

"Well, *I'm* freezing and *I'm* the one who's dying and *I* want the heat on." This was the first mention I had heard from anyone that she was dying. I chose to dismiss this idea as yet another delusion. I was now officially late for my baby-sitting job and called the Glendalls to apologize.

Dr. Roth made it over in less than half an hour. "Is she going to be okay?" I asked.

"She's okay for now. She's just very sick."

No duh, I thought.

"I gave her some morphine. And some xylocaine. She has several open sores in her mouth, from the chemotherapy. The xylocaine will help numb her mouth and her—"

"Is she going to die?" I interrupted, the question fueled by his frankness.

Dr. Roth ignored me and continued. This was a house call, and there was no time to indulge emotion. "The xylocaine will numb her gag reflex, so if she eats, she could choke to death. You got it?" He looked at me as if to say, "I'm counting on you." I hated being the oldest.

I saw him to the door. There was nothing more I could do for her, except for giving her xylocaine and taking away the crackers by her bed, so I did. I phoned the Glendalls to let them know I was on the way over. I called the Glendalls the Oddballs. Because they just were. The kids ran around naked, the mother threw their trash, including her used sanitary napkins, into the fireplace, and they had a diabetic poodle that liked to hump my leg. Mr. Glendall was a teacher at the high school. He was small, maybe only five feet tall, and thin, not pudgy like the other dads on our street. His wife was closer to six feet tall, and really fat. I tried not to think about how they had sex.

Their kids were already in bed. Tim and Beth were skinny children. I didn't know how one person in the house could be so fat, and everyone else be so skinny. When Mr. and Mrs. Glendall left, I started to rummage through their stuff. I don't know why, really, other than to try to find out why they were so weird.

I began in the rolltop desk, where I had found some stamps and some money last time. This time I found some bills and the annual town report. I knew the town report contained information about property values—my father checked it every year to see that we were being taxed properly. I wanted to find out more about kids at school, kids like Sue Paseka.

In junior high, it's not uncommon to hear about someone months before finally meeting that person, as if their legend precedes them. Like with Sue Paseka. When I began seventh grade, I was bombarded with graffiti like: "KISS LIVE," with the *s*'s in *kiss* etched in smudged pencil like a stubby pair of thunderbolts, usually next to a similarly smudged, stylized rendition of an erect penis, perfectly round testicles in tow. More complete phrases like "Bill Noeth is a pud" or the ones I saw scrawled everywhere about Sue, appeared around the school with less frequency but with considerably more venom.

I was fascinated by the sheer volume of graffiti devoted to Sue Paseka, certain that she was one of those loudmouthed girls who wore a drippy, long corduroy jacket and smoked cigarettes outside under the overhang. "Sue Paseka gives good head" appeared on lockers, on the chair-desks, on the backs of school bus seats—I found myself reciting *Sue Paseka*

Sue Paseka, Paseka Sue Paseka Sue over and over on my way home from school. I loved how *Sue Paseka* rolled fast off my tongue, the outright badness of her name, as if this mantra had somehow replaced all other swear words.

Then one day I was introduced to her by my friend Paula. "Regina, this is Sue. Sue, this is Regina."

"Sue, as in Sue Paseka?" I joked, assuming it was everyone's joke.

"Yeah. How did you know?" She seemed annoyed, as if I was the fifth person that day to guess her last name.

"Uh. I dunno. I guess Paula talked about you before." The funny thing was, she didn't look like *my* Sue Paseka. She was tall, with incredibly good posture, perfect hair, and crisp clothes—a new Fair Isle sweater and designer jeans. She did have a huge head, so I figured the giving-good-head part wasn't a bad thing. It just meant she was smart.

I wondered if she had seen any of the graffiti. How could she not know about it? "Nice to meet you," I said. I resorted to the standard line for awkward situations—"Got to get to class"—and walked away, stiff with embarrassment. I decided having horrible graffiti written about you was a sign of popularity.

I opened the town report, found the listing for the Pasekas' house, and compared it with the value of ours. I looked up a few other neighbors, then flipped to the back of the book. Here I found a section with names and addresses of teachers. I looked up Ms. Tryon.

I went to the T's and inhaled: Maida S. Tryon, M.Ed., University of Michigan. *Michigan,* I thought. *Of course.* I had no idea what it meant to go to school in Michigan, but somehow this information fit nicely into the imaginary file I kept on her. I would need to find out more. I wrote down her address and phone number and stuck the town report back into the rolltop.

I went to Kmart to buy a hooded sweatshirt. I fished around through the sporting goods section and found one that didn't have the word *MacGregor* on it or the fishnet insulation on the inside. I went to the dressing room to try it on in front of a mirror.

"You can't go in there," a clerk said. "This is the *women's* dressing room."

"But I'm a girl," I said back. She knew I was about to cry and let me in the dressing room without an argument. I tried on the sweatshirt, and cried. I hated Kmart.

In my room there's something I like to stare at. It's a see-through decal of a troll, and it says, "Made in Trollhattan. By Trolls." When we first moved into our house, I didn't get the pun. And then one day I got it. And then I didn't get why it was funny enough to remain on the windowpane. But as much as the troll decal seemed really stupid, I never bothered to peel it off. I liked to lie on my bed and think about who lived there before me, and wonder if they stared at the troll decal the same way I did, and what good-enough reason they found for it to remain.

Other times I would listen to music late at night with the radio under my pillow. I would spin the radio knob to find a favorite song, wait for the song to end, then spin the dial again and again, until I became either too bored or too tired to continue. Most of the songs were stupid—a boy could not go on without his girlfriend, a girl would be angry at her boyfriend, or everyone would call each other "babe." Late at night, when kids my age should already be asleep, I would listen to "The Low Spark of High-Heeled Boys" and knew that this was a song that didn't get played during the day for a reason. I thought of some boys I knew and how it would be okay with me if they wore high heels.

But lately all the words carried more meaning—I don't know what exactly, just more. I became one of the people in the song, and Ms. Tryon would be the other. I would become the distraught one, working my way back to her, holding on, with one less toothbrush hanging in the stand. Ms. Tryon would reassure me that love would keep us together, or that we would somehow grab some afternoon delight.

I spent hours in my room this way—staring at the troll decal, listening to the radio, thinking of her, and not completing my homework. These songs became strung together in my mind and formed an entire soundtrack for our strained relationship. I would wake to the alarm-clock radio and start the day's mock dialogue between us with whatever song was playing. I made a game of staying in bed as long as I could before making a mad scramble to shower, grab my books, and run to the bus stop with wet hair and a banana or a doughnut for breakfast.

On Saturday morning I called. Just to see if she was home. I fished for the piece of paper with her number on it and dialed. Three rings and then, "Hello?"

Only it was a guy. I paused. "Hello?" he said again.

"Uh, hello," I fumbled. "Is Maida there?" I was saying her name out loud. Please be Ms. Tryon, I thought.

"Yes. Just a minute. Who's calling?"

I froze. Just who would be calling her on a Saturday morning? My mind drew a blank. "Oh, I'm sorry, I think I have the wrong number," I said, and hung up the phone before I could catch my own faulty logic. God, was I stupid.

So, there was a *man* involved. A boyfriend or husband. Who else would be there so early on a Saturday? And why didn't she answer the phone first? Maybe she was in the bathroom. Or doing laundry in the basement. These ideas pleased and surprised me, as I had never before considered teachers—especially Ms. Tryon—as humans having either physiological functions, dirty laundry, or basements.

I waited until later in the day, when I would be alone in the house, and called again.

"Hello?" This time it was a woman. I kept quiet.

"Hello?" she said again, impatiently.

It was her. She had the same sultry voice at home on a Saturday as she had in class Monday through Friday. There was music playing in the background. I wanted to hang up, but I wanted to know what song was playing first. I couldn't recognize it.

"Hello?" she said one more time. I hung up. My stomach had fallen the way it did on elevators. I could feel my face getting hot. I was doing something evil, and I was loving it—her voice, the annoyed quality to

it, the music in the background—what was she doing that I had interrupted?

I pictured her in her house on a Saturday—her hair in a kerchief,
spider plants and their babies dripping off the windows, and a Beatles
record warbling in the background, while she dusted or vacuumed and
tried to forget about her boyfriend/husband. Her grocery bags sat un-
packed on the kitchen table—fresh scallions and celery and aromatic
French bread wedged upright between L'eggs panty hose containers.
The phone would ring, and she would hear it above the shrillness of
her life—the cranky children, the vacuum cleaner, or the teapot whistle.
She would abandon everything and forget all that pulled at her to answer
my frantic, empty call—one with no demands, expectations, or dead-
lines—just space and time and longing. My calls would be the well-
deserved break from her day's routine and would add an element of
intrigue and curiosity to her regimented life. I vowed to call again later,
to hear what she sounded like after a long, chore-filled day.

School had become unbearable. Junior high was an obstacle course of
rude boys, or of girls with hair, or both. Boys snapped the bras of girls
who annoyed them—it was their way of owning a section of hallway.
Finding a bathroom between classes that wasn't filled with Sue Pasekas
feathering back their hair was impossible. I longed to snap their bras,
just to navigate my way to a stall.

I spent study hall in art class working on my projects with other girls,
to avoid the boys flicking footballs made from wadded paper triangles.
My latest project was a copper foil of a mouse with an umbrella in a
rowboat. I would trace the outline of the mouse with a burnisher, flip
the foil, and trace the inside of the picture on the reverse. By the end
of the class, the copper would stiffen from its limp foil beginnings—I
liked how it hardened so quickly without very much effort. Other girls
chose pastels and worked on their drawings of flowers from seed cata-
logs, always smudging and erasing, smudging and erasing. Weeks would
go by, and it seemed like their pastel flowered drawings were the same
as when they started. The other girls seemed delighted with their "progress" and saw nothing wrong with the endless erasing and smudges. I

wondered why I noticed what they couldn't and what was making me unlike them.

But everything made me think of Ms. Tryon, especially while working on art projects. I would try to think of other things, things where there was no place for her to invade my thoughts, like church or mowing the lawn, but no matter what I thought about, Ms. Tryon found a way to enter.

I kept calling and hanging up. I was accumulating the range of emotion in her "hellos" by calling at different times of the day—even on holidays or school vacations. Sometimes the boyfriend/husband would answer. I became fascinated with him, too, and tried to fit a face to his voice by refining one of his features, like a police sketch artist, with each new hello.

I had a French test. I hadn't studied for it. Before I left for school, my mother called me into her room. "Gina, get my beads," she said, motioning to her night table. "My beads." Her breathing was shallow.

I got the beads and put them in her hands. Her wastebasket was filled with wads of surgical tape and gauze pads soaked with a pus that looked like warm marmalade. She was looking up at the ceiling, not at me.

"Say the Beatitudes." I didn't. I was hoping she wouldn't recall what she just said, and that I could leave. "Say them," she said, looking away from the ceiling and directly at me. Drool had dried and crusted on the corners of her mouth. She started for me: "Blessed are the . . ."

"Blessed are the poor in spirit," I filled in the blank, "for they shall inherit the earth." My mother nodded, mouthed along with the words, and closed her eyes.

"More," she said. "Blessed . . ."

I didn't know any others, so I just repeated the one I knew. "Blessed are the poor in spirit, for they shall inherit the earth." She smiled. My throat got tight. She was totally out of it.

I thought of the French test. "Ma, I want to stay home today. To take care of you. You don't look too good."

She shook her head. I looked around the room for her New Testament but couldn't find it.

"We can say the Rosary together." She shook her head again and grabbed me by the shoulder.

"I have cancer," she whispered. "Don't tell the children." But I *was* one of the children.

"Please Ma," I begged. She shooed me away with her hand and the beads. I could have stayed home—she wouldn't have noticed—but I went to school instead, sick with myself and the image of her just lying there.

I got an F on the test. I was done but couldn't remember whether a word had an *accent grave* or an *accent aigu* over it, and I looked over at Jason's test to see which way the accent mark went. Ms. Tryon saw me and grabbed my test. All I could say was, "But—"

"That's called cheating," she said. I left class vowing to hate her. *That bitch,* I thought. I wasn't cheating—I had already finished and was just checking an accent mark. Ms. Tryon was going to be sorry she had ever caught me cheating in the first place.

I called even more often now—sometimes two or three times a day. I knew what I was doing was wrong—and sick—so I didn't tell anybody. But I couldn't stop. Every time I was alone at home, or baby-sitting, or at my grandmother's house, I would call her and hang up. A few times I meant to dial other numbers but called Ms. Tryon's by mistake, almost saying "hello" back and giving it all away for good.

On the weekends after chemotherapy treatments, we would stay at my grandmother's house in Boston. My mother would throw on a bathrobe and drive us to the train station. The train would take us within five minutes of her house—the only one on the block that didn't have aluminum siding.

I loved visiting my grandmother, mostly because I felt like there was a grown-up who was paying attention. My sisters would head to the basement to find the Monopoly set. I would start in the kitchen, drinking whole milk or regular Coke and eating English muffins with real butter. My grandfather stayed upstairs in bed, just like my mother.

I liked to poke around in my grandfather's office. I was always poking around, I guess, whether it was at the Glendalls or in his office, flipping through medical journals or textbooks. I was convinced there was something large that adults weren't telling kids my age—about sex or love or about how things pretty much never changed despite money, love, accidents, or winning the lottery. Adults were complicit on these points, the way they were with Santa Claus, but to tell us the finite truth so young would be to ruin everything. Hope was a number line, I thought, only the end points were open, not solid.

I would spend hours with my grandfather's medical books. One particular volume on anatomy and physiology had a section on genital deformities, with color plates of hyperextended clitorises, undescended testicles, and pseudohermaphrodites. I tried to decipher the medical language, to see if I fit into one of these categories, and squinted at these photos of near-boys and -girls, trying to make them look like me. I read beyond this section and the color plates became even more grotesque, with vaginal and penile lesions and postmortems of faces disfigured by syphilis. I thought of the number line again, and the elusive medical book that would expand its end points to include me. As much as I read, though, I thought I would never find the book with me in it.

When I visited my grandmother, I always brought all my money with me. I would take the trolley to Harvard Square and buy records—sometimes nine or ten at a time—because I could spend this kind of money visiting my grandmother and not get yelled at. I had heard from kids at school that leaning up against the front of the Coop with one leg up against the wall meant that you wanted to buy pot, and that within minutes you would be approached by a drug dealer. After I bought my records, I went outside and leaned against the wall for fifteen minutes. No one offered me anything. I saw lots of freaks.

Ms. Tryon handed back the French tests. As she gave me mine, she said "So close, and yet so far. Right, Regina?" At first I thought she was talking about the hang-up calls. She had figured out it was me. I was so close to her and yet so far away. And then I looked at the test. At the top there was a large F written in heavy, red Magic Marker. Next to it and much smaller was "103%." I had gotten every question right, even the extra-credit ones. Why had she bothered to check my answers if I was going to get an F anyway? She was playing her own game with me, which I had yet to decipher.

On my way home from school that day, I practiced how to tell my mother I got an F. But when I got to the house, I saw an ambulance pulling away from our driveway. Lazy, deliberate lights and no siren. I went inside and waited for someone to tell me she was dead. A neighbor came over and told us to stay in her house until my dad got back from the hospital. No one looked us in the eye—I knew she was dead but didn't want to ask to know for sure.

My father left work early, went directly to the hospital, and arrived home a few hours later. She wasn't dead, because he didn't say anything to us. I got the elevator feeling in my stomach again but knew it would get worse if I talked to him about her.

It was late afternoon. Everything was awkward. I went outside, fig- uring the geographical and physical distance between me and my father should somehow match. I saw some baby toads peeping through the neighbors' freshly cut grass. I picked one up and brought it out back. Mary, one of the neighborhood kids, came around back to see what I was up to. "Do you want to play badminton?" I asked.

"Sure," she said, picking up one of the racquets leaning against the garage. "Got a birdie?"

"Oh, I think the last one we had got chewed up by the lawnmower," I said. I still had the toad in my hand. I pretended to look for a birdie. "Here," I said, bouncing the toad in my hand. "We can use this."

Mary laughed. "No way." But it was too late, I had already placed the toad in front of the racquet and *ping*ed it over to her. Mary shrieked and raised her racquet in self-defense, more afraid of the toad plopping on her than of swatting it back at me. We rallied the toad back and forth a few times, unable to contain our laughter. I was being mean to some- thing, my mother was tucked away in a hospital, and my father was too steeped in the day's drama to even notice. Even the toad didn't seem to mind. But the idiocy of this newfound toy wore off quickly. I let it hop away into the taller grass and looked around for a real birdie.

*   *   *

That night I found the town report again at the Glendalls and wrote down the phone numbers of all the other teachers I had. I was not a pervert, I told myself, and began calling the new numbers that night, telling myself it wasn't about Ms. Tryon at all. I hated her now.

The "hellos" with these new teachers grew more frantic over time, just as Ms. Tryon's had become. The composite sketches of homes and families grew larger and more elaborate. Sometimes small children would answer, but I never used any of these unexpected moments to find a reason to stop. Instead, the more surprised I became by sounds of pots and pans, of loud rock music or teenage boys, or of dogs barking in the background, the more necessary it became for me to find out everything about each of them. It wasn't about her after all. I was not a pervert. *Not a pervert, not a pervert.* This thought replaced the Sue Paseka jingle I had invented earlier, and I invoked it with equal urgency.

My mother was out of the hospital a few days later. I came home from school one day to find her gone and thought it had happened again. I called Ms. Tryon and hung up as usual. Then my dad came in the door.

"Get in the car," he said. "We're going to school."

I got in the car. Both my parents were quiet the whole way. My mother had summoned the strength to put on clothes, shoes, and makeup. We went into the principal's office. I had no idea why we were there. I thought maybe they had realized I was smart and were asking me if I wanted to skip a grade.

The principal's name was Clifford A. Card. He was tall with hunched shoulders, like Lurch from *The Addams Family.* I never understood why he used "Clifford A. Card," and not just "Clifford Card." Probably to distinguish himself from all those other tall, hunched-over Clifford Cards in our town, I thought.

He spoke for a few minutes in sentences that didn't say very much, like a senator on *Face the Nation.* Then he leaned over and asked, "Regina, are you giving your teachers crank calls?"

"No," I said quickly. I could feel my face getting hot. I couldn't look at him or my parents. They were just sitting there, arms folded, not saying anything.

"Well, I have reason to believe that you did. All of your teachers are getting crank calls, and you are the only student in the school with this set of teachers."

"No, I'm not." I had no idea if this was true.

"Who else is in all your classes?"

I thought quick. "Lars Jorrens," I answered. He was one of the boys I thought would look okay in high heels.

"But the thing is, Lars wouldn't do something like that."

I surprised myself by agreeing with Mr. Card. "Maybe somebody doesn't like me and is doing this so you'll think that it's me," I said.

"Like who?"

"I don't know. Someone."

"Do you have any friends?" he asked. This question took me by surprise.

"Yes." I didn't name any, in case he was going to check with them, and because I didn't have that many anyway.

"Well, perhaps I can call each and every one of your friends into my office and see what they know about you and these phone calls." This tactic was the scariest of all. None of my friends had any idea what I was doing, but they would find out if Mr. Card had his way. He knew I was behind the calls and was going to humiliate me one way or another, with or without a confession. He continued: "This kind of harassment is a crime, and I will find out who's behind it, even if I have to go to the police."

I asked rhetorically, "But why would I do this? It would have to be a pretty sick person to make a bunch of phone calls to teachers all the time."

Mr. Card was silent for a moment and then looked straight at my parents and said, "Well, as the good Lord said, 'From the mouths of babes comes the truth.'" My mother closed her eyes and nodded *Amen* in silent agreement. Mr. Card was good at this—he had her pegged for a Jesus freak in only one meeting. That meant he had me figured out, too. I stayed firm in my denial of the phone calls, and we went home, quiet the whole way in the car. I couldn't stop now, I thought, or he'll know for sure it's me.

*   *   *

It wasn't long before I got caught. At Mr. Card's insistence, my dad requested from the phone company copies of all of our phone bills for the past year. Only one call to Ms. Tryon in the year of hang-ups to six different teachers appeared on the bill. I guess I was hanging up before it registered with the phone company.

All my mother could say was, "Why, Regina? Why?"

"I don't know why, Ma." This answer wasn't enough. "It won't happen anymore. I promise. Please don't tell anyone. Please don't tell Grandma." I don't know why I added my grandmother to all this mess.

"I won't," she said. I was surprised by her allegiance on this point. "We—you—need to tell Mr. Card it was you. Tomorrow morning. I'll call him to let him know you have something to tell him." This was the most coherent she had been in over a year. I began preparing my confession in my head.

The next day I walked into his office and he shut the door. "Well?" he said, hoping to make it quick.

"Well," I mimicked, then paused for a minute. My heart was in my throat. "It was me. I made the phone calls. No one else, just me."

I was expecting a lecture and punishment, with more quotes from the Bible. Instead, Mr. Card said, "It's because your mother has cancer, isn't it?" Cancer. I couldn't believe he knew this about me, too.

I thought about it. Conflicting emotions surged up from my stomach and into my throat. I wanted to throw up, or cry, or yell at everyone, including my mother. I wanted to tell him—anybody—all of it: how Ms. Tryon looked like Jesus, the graffiti about Sue Paseka, the clerk at Kmart, and how I understood "The Low Spark of High-Heeled Boys"; how boys snapped the girls' bras in the hallway and always got away with it; the toad—that poor, poor toad; the pastel drawings that never got finished, the Beatitudes and the F on the French test; the hyperextended clitorises and my imaginary number line; how I hated the name Gina, how my sister called me Greg and how I let her; and the ambulances that pulled slow out of the driveway. I wanted to tell him everything, but the words came up all at the same time and fought with each other to be the first ones out. I just slumped over shaking, crying so hard that no sound came out.

*　　*　　*

"Well, isn't it?" he asked again. *What a bastard,* I thought. "It's because she has cancer, isn't it?"

I stopped crying long enough to answer. I said yes.

The Beginning of My Worthlessness

Justin Chin

My guardian, Aunt Jessie, or Jamesy as we called her, was the self-appointed disciplinary mistress of Sunday school, the one to whom errant children were sent to be punished for misbehaving in the house of the Lord. The mere mention of her name was enough to send some of the younger children into tears. She was a confirmed spinster, and the only man I ever remember her going out with was Stephan, a dull idiot with a Beatles moptop and Englebert Humperdinck sideburns, who came to pick her up on his scooter to take her to choir practice every Wednesday evening. But soon he faded into the woodwork and Jamesy filled her evenings with crafts.

We were living in the postmacramé age, and découpage was the in thing. Every night she would select pictures with inspirational verses that she clipped out of *Moody's Christian Monthly* and glue them to pieces of plywood. The wood was painted black, the plaques were then varnished, the edges were filed into patterns, and finally a small hook was jammed on the top of the picture. The découpages didn't sell too well at church fund-raisers, so she tried her hand at cake making, learning how from a class at the local community center. Jamesy's cakes were a hit. She made sponge cakes topped with a ring of mice created out of tinned pear halves, maraschino cherries, and peach slices. The mice would sit on a layer of cream, Tupperwares of which would take up whole shelves in the fridge. If her cakes did not rise or if they turned out wrong, she would be in a foul mood and the kids would all be on guard, waiting to be scolded for even the slightest offense, harsh words to send us to bed. I was always told that Jamesy had a thyroid problem, which accounted for her irritability. There was a scar across her neck, which she once showed me, where the doctors cut in to dig out the oversecreting gland.

Jamesy scared the multiplication table into me in Primary Two (second grade), months before it was even taught in school. She made me recite the times tables from two all the way up to twelve while the bamboo cane hovered over me, ready to rain stinging blows on my arms, legs, back, and buttocks if I should falter or hesitate. I learned spelling and vocabulary, synonyms and antonyms, similes and grammar with the threat of being caned. She told everyone that I was the lazy one and I had to be pushed.

Every Sunday morning we were roused out of bed at seven o'clock. A breakfast of milk and bread or cake was chugged down, before we were made to go practice our music. This was Singapore in the eighties, a country racked with overanxious parents who demanded that their children excel at both academics and music, and we all had to take up violin or piano lessons. Sunday morning was the worst time of my week. Each of us would take one room, in which we were expected to practice. Being the youngest, I would always end up in Jamesy's room, practicing my violin while she prepared for church. Occasionally, she would look away from makeup, hair curlers, and blow drying to scold me for my useless, worthless talent. No one cared that my brother played two scales, maybe an arpeggio, before ending up on my grandmother's bed to read the sports section of the *Sunday Straits Times*. I was horribly tone-deaf, and I could never really tell if I was playing the right notes. All I tried to do was put my fingers where I was told they should be and hope it was right.

I was reasonably good at faking it, but when my fingering faltered, Jamesy snapped, "Play properly." I tried, but I was scared and made more mistakes. "You need to practice more," she yelled. I made another mistake, a caterwaul issuing from the bow pulled across those four strings. "That's not the right fingering," she screamed at me, crossing the room and cracking my knuckles with the edge of the metal ruler that she had nicked from her office. My fingers bled and I started crying, which made her angrier. "You just never practice, all week. What have you been doing?" she demanded. "Did you practice?"

"Yes," I whimpered. She returned to her makeup mirror and let me go wash the blood off my knuckles and dab some disinfectant on them; my cousin Karen had to tune my violin because the blow had knocked it out of tune.

If Sunday mornings were terrible, Saturdays were no better. Roused out of bed at an equally early hour, we were made to do housework. We didn't mind doing our share of chores, but Jamesy's idea of housework went beyond that. Every week, she made my brother and me get down on our hands and knees and scour the driveway with coconut-husk brushes and Vim. She would occasionally come by to check on us. If she saw any discoloration from the even gray she expected the driveway to be, she would blow her top. Her greatest vexation was the small black stains, no bigger than fat periods, left by sap from the fruits and flowers of the sea-almond trees that lined our cul-de-sac. If these were not properly scrubbed off, she would threaten a caning, ranting about how lazy, useless, and good-for-nothing we were. After the driveway, we were to wash and wax her car to her satisfaction.

Jamesy had this notion that we needed to be properly nourished, which meant we had to finish all the meat and vegetables that were on our plates. She hated to see "good food go to waste." Apparently, there were all these starving belly-bloated people in India who would gladly eat our French beans, steamed okra, and liver if they were given half a chance. My brother and I had a barter system: He would eat my French beans and I would eat his beef liver. My brother also developed a system of hiding food under his plate. We sometimes piled on a huge mound of rice to hide the food we didn't like. It was okay to throw out plain rice, but all meat and vegetables had to be eaten.

One evening, we had boiled carrots in a horrid cabbage stew. There was something about the taste and the consistency of those boiled carrots; I just could not keep them down.

"Can I not eat the carrots?" I asked hopefully.

"You better finish it," Jamesy snapped. The rest of the table was silent. My brother, cousins and grandmother ate in silence; they knew what was about to happen.

"I don't like them," I said, again hoping for some reprieve.

"Sharon, go get the cane," Jamesy ordered. My cousin Sharon hesitated. "Didn't you hear me?" Jamesy's voice became a loud screech. Sharon reluctantly went to fetch the bamboo cane.

"You better eat your carrots!" Jamesy repeated to me. I tried to eat them by dulling the taste with some rice and meat; with the cane hovering, I dutifully put spoonful after spoonful of boiled carrot into my mouth. Then I did the unthinkable. I vomited. A rush of chewed-up mucus-covered carrot mush spewed out of my mouth onto my dinner plate, trailing to the floor.

Jamesy exploded. With her left hand she grabbed me and pulled me off my stool, and with her right she swatted me repeatedly with the bamboo cane. She dumped me back on the stool, then took the spoon, scooped up some spewed carrots from my plate, and held the spoon to my face.

"Open your mouth," she screamed. Through heaving sobs, I tried but just couldn't. "Open your mouth, and this time, you better eat it." She swatted at me again but missed, hitting the metal legs of the stool with a loud clang.

I opened my mouth and swallowed the spoonful of slimy, bubble-coated carrot mush. Jamesy then scraped what she could off the floor and I ate that too. The rest of the table was quiet. We finished our meal in silence.

My cousins Sharon and Karen later told me that I had it easy. Before I came to live with Jamesy, they were forced to eat a whole can of Spam each, and again, anything vomited up was shoved back down their gullet.

Jamesy was instinctively good at violence. She'd beat us and then go to her prayer meetings and Bible studies. Soon I realized that I was the only one getting beaten. All the other children had gotten older and were spared the rod if not the harsh tongue lashings, but the stinging swats of the cane, the belt, and the back scratchers were reserved for me until the final days of my thirteenth year.

*   *   *

At the start of every school year I had to get a set of passport-sized photos taken. These were used for bus passes, library cards, report cards, health reports, and other documents. I would comb my hair, put on my school uniform, and set off to the Cathay studio, which was run by four old men who always seemed to be in their pajama trousers and white undershirts. The equipment in the studio was as old as the proprietors. The photographer would put me on the stool and make me hold up a stick on which the serial numbers were composed out of wood chips, then he would putter around to adjust the golden umbrellas that were strategically placed to reflect light. The old, old camera was huge, on a trolley and covered with a black cloth—the kind you see in movies of the thirties. The old man would crawl under the cloth and try to adjust his equipment. Usually I was made to sit at a slight tilt to match the tilt in the camera. Then, with a final admonition to hold still, there was a massive supernova and the pictures for the year were taken.

All this has given me a record of myself growing older in bits, year by year in the same pose, same frame, and a similar white shirt, not unlike the evolutionary table found in biology textbooks. Looking at the photos of myself at thirteen, I am amazed at how very young I look. Baby fat, chubby cheeks, doleful eyes, crooked teeth—braces would come the next year. Sure, puberty had hit, my voice had changed, and I was finally granted divine reason to quit the Sunday school junior choir. Small scraps of hair had started to peek out of my pubic region and under my arms. But in the photo I look ten. The only giveaway is the school uniform—I'm wearing a school badge instead of a patch.

I was in Secondary One (seventh grade). It was to signify a Great Change in my life. "You will no longer be spoon-fed! You are no longer children, you are all young adults and you will conduct yourselves as such!" boomed principal Ernest Lau over the P.A. of the auditorium on Orientation Day. Secondary school was difficult: a new series of subjects, a new environment, new expectations. I did not feel any older or more mature even though I was constantly told I was.

One day, on the bus to shop class, this ugly fuck of a man sat behind me and put his foot in the crack of my seat. He was skinny, with a patchy, pencil-thin mustache that besotted his oily face. I ignored him for most of the trip. I did notice that he changed buses when I did, but this time he sat beside me. He tried a little small talk, but then he

suddenly and very nervously put his hand on my crotch. It never occurred to me to tell him not to. I'm not sure if I agreed to it or not, but
he managed to get me to follow him to a nearby rest room at another
secondary school "to play." In the bathroom stall, lit by two scant rows
of fluorescent lights, half of them burnt-out or flickering, he tried to kiss
me, but I was too nauseated to do that. He sucked my nipples and
played with my cock. I had no idea what to do. He then tried to get
me to suck his. Somehow I knew this was expected of me, but I just
could not put his ugly, foul-smelling penis into my mouth. When he
forced it in I gagged so hard I started vomiting. Undaunted, he tried to
put his cock in my ass. Thankfully, he came prematurely. He pulled up
his trousers and left me in the toilet stall confused, frightened, crying,
and praying to God for forgiveness of my horrible sin. I spent a good
deal of time locked in the stall, trying to clean up, trying to wipe the
smell of that act off with wet toilet paper, but I was doused in the stench
of that man and what he had done.

This incident should have soured me on men, but it only made me
more confused and needful. One day later, something accidental happened that would change my life. I discovered that at a urinal I could
actually see someone else's penis. I was ecstatic and fearful, but I wanted
more. One day, at a local shopping mall, as I was trying to sneak a peek
at penises in the rest rooms, a man at the urinal actually turned to me
and started playing with himself. He flashed me a gold-toothed smirk
and motioned for me to come over. Shocked, I zipped up and ran
out, but the seeds had been laid. The whole world of rest-room sex had
opened itself up to me.

Soon I was spending a great deal of time hanging out in shopping
malls and cruising the rest rooms for sexual encounters. My rest-room
exploits started to be a great burden on my mind. The better part of
the year was spent making deals with God, asking for a sign, then ignoring and rationalizing everything I perceived to be a sign, praying for
forgiveness, and being obsessed with raging hormones and a seemingly
endless supply of dicks. I believed that it was all part of a test by God
to see if I was a sinner. I was.

I had known before that something was up, and that I was attracted
to men, but this toilet thing was a whole new realm of sin and Satan, a

new level that I had never before imagined. The following years were spent praying for forgiveness and trying to purge my homosexuality through prayer and Bible study. While my classmates wondered what sex was like, content to masturbate over pinups, I was out there having my cock sucked and my ass fucked. These were grown men I was tricking with. Some were nice, grateful for a young boy to have their way with. Some were harsh and mean. There were a few nasty encounters, brutal and painful experiences, near-rapes, but through it all, I never thought that I had the ability to say no.

I was scared about what I was doing, scared of God's judgment and of being caught in all those rest rooms and parks, but I really did enjoy those sexual encounters. That feeling of doing it to them and them doing the same for me was just too damn good.

This is what I knew of homosexuality: That it was a sin. That gay men wanted to have their penises cut off. That they all wanted sex-change operations. That the transvestites on Bugis Street and Rochor Canal were bad people. That poor transvestites who could not afford the sex change and hormones had crumpled-up newspapers for tits and hung out in dark parking lots at night whoring. That you had to be effeminate. That it was to be made fun of. That the boys in the Drama Club were. That they could never have children. That in a gay couple, one would play the woman and the other the man. That it meant a life of suffering, loneliness, fear, secrecy, shame.

This was the year I realized I was helpless, different, wholly alone and defenseless. This was the beginning of my worthlessness. It was always pointed out to me that I wasn't good enough and that there was always someone somewhere doing better, and that no matter what I did, I could still have done better.

The adults in my life held my brother up as an example for me to emulate. He excelled in mathematics and the sciences and had no problems with his second language, even taking on a third. He got good grades and was always in the top classes. He competed in chess tournaments on the state level. He played football for the school. I got how-to-play-chess books for my birthday, in the hopes that I'd learn to use my brain. I was content to whip out the drawing block and paint, but this was frowned upon. Every time I was caught laying out newspaper for an art project, I was chided and lectured about how I was wasting my time, better I should go and study or play football. Reading was also frowned upon. I enjoyed having my storybooks: I loved the fantasy worlds of Enid Blyton and progressed from Nancy Drew mysteries to Agatha Christie. I thought Hercule Poirot was so cool. But these were not school-related, and so more scoldings followed. And if I spent too much time on my English-literature work, I was admonished for wasting time that should have been spent on "more important subjects."

Dad was a doctor and Mom was a nurse. It was expected that my brother and I would end up in the medical profession. I faked an interest in biology and zoology. I told everyone I was going to be a veterinarian. I was always referred to as the Artistic One, but what good was that? An artistic bent should lead to a career in architecture. "You like art, why don't you consider architecture?" my mother said repeatedly at dinner, and Dad nodded.

It wasn't just the adults in my life, it was the whole damn nation. Everyone was defined by academic achievements. So much emphasis was placed on education, and I was a royal fuckup. At certain points, I'm sure my parents thought that I was the most worthless thing that had ever happened to them. They couldn't brag to relatives and friends about my grades. I was just not trying hard enough, I kept hearing.

While my brother's later failures in school had to do with bad choices, girlfriend problems, and other distractions, mine had to do with myself. While my parents saw glimmers of hope radiating from my brother, they saw in me a challenge to make something of my inadequacy. My father, who was the silent sort, was seething in anger and frustration under his quiet exterior.

My brother was also constantly told that he was good-looking, and he embraced the compliment wholeheartedly. He filled photo album after photo album with snapshots of himself. I had no interest in filling a single one. By no fault of his, my brother had helped to make me feel stupid, ugly, and worthless.

In school, I was nobody. I wasn't smart enough to be one of the smart kids, not artsy enough to be one of the talented kids who sang and danced at the annual Drama Club productions, not rebellious enough to be one of the bad kids, not hip enough to be one of the cool kids. I was beige, a dull gray, sitting behind a desk passing each day in no exceptional way. Everyone around me seemed to be in school plays and national choirs, competing in sports competitions, going on fabulous holidays, and plotting brilliant careers. I had friends, but for some reason my friends and I never got to those scrappy boyish adventures everyone else seemed to get up to. All I had was a secret that I dared not share with anyone.

At home, the beatings and canings had stopped, only to be replaced with shouting. Loud arguments between my grandmother, my cousin Karen, and Jamesy were as common as the beetles that flew into the bug zapper. Every day there were bursts of angry words that engulfed the house and reverberated through all its rooms. Arguments would last for hours. I learned to be as small and as inconsequential as possible to avoid all the shouting.

I pretended to be a snail. I wanted to curl up into a small ball and not move in a place where no one could see me. I dreamed of being abandoned on a deserted island. I can't remember much detail about that time except for an endless stream of school and homework. It was also the last few months that we had to tolerate Jamesy. Years before she had applied to emigrate to Australia, and now she was actually going to go. I was so incredibly happy when Karen told me, I just couldn't believe it really was happening.

Home without Jamesy was so much more bearable, it seemed like an answer to my prayers. It seemed that some semblance of life had crept back into the house. My grandmother tried to maintain some of Jamesy's discipline, but the most she ever achieved was an annoying nagging. I stayed away from home even more, hanging out at shopping malls, the public swimming pool, or the library, pursuing my queerness with equal parts apprehension and zeal.

For a long time, I was angry with my mother because she chose to believe her sister over me, never even flinching at my tales of Jamesy's terrorizing and cruelty. "Oh, never mind, discipline is good for you. She loves you and this is just the way she shows it," she said. How we were disciplined in our family was a matter of pride; the adults bragged about it at family dinners and at church. My cousins Kevin and Sylvia endured canings on their tongue when caught telling a lie. And when these canings or forced eating of vomit were brought up at social gatherings, the adults laughed about it, proud of their child-rearing skills, and the kids were expected to laugh along, grateful that we, unlike half the brats at church, were disciplined.

My mother refused to fault her sister for anything. She really did believe that Jamesy did what she did for our benefit and that by any means necessary I would excel in academics and become a neurosurgeon. I blamed myself. I was the *hum-bau,* the crybaby, the overly sensitive one. Something was seriously wrong with me; I was wholly ungrateful and selfish not to appreciate my upbringing. After all, didn't Jamesy teach me how to ride a bicycle one Sunday family outing at Marine Parade Parkway? Didn't she take me to go see the new Spiderman movie at the Capitol after school one day?

I keep those childhood I.D. photos in my desk, and look at them from time to time, and I'm amazed at what that young face staring back at me endured. I tell myself it wasn't all that bad and that many children all around the world have had it much worse—it's not like I was starving and chained to a sewing machine to make discount fashions, or living in a war-torn country having my limbs blasted off by land mines. Sometimes I try to think about what it would be like if it had all somehow been different, but I just can't seem to come up with a vision or a fantasy of what that would have been like.

This is what I now know of homosexuality: That it is okay. That it is a sin if done wrong. That it is a better sin if done just right. That the boys who join the Drama Club now are still gay, and the ones before them are doing all right for themselves. That it means a life of fear, not for being found out, but for being bashed and killed. That it means a life of courage, of struggle, of real family. That it continually tests what I know of love. That it gave me back some semblance of myself. And that it brought about the end of my worthlessness.

 **Train**

Gabrielle Glancy

Arthur Ernst picked at the gums between his teeth until they bled, then sucked the blood, which, when someone finally asked him about it, he said he liked the taste of. He had a swastika decal pasted on his notebook. You would think, my being Jewish, this would have turned me off to him. But in fact, I asked to be his campaign manager in seventh grade when he ran for class president. My job involved making posters with stars and stripes on them that said EARNEST ERNST: HE'S YOUR MAN! I thought since he had sent me a valentine—his name signed on the back of a red store-bought paper heart—he liked me. I found out later his mother had made him send them to all the girls in the class.

Arthur Ernst's mother was German or Swiss and seemed older than all the other mothers. She had an accent and looked like the baroness whom the father in *The Sound of Music* leaves for Julie Andrews—tight blond bun, high cheekbones. She was clearly from a different world. And it made Arthur different too. His father looked exactly like his mother only in male form, like the German incarnation of Dr. Strangelove, with blond, thinning hair. The skin over his jaw shined uncannily and seemed to pull just a little too tight.

So since Arthur had sent me a valentine and I was trying to like someone besides David Gittleman, who I would be nearly obsessed with until I was seventeen, I agreed to work for him. But Arthur Ernst was weird.

One day I convinced him to play tennis with me, which was the closest thing to a date we ever had. Tennis is how I had met David Gittleman. In the waning sun of a warm June day on courts I would come nearly to own, Arthur split his pants climbing the fence to retrieve the balls (one by one, he had hit them all over). His racket was warped; it was his mother's. I tried to hit to him, to slow the pace, finally to give him some tips, but it was no use. Even with his blond, boyish strength he was no match for me. Later we rode our bikes back to my house and went down to the basement, which was damp and cold even in summer. Arthur sat on the red plush velvet couch that used to be in our living room, and I walked around nervously, afraid to sit down next to him. At one point, I put on Carole King's "I Feel the Earth Move." I remember studying the black, grooved surface of the record, the only one I owned: its slightly warped spinning seemed a reassurance to me in this already dampened whirl of expectation. I felt secretly triumphant that I had a boy in my basement even if I wasn't sure I liked him.

In fact, Arthur Ernst smelled bad, his blond hair was greasy, his lips didn't fit over his gums enough to conceal the bloody edge of his obsession, and he wore red pants. True, they were a bit faded. But red? When they split he was only halfway up the fence, and I could see his white jockeys stretched over the crack of his butt. Of course, that was the end of tennis for us. I had seen more than I bargained for. Arthur lost the election, which was no surprise. He was more than unpopular— though probably the smartest kid in the class—he was a kind of freak. And I gave up trying to make Dave jealous—for the moment.

That year the kissing parties had dissolved from the jittery boredom of spin-the-bottle—which seemed an odd and short-lived formality—to a game we invented called "rotation." In this game, the boys got in a line and the girls "traveled," kissing one boy after another, until they got to the end of the line and then started over. There were always traffic jams, especially between Denise Koster and Rickie Gilbert, who would still be dating when they graduated college. Nonetheless, rotation was energy-efficient and got right to the point. Why we went to the boys and the boys never came to us I never thought to question.

David Gittleman was the shortest boy in the class, and even I had to bend over to kiss him. He was thin, hardly more than a vertical line with hair—which was stringy and black and came to points on his forehead. He had these soft, tapered lips, and he kissed me in a way that could be construed as meaningful. Or at least that's how I would come to describe it.

This was the year my mother and I made a pact to join Weight Watchers after Thanksgiving. By spring I was as thin as I would ever be as a teenager and I felt not exactly "in my body" but, for the first time, like I had one. When I descended the basement stairs that spring wearing a white-and-gold tube top, navel showing, I distinctly imagined David Gittleman, who was behind the pool table, elbowing his friend Michael as if to say, "Hey. Look at her!" I say *imagine* because I was a dream to myself then, the world of sex and boys a kind of invention of adolescent imagination as real as "the stairway to heaven" I thought I would, in blissful heterosexual union, someday climb.

That year, Miss Jalovick, our home-ec teacher, had us cooking omelets. She was an extremely petite woman, always very tidy, and she wore these straight, tight skirts that pulled across her ass in a way I had not imagined possible. If she were any smaller, it would have been unnatural. She was perfectly proportionate. It seemed to me she was middle-aged— perhaps she was twenty-four—and she wasn't married.

I was incorrigibly and deliberately inept at all things domestic. I ate brown sugar out of the box with my fingers, burned the pancakes, and was overwhelmingly delighted when the omelet flipped out of the pan and onto the floor, where it seemed to keep cooking in the absence of the fire. Miss Jalovick was always exasperated with me in this way that I liked—she seemed to find my mistakes funny.

Miss J., as we called her, once had me carry her books out to her car for her. As she bent over to flip the bucket seat so I could put the stuff in the back, I saw the edge of her slip come out from under the hem of her skirt. Bucket seats, I had recently learned, were a problem because they made if difficult to fool around in the car. And yet I found the bucket seats, the Trans Am itself, sexy. I couldn't help imagining some big brute of a guy leaning over those seats and kissing Miss J. She lived with her parents, someone had told me, which I thought was strange enough. But that her father had given her this new silver bullet to drive around in seemed almost perverse.

Before Patty Shell's birthday party I had a fight with my mother. She seemed slightly sour about everything I put on. "How about this?" I would say, running into her bedroom. By the time I got to the party— I had already been crying—I was late. When I walked in, the boys were passing around pretend marijuana, actually oregano, in a plastic sand-wich bag. Then they asked if I wanted to play train. This consisted of a line, boy-girl-boy-girl, everyone's hands on the next person's shoulders. The boy would kiss the girl behind him, the girl would kiss the boy behind her, and so on. Arthur Ernst was in front of me, and I was dreading the moment he would turn around. What happened, though, was worse than I expected. He received a kiss from the girl in front of him, and as I leaned my cheek toward him, he slapped my face. The slap was hard; I was shocked. I found myself unable to hold back tears. The line dissolved in laughter. Apparently, they had all played a round of train before I had arrived.

Of course, I had girlfriends. Diane McCann I would love side by side with David Gittleman until the day she started dating Jeff Rexler, who would turn out to be her first serious boyfriend. Diane I loved with an intensity I understood only after I actually made love to a woman. That place between her hips, that dark triangle of her that had drawn me so would prove to be central to what I desired. My jealousy often drove her to tears. Once, on the curb in front of my house, I tormented her until she said she couldn't stand it anymore. I bought her gifts, mastur-bated in her single bed next to her as she slept, made her kiss me on the lips after she said her prayers.

The strange thing is, I was never embarrassed about my attraction to Diane. I felt I had a right to her somehow. It was how much I demanded of her and how much suffering I put her through that pained me. In fact, I was unable to speak about her to anyone for nearly fifteen years after the last time I saw her.

I met Diane the first week of sixth grade. She had picked up a Number 2 pencil I had dropped at her feet. It was her shyness I was attracted to, her Irish good looks, her devout Catholicism—and her father. Frank had this full head of wavy hair, graying at the temples. There was a bounce to his step—he walked on the balls of his feet and his heels seemed to never touch the ground.

My shame about Diane centered around one particular incident a few weeks after I met her. Linda Erdich, a tall blond girl a grade ahead of us who lived next door to the McCanns', was teaching Diane how to ride a bicycle. Diane had grown up in the Bronx and had never learned to ride. So we hoisted her on the bike and pushed her down the driveway. Just when Diane got some speed, she'd get afraid and stop pedaling. The bike would wobble and eventually fall. "Pedal! Pedal!" Linda shouted down the street. But over and over, Diane would freeze. Finally, we ran after her. Straddling the crossbar in the middle of the street, she whined, "I can't. I can't. I give up." Linda looked at her, exasperated. Suddenly, feeling like someone needed to take control and do something, I slapped the inside of her thigh. She was stunned. I felt the sting in my hand, and her bare thigh—she was wearing shorts—grew instantly red. Tears began to fill her eyes. I felt oddly justified, though I had surprised myself. We remained friends for six more years, until we graduated high school; we never spoke about this incident.

One day, in seventh grade, when Diane was baby-sitting her three younger siblings, I found her crying on her front steps. The McCanns lived four houses down, and I would often ride my bike to their house. It was the beginning of May. The mimosas that in August would flourish with delicate pink cocktail-like flowers were not yet in bloom. The lawn was thick and trim like her father's hair. When I reached her, she explained that she couldn't get the kids to listen.

"I'll take care of it," I said in a tone that even then sounded manly to me.

One by one I grabbed her two brothers and one sister and tripped them on the lawn. I had mastered the art of tripping people in my years on the streets of Brooklyn. So then all four of them were crying. Once again, in the name of some unknown, undefined role I seemed compelled to inhabit, I had gone just a little too far.

That spring, I saw more of David Gittleman and less of Diane. I was falling in love with him after all. Every evening after tennis, just as the sun was going down, I would invite him back to my house to "sit on the porch." My stepfather kept his beer out there in our extra refrigerator, and night after night I would sneak Dave a Bud. The locomotive drone of crickets outside the screen, fireflies shooting up from the lawn, the buzz of half a beer—all this would make me want something to happen between us. "Do you want me to turn the lights on?" I would ask Dave as it was getting dark. Barely visible across the room, he would say no.

For the first time in my life I had a boy I liked, and here he was, all promise and disappointment rolled into one, sipping a beer in my screened back porch. My body seemed at once a lure, a hindrance, a half-awake, expanding thing. The nights were never long enough, the kiss always about to happen.

The following summer, the summer between seventh and eighth grade, my mother would spend in jail. She had been sentenced to six months for leading a teacher's strike. My grandmother, who had raised me until my mother married her last and final husband, would come to live with us again, returning me to the salmon patties and *New York Post* of my childhood. One July day I would convince my grandfather to let me drive my mother's brand-new Ford Pinto, which I crashed into a pole (my stepfather had bought it for her the day before the paddy wagon came to pick her up; she had never driven it herself). And one night after a nightmare, I would crawl into bed with my stepfather, and as he fondled my newly forming breasts, I would say over and over: "I'm not Mom. I'm not Mom."

But this was seventh grade. This was a good year.

Outtakes

Clifford Chase

Chris thought my friend Roger was weird. It was one more thing that separated me from whatever it took to be the kind of boy who was Chris's best friend. Whenever Roger and I were together, we would begin to speak in our secret baby voices, and we couldn't stop. This was okay if it was just Roger and me, but it was not okay if Chris was also there.

Chris's lean Polish father took the three of us one Saturday to the airport to watch planes land. I didn't understand the activity, presented by Mr. Studzinski as a major treat, but I went anyway. Roger barely looked up at the sky. He made one joke after another in baby talk. "Poo-poo plane!" At first I glanced sideways in embarrassment at Chris and his father, but the game compelled me irresistibly. "Oooh! I need to go bad pee-pee!" Roger cried. Once again I grew giddy with our private, forbidden language. "Oh, me too," I cooed. We went on like this for more than an hour, until my head hurt, my own twelve-year-old voice lost to me. Later, walking along the runway embankment back to the car, Chris whispered that his father disapproved. I stared down at the dry, pebbly ground. "It's Roger, not me," I said.

That summer, Roger and I needed an elaborate control-room set for our movie *The Spy Called Muppet*. Chris knew how to wire tiny blinking lights, and I was delighted when he said he'd help us. Our friendship was beginning at last to blossom, and maybe he would grow to like Roger after all. I made the cardboard consoles and construction-paper chairs for the puppets to sit in, and Chris fitted the pointy lightbulbs into the little holes I'd made. It was the first time the two of us had joined in such an extensive project, and together we made a magnificent spy control center. The banks of colored lights blinked in succession— pink, yellow, blue. A motorized wave pattern, Magic Marker on adding-machine tape, scrolled past a rectangular opening like a screen.

The set was created to be destroyed. "We're under attack!" the muppets shouted. After they had fled, it was time to set fire to the control room. I had made sure my mother wouldn't be home for the filming of this scene. We took the intricate set from the card table and placed it out on the patio in the sun. Gleefully Roger and Chris poured lighter fluid on the cardboard, and I loaded a fresh cartridge into the Bell & Howell. Often I had secretly burned model cars and ships in corners of the backyard, savoring the plastic and rubber fumes, but filming the event took nihilism to a new level. We lit the control room in several places, and I aimed the camera. I had argued with Roger for the right to film this moment, since Chris and I had built the set. Though Roger was codirector, this scene was just Chris's and mine. The lights popped and fizzled, the little flames wavered from the consoles. "Bitchin'," Chris said. "Get a shot of that!"

I zoomed in and out, slowly dialing the camera's little silver lever; I panned from one flickering cardboard panel to another. The dazzling effects of blue, green, and yellow fire seemed infinite in number. Chris and I had worked together so well creating this masterpiece, and now with its destruction we seemed to discover the meaning of ecstasy. It would all be captured on film.

Almost too quickly the flames died down, and nearly every inch of cardboard had curled and blackened when I noticed that the film-footage indicator hadn't moved at all. Until then I had taken no heed that the camera was making a funny noise, a high, sped-up whining instead of its normal ticking. That overexcited mechanism must have seemed only one more sign of my own enchantment.

"What's the matter?" Roger asked.

I was fiddling with the camera. "The film is stuck," I said at last. I eyeballed the disloyal footage indicator one last time. "I don't think I loaded it right."

Roger threw up his hands. "What?"

But it was Chris's disappointment that seemed most damning. He groaned with disgust, staggered around the patio. He wouldn't look at me. Though we would remain friends for perhaps another year, well into junior high, somehow I placed that particular failure as the beginning of the end. "It's okay, it's okay," I murmured sadly. "We'll just shoot this part." I reloaded the camera and doggedly panned the control room once again. But there was nothing left to record except the ashy, smoldering aftermath of our brief, profligate communion.

The year before, in sixth grade, I had somehow, inexplicably, entered a realm of humiliations. Before then, the other kids rarely called me names, and my teachers admired all the tiny paper clothes and props I made for my muppets, the elaborate stories I wrote about them. I put on shows for the class, kneeling under a card table listening to the kids' laughter, wiggling the muppets' bodies above my head and speaking in funny voices. The muppets danced to "Lady Madonna," and the tiny tinsel wigs I'd made for them flew up and down, glittering. In fifth grade Mrs. Smurthwaite let me go ahead in math, and when after a few weeks I'd finished the year's lessons, she let me write stories and make collages from women's magazines until June.

But Miss Squire, my sixth-grade teacher, made it plain from the start that she would brook none of this child's play. "It's time you grew up," she said, as if the meaning of that were self-evident. I had been spoiled, she believed, in being allowed to work independently. I learned that in every respect I would have to keep in line from now on, that I must no longer be unusual at school. I got in trouble for things like mumbling, or for writing my name on the wrong corner of my paper. We had a separate math teacher that year, Mr. Lang, and he wouldn't let me go ahead. He told the class that the muppets were like dolls and a boy shouldn't play with them.

Indignities such as this seemed to have become as much a part of me as the shiny, too-smooth silver of my capped front tooth. I kept hoping to cross some barely visible border and leave them behind. I wanted to be more like my friend Chris, who was smart but somehow never stuck out too much. Maybe it really was a matter of growing up, I thought. Seventh grade, which meant a new and bigger school with all new teachers and lots of kids who didn't know me, seemed to offer dazzling and perilous vistas of self-revision and renewal.

I had to pass my old grade school and cross the whole of the green field, diagonally, then the blacktop courts, to reach the junior high each new morning, swinging my lunchbox in one hand and my flute case in the other, humming, daydreaming nervously under the morning clouds. Seen from the field, the school's low roof went in short decorative zigzags, like the peculiar stripe on Charlie Brown's shirt. In the distance, cloud shreds would be sitting up in the ridges of the blue mountains, though this was a detail I'd fail to notice until high school, when I discovered that a love for nature could protect me. It was September. I still had my metal lunchbox from sixth grade, with Snoopy cartoons on it, edged in battered orange. This morning a group of hard guys, eighth-graders, loitered in dark jackets and bell-bottoms by the green-gray wall of the school. I would have to pass through their midst to reach the chain-link gate.

Humming an intricate flute solo, approaching their blacktop territory, I began swinging my flute and my lunchbox higher and higher. Just as I reached them, the lunchbox flew open, my sandwich and "Peanuts" Thermos spilling at their feet.

"Whoops!" I cried, involuntarily, exactly as my mother had done since I was a toddler. I would have given anything to erase that unbidden mommy's exclamation, but now I could only continue bravely the abject performance I'd begun. Simpering in apology, gripping my flute, I bent to gather my lunch. A black boot moved aside in disgust.

"____"

I won't bother to record the name-calling and snickering, since its contents are predictable, and anyway in that same instant I blotted it out. I pushed my horn-rims up my nose. I picked up my sandwich and Thermos.

Or maybe they said nothing at all, and I filled in the blanks myself.

In any case, I wasn't kicked, nor was my flute stolen. I understood with a pained relief that I was beneath even bullying. Each subsequent action was ever more bumbling and girlish: nervously shutting the lunchbox, which opened again, shutting it once more, stumbling on my stubby, unathletic legs to the big open gate. The blacktop here was weathered gray and littered with candy wrappers and dirt; dust devils cul-de-sacked into this corner from time to time, leaving here what they had gathered. The hard guys had already forgotten me. The incident had left no trace, and I would not have to tell Chris what had happened. Inside the gate, the corridor was deeply shadowed and, I hoped, cool with forgetfulness.

"Dress-and-run" meant we had to change frantically into our P.E. clothes and run the six hundred yards around the perimeter of the field. We got points for how quickly we finished this grueling exercise. The dressing part was almost more important than the run. Mr. Amaya believed that boys had to be taught with severity not to dawdle with their jockstraps. It's true, my jockstrap was a strange and seemingly useless item that fascinated me; I would have liked to take my time and contemplate it, try to fathom how my balls and my crotch and my butt felt strapped and cupped in elastic. Instead, the words "Dress and do it, boys!" flooded me with panic, and the locker room became a delirium of limbs, red shorts, stuck socks. If you were a slow runner, it didn't matter how fast you dressed; whether you lingered or not, you'd always get a six, never a ten. I usually got an eight. We never knew which day would be a dress-and-run, and each morning Mr. Amaya smiled just slightly at our dread.

Mr. Amaya liked to make pronouncements like "A fine specimen!" when, say, we watched a film about gymnasts. Somehow he was allowed the luxury of observing and evaluating the male physique. I never experimented with phrases like "A fine specimen!" perhaps because I knew I couldn't carry off Mr. Amaya's manly tone of cool appraisal.

Was his gaze so disinterested? Once, after gym class, he singled out a rough boy whose locker was next to mine. The boy was stocky, and you could see clearly the outlines of all his muscles. "We're starting an after-school workout club," Mr. Amaya said. "For boys like yourself"—

how did he put it?—"boys who we can see have athletic potential." This boy never tried in P.E., hanging back in football and soccer, scoring a six regularly in dress-and-run; so this "potential" could only mean his body itself. I blushed to hear Mr. Amaya betray aloud the assessment I couldn't help but make to myself each day in that locker room.

One week we had physical fitness tests: how many pull-ups you could do, how fast you ran fifty yards, how far you could run in six minutes. After each test, Mr. Amaya stood with his clipboard shaking his head as he marked down my score, which was always low.

We did the six-minute run in groups. After I'd done my paltry best, less than half a mile, I stood in the center of the track trying to get my breath, slyly watching Chris chat with his own group at the starting line. Mr. Amaya barked "Go!" and Chris began loping around the track in long, goofy strides, his ankles kicking outward almost like a paddling duck. I secretly hoped this peculiarity might place him after all in my own oddball category, but he was fast. In his own way, he was graceful.

Mr. Amaya now stood shaking his head for a different reason, with admiration. Chris sped in red shorts around the track, his slender, nut-brown legs flying side to side, kicking further and further ahead of the pack, already lapping the stragglers. When at last in the dusty sunshine Mr. Amaya dropped his arm and called out, "Stop!" Chris was just about to cross the one-mile mark.

Mr. Amaya sighed, glancing at the other coach. "I don't think I could've done it myself," he said.

Although I was glad to see Mr. Amaya beaten, for once, Chris's prowess made me not proud but uneasy. I saw him accelerating away, his quick heels striking neatly side to side, mile after mile, until I was just a dot in his landscape.

At lunch, Chris fed the seagulls and pointed out favorites. We sat cross-legged way out on the edge of the green field. The sky was overcast, and two or three gulls flocked above us, fluttering white and gray, calling. Games of basketball and four-square were played on the distant blacktop. "Look at that one," Chris said. "He's really smart." The bird drifted above us, wings motionless, hovering in the wind, considering us. His white body was plump, streamlined, and palpable. I watched his small, wise eye, how he looked this way and that, directing his beak here and there, waiting for a sign. And with a flick of his long arm, Chris pitched balled-up pieces of bread across the grass, and sometimes a quick gull caught one right in the air.

If the sun was out, we played a game with their shadows. Chris, his friend Chuck, and I ran and dodged under the dozens of circling birds, and if a gull's curved shadow crossed your body, you fell down dead in writhing agony. I lay then on the fragrant lawn, spying the other two boys run until they, too, fell, first Chuck with a short cry—"Aghh!"— and then Chris, tumbling over and over with a long, rolling scream.

We lay still, each in his own grave, while the seagulls continued fluttering white and gray overhead. In the lush solitude of grass I heard Chris softly singing his joke song:

Ride, captain, ride!
Upon your mystery shit.

Months passed. One spring day I would look at Chris, slender and tan in his white T-shirt—perhaps I was following him into his dark garage, perhaps watching him hammer nails into the walls of the fort— and I would think to myself, "It's a good thing he doesn't turn me on." I had recently figured out exactly what homosexuality was, by looking it up in the *Encyclopædia Britannica*. Being with Chris wasn't like my furtive glances in the locker room, so I believed I'd chosen my friend well. He and his body weren't encouraging arousal on the wrong path.

This was not exactly a system of sin and temptation. It was far more private than that, more unique, and never spoken in the world. It was entirely my own theory.

I believed I could prevent the homo self in me from going through puberty. The straight boy would develop and grow "normally," but the homo boy would not. I believed, for instance, that if ever I masturbated thinking of men, then my homo self would begin to develop, to sprout hairs as it were, and make his way toward manhood. Each step along that path was probably irreversible. So, it was as if there were two boys in me, the straight boy and the homo boy, and I had to encourage the one to grow and the other not to. Each glance, each thought, each action could move one or the other self forward, like a token on a game board, closer to a wonderful or disastrous maturity.

I was the only boy in Band who played the flute, but I hoped to turn my faggy instrument into something cool and up-to-date by branching out into rock and jazz. My friend Todd played the drums, and a neighbor of his, Jeff, was learning electric guitar. This Jeff, who also played football and was already in high school, had been eager to get together with me and Todd to try "Color My World." "All right!" Chris had said. For that brief moment it had seemed a surprising plus that I played the flute.

The jam session was after school, at Jeff's house. But I had only just put my flute together when Jeff announced that he had heard I was a fag. "Is that true?"

My head tingled darkly. At the other end of the room Jeff began twiddling bits and pieces of a solo, not looking at me. Todd only continued tapping on his snare drum, and Chris, who had come over to listen, read a model-car magazine.

"No, it's not *true*," I said. With a too careless toss of my head I began my warm-up scales.

My lips absurdly pursed, the delicate silver wand shining with stigma under Jeff's low rec-room ceiling. I dipped and bobbed expressively, as my flute teacher, Cynthia, always did. The very tip of my tongue articulated each note—*tah, tah, tah,* I played; *tikka, tikka, tikka.*

Jeff continued his fragments of hard rock, paying no attention to me, swearing when he missed a note.

"Aren't you guys gonna play a song?" asked Chris, who also lived on this block. I had wished that through "Color My World" and perhaps Jethro Tull songs to conquer Daffodil Lane at last, but this was not to be. Who had told Jeff I was a fag?

"Whatever," said Jeff, shrugging, and with little enthusiasm he began the arpeggios of the slow dance. Raspily and without conviction he sang of realizing, at last, just what his lover meant to him. I remember this scene with both the intensity and incompleteness of a dream. When it was time for my solo, I couldn't find the key. I tried one note after another. A hundred times before I had played along with the record—transported, the headphones cupped tightly over my ears so that I could scarcely hear myself. But I had never played the song with another actual person.

Jeff broke off in disgust. "I thought the little pussy said he could play this."

"Let me try it again," I replied, ignoring the insult. But the session was over.

I stood alone by the front windows, cleaning the spit out of my flute with the little blue cloth. Out there in the sunshine, behind one of the tall redwood fences, I'd heard, two boys on this block were found kissing the other day. By the stairs, Jeff was bragging to Todd and Chris about making the high school football team. Jeff was tough, but he was not smart, I knew.

"Look at that two-hundred-pound bench-press muscle," Jeff said.

Like a button on a remote control, the word *muscle* made my head turn. I saw him flexing his right arm—the round, pale, hard biceps bulging from the sleeve of his faded T-shirt. "I did two hundred last week," Jeff said.

"No," said Todd.

Is it possible that Jeff called out to me, "What are you staring at, faggot?" Maybe I only feared he would say something like that. Or maybe even now I wish that he were, in fact, showing off for me.

I turned away quickly. I began cleaning my instrument again. "Skin flute," certain boys at school had taunted, pleased by their recent discovery of sexual metaphors. I pressed the lump in my pants against the edge of the small table, trying to make the lump go away. I placed the flute's three pieces carefully in the blue velvet indentations. I folded the spit-soaked cloth and shut the case as slowly as I could, to give myself a little more time.

I was a femme and a fag, it was true, and I didn't know how to fight, but was that the only thing that divided me from the likes of Chris? In fact, no one at school could match my cynicism, the love of parody I'd cultivated with my older brother for years before he went away to college. So far Roger, who attended the junior high across Saratoga Avenue, was my one cohort in humor.

In a box in my closet, in an old photo album, I have a small photo of Roger in a fright wig with a blanket on his knees, seated in profile, which I snapped with my white Swinger Polaroid. He had wanted a takeoff on *Whistler's Mother* but the joke disappointed: The photo's frame was bigger than it had appeared in the viewfinder, spoiling the fiction. You can see the edge of the blanket, Roger's tennis shoe, my bedroom curtains; and Roger's face is freckled and hopelessly childlike. We were nine or ten.

Roger and I had known each other from when my family first moved to San Jose. Now we lived just barely within biking distance, and we saw each other only on Saturdays, or we talked on the phone. Since the control-room fiasco, I don't think Chris ever wanted to see Roger again, even though the misloaded film had been my fault. My friend Todd didn't like Roger either, nor did I like Roger's friends at his own school. Our friendship therefore lost all connection to daily life, which left us free, at least for a time, to create an even more rarified world.

Like all our projects, *The Spy Called Muppet* was a comedy, but our art culminated in seventh grade with *Turning On Is Copping Out,* our parody of an antidrug film. It wasn't that we used drugs or wanted to; we objected to antidrug movies on purely aesthetic grounds. I enlisted my new friend Wayne to costar, since an openhearted, conventional boy like Chris could not possibly have related to such an undertaking. Wayne played the drug pusher, Benny the Eel; I played the pudgy boy he corrupts.

I still have the movie. The opening subtitle: "It could happen any-where, even here . . ." We chose the one pink house on my block for the exterior shot; it seemed the most all-American, the most tasteless. Inside, I lie sleeping on the couch. Roger and I Scotch-taped a little flagpole and American flag to the coffee table, and we placed a small fan next to it, blowing the flag out to the side. You can see the fan.

After I have a fight with my mother (played by my mother), Benny/ Wayne ends up injecting me with LSD. I spend the rest of the movie tripping. At this point our sense of humor gets somewhat lost in the

wonder of blue and red lens filters and crooked camera angles. I contemplate a dandelion; I jump off a set of bleachers in a parody of thinking
I can fly. *Turning On Is Copping Out* was never completed. In the final
moment, I stagger to the entrance of a hospital. The end of the reel is
slightly damaged, so that just as I fall, "blacking out," the frame freezes.

That year Roger and I had fixed our ironic gaze on a new, especially
saccharine show called *The Smith Family,* starring Henry Fonda as a
family man and cop. Roger and I called each other during each commercial break to exclaim over the latest white-bread TV wisdom. Soon
we were talking on the phone during the entire episode.

But something about these conversations began to scare me. Just as
Roger's baby talk had both repelled and mesmerized, now I wondered
about such extensive giggling over a television show. On nights when
The Smith Family wasn't on, I lay on the floor of my brother's vacant
bedroom, laughing on the phone with Roger, building our sugar-cube
edifices of cynical comedy, staring at the empty ceiling. My brother
had taken all his things with him to college, and the room was bare,
echo-y. The beige phone hurt my ear, we talked for such a long time,
and my throat ached from laughing.

The next morning at school, under the low clouds and the circling
seagulls, I would try to explain our jokes to Chris, and he would just
say he thought it was weird. It seemed I was getting weirder and weirder
to Chris.

I began to step back from my phone conversations with Roger. Perhaps the particular refuge from conformity he offered was one I couldn't
afford. I tried not to laugh so much at his jokes. I tried not to get so
carried away.

Then one night Roger told me about a new gag he liked to play at
school. "I sit down and cross my legs and make my wrists go limp, and
I say, 'Hi, fella!' "

At this moment a kind of electrical switch clicked inside me, a spark
of fearful judgment, a conclusion. Jests in passing about faggots, even
brief imitations, were normal; but extended enactments surely were not.

So, I thought, *Roger is a fag*.

This observation did not square well with a penchant for *Playboy* magazine that Roger had often expressed to me, in baby talk, as we passed by newsstands in 7-Eleven and Thrifty Drug. But this fact did not concern me. I had solved the case.

"That sounds weird to me," I said sternly.

"It's a joke. No one is going to think you're serious," Roger replied. "What's the big deal?"

But I had decided: Everything added up, and I had to save myself. "I think it's really weird," I repeated.

"Why?"

"It just is," I said with finality. There was a silence. "Well, bye."

I was still staring up at the stippled, cobwebby corners of my brother's ceiling when I hung up the phone. Nothing more needed to be said. Roger and I scarcely spoke for the next four years.

That spring of seventh grade seems especially blank, a search for friends, a number of candidates but no one in particular. Losing Roger did not, of course, mean gaining Chris or Todd. Soon after that I got into trouble with Todd's mother and was forbidden to see him. Chris was fading quickly into a glittering, crimson cloud of soccer, track, and popularity.

For a little while I tried playing soccer myself, after school, and for a moment or two I was almost good at it, or at least I could run down the field with abandon, losing myself to the grass and the wind. Anyway, that was how it was described to me by another kid with big plastic glasses even thicker than mine. I don't remember his name. In the locker room after the game, he told me how I looked sprinting down the field that day, how my hair flew out straight behind me, I ran so fast. Each time thereafter I tried to recapture that all-consuming, carefree concentration, and each time that kid with thick glasses, who maybe could become my friend but never did, would say, "You ran pretty fast today, but not like that one time."

Though Roger had been the cameraman for all our movies, I owned the editing machine. In my darkened bedroom I'd watch a scene glint frame by frame as I carefully cranked the two reels, forward and back again, searching for the flickering moment to splice. After Roger and I parted, and there were no more films to edit, I would thread the old ones into the machine anyway. I liked it better than the projector, how you peered down into the little grainy, glowing screen. It was a game to turn the crank at just the right speed, pleasing to see the mistakes edited out, the fluid movements from one shot to the next.

But I also had a weakness for outtakes. I saved them on extra spools labeled "crap," sometimes splicing them onto the ends of the finished movies. Recently I projected *The Spy Called Muppet* on my kitchen wall. I hadn't seen it in twenty-five years. It's nearly half an hour long, and there are no people in it, only puppets, cardboard sets, animated Matchbox cars. But at the very end, after the crooked, hand-lettered credits, Roger himself suddenly appears: his freckled, twelve-year-old face. I must have been the one who filmed it. He's laughing a little wildly, open-mouthed, braces flashing in the home-movie silence. He can hardly contain himself as he pretends to pull strings of boogers from his nose and eat the results. The camera shakes, the end of the roll is about to go white, and Roger squirms with the purest enjoyment possible—a transport of giggling, goofing around carried to ecstasy.

Notes on Camp

Robert Marshall

The summer after seventh grade Anna Voigt, my teacher and mentor, went to the Naropa Institute. After attending the Jack Kerouac School of Disembodied Poetics, she took a bus through Nevada to San Francisco. Along the way she wrote to me. I was at camp.

Her letters were short and filled with images. The cowboy she had met in Reno. The drunken woman next to her on the Greyhound. They weren't like my family's letters. They were show, not tell.

At the rest stop, out of Vegas two hours,
a woman screams at a lizard as she steps off the bus.
Johnny Cash on the jukebox in the "Hub Cafe."
My drunken friend from the bus bemoans lost man.
Dust on everything.
More ideas for Goddess poems!
Write to me at the Y in San Francisco.
Want to hear about you.

I didn't know how to reply. I was used to writing a certain sort of letter, the kind I would send to my grandparents, which always began,

"How are you? I am fine," or sometimes, for variety, "I am very well." I would then go on to list my recent activities. I would comment on the issues of the day that they had asked me about, and I would conclude with hopeful sentiments about upcoming events. Anna wouldn't want that. I needed a letter with images like the ones about the bus.

I had resisted going to camp. I doubted I would survive. But my parents prevailed and I went. They went to the Vineyard. They sent postcards with lighthouses. My mother wrote about how they had met a woman who had known Eleanor Roosevelt. Dad wrote about the beaches, the weather, and whether Nixon would be impeached. He had enjoyed meeting Mr. Nadler, the camp's director. "I hope your summer is not turning out to be as awful an experience as you thought," he would add. I tried to be stoic in my response. There was no point in arguing anymore. Still, I didn't want them to think I was having a good time. I complained a little about the food, and the absence of TV, stuff like that. I wrote, "I am REALLY frustrated I am not getting to see any of Watergate." I was, a little. On one of the first nights, I imagined, as if within a crystal ball, the meetings that often took place in our living room—my father, in front of the fireplace, in his white shirt and tie, discussing politics with other intelligent community leaders. Lying on my cot, in the camp's darkness, I contemplated this crystal ball with longing. It gleamed, like my father's head in the imaginary fireplace light.

I only thought of this one night.

There were twelve boys in my cabin. One said he was part Cherokee. He had dark eyes and wore a headband. I often glanced at him. One was from New York. He lived near my grandfather. Another had the face of an angel. He was from New Jersey and slept in the cot next to mine. I was the youngest. The cabin was a few yards from a lake in which we swam, in which some boys fished.

I tried to befriend the boy from New York. His name was Ira. He wanted to be called Houdino, after the escape artist he admired. Houdino was not athletic. His mother had had rubella, and he was missing several fingers. He said when he grew up he was going to be a counterfeiter. He had books at home on how to do it. He hadn't brought them with him—he was afraid they might be stolen. If counterfeiting didn't work out, he was going to design stamps. He got short-sheeted. He was called Houdino but with derision. I felt sorry for him, but after the first week I realized we didn't have much in common. Ira was, as Anna would have said, very "left brain." He didn't listen when I tried to discuss my ideas on spirituality. I remained a little bit friendly with him, but not too.

My mother had sewn my name into my undershirts. She had written it with a felt-tip pen on the inside cover of the many books I'd brought with me. These included *The Teachings of Chuang Tzu,* Carlos Castaneda's *Journey to Ixtlan,* and *The Catcher in the Rye.* I'd brought *The Catcher in the Rye* because I feared the other books might appear too peculiar. I tried to read it on the plane heading east, but I kept wondering what Holden Caulfield would have thought of me.

I wanted to read books that had something spiritual to teach me. But I wasn't sure how I would explain *Zen and the Birds of Appetite* if someone were to ask about it, so I kept it under the cot all summer. I kept *Journey to Ixtlan* on the ledge above my pillow. It was, after all, anthropology. I was comforted each time I opened it and saw my name in my mother's writing. Before I went to sleep I would read about Carlos Castaneda's discussions with his mentor, don Juan.

" 'You cannot leave these desolate mountains without saying your thanks,' he said in a firm tone. 'A warrior never turns his back to power without atoning for the favors received.' "

Kevin, a counselor from another cabin, saw me reading this book and called me the "resident intellectual." He sort of liked me but said I was weird. He went to Amherst. He was reading *A Portrait of the Artist as a Young Man.* He talked with John, our counselor, about which of the girls they'd like to fuck. It was rumored John had done "it" in our cabin the previous summer, while the boys, supposedly asleep, were listening.

*   *   *

I tried to think how to describe camp to Anna. When I sat down to write, on the steps of Cabin Seven, I never felt centered enough. I watched the squirrels dart past on the grass. I rolled pine needles along the wooden slats. I wanted to just be there in the moment. But other moments kept rushing in. I was missing the immediate Now. I was too self-conscious. I didn't like the sound of the letters I began. They weren't like Anna's. They didn't have the right tone. Perhaps, I thought, she wouldn't care about this as much as I thought she did.

The sun was setting. The lake, I thought, was a flickering jewel. Was this image too forced to put in a letter to Anna? I heard the shouts from the water. I looked at the trees' reflection in the orange water, which merged with the real trees, as if they were the two sides of an inkblot on a folded piece of paper.

My grandfather wrote to me on his law firm's stationery. I had sent him a copy of the *Amethyst,* the literary magazine I had worked on with Anna. He commented, "The poems are quite good. However, I do wonder why you insist on referring to yourself as 'i'? Why not 'I'?" He corrected some of the spelling errors in my letter and reminded me of Cicero's advice about a sound mind in a sound body.

I argued with him internally about the importance of the body. Wasn't it just a part of the illusory world? Didn't it exist, in a sense, in the mind? I knew that if someone were to listen to me carefully and patiently, I could sort of prove this. I wrote a carefully worded response about "i," saying that I did not want to give too much importance to the self.

I had to fill up the page. I told him how sorry I was to be missing Watergate.

Although at home I always sat when I went to the bathroom, at camp I knew I had to stand to pee. "You're the only person I've ever known who shits and pisses separately," John, our curly-haired counselor, told me, quite amused. Anna sent me a note describing her arrival in San

Francisco and the graffiti on the walls at the YWCA. She enclosed a sheet of white bond paper with advice typed from the *Tao Te Ching:*

Yield and Overcome
Bend and be Straight.

It took two weeks before I heard the word *fag.* It was the word I feared most, as once I had feared *weak.* "How ya doin', fag?" a boy said, for no apparent reason, as I sat beneath a tree during free time, writing to my parents. He did not say it again. It was odd how this word had followed me, all the way across the continent, the way the moon had trailed us past the airplane's silver wing. Somehow I *knew* this word would follow me. But actually, at camp, it didn't shadow me as closely.

Everyone was excited about the upcoming canoe trip, but I was afraid to go. I had never canoed. It would be uncomfortable, and I would be made fun of. I didn't want to think about whether or not I should go. But during the days preceding the trip, I could hardly think of anything else. I wondered why I couldn't control my thoughts. I would decide I should go. I should go because I was afraid of going. Then I thought that my father would want me to go, and I shouldn't do something in order to please him. Then I thought that not going because he would want me to go was also a way of letting him control me. I ought to do what I wanted. I should listen to myself and follow my instinct. My instinct was to not go. But wasn't that *fear*? How could I grow without conquering *fear*? I knew this decision wasn't that important. But I felt like the universe was watching me. I signed up for the trip. I began to imagine what the day would be like—the discomfort of crouching in the canoe, the humiliation of mishandling the paddle, the sunlight, the shouting. I ought to have the inner power and sense of detachment to cope with these possibilities. But why should I have to prove this? After all, not everyone was going. On the morning we were to leave I told John I wasn't feeling well. He shrugged his shoulders, indifferent. After everyone had left, with the camp nearly abandoned, I felt glad I hadn't gone.

I stayed in the cabin and read. In the afternoon I began to feel melancholy. I should have gone. I went down to the meadow and did some drawings of the dandelions and the Queen Anne's lace. I walked around the lake. It was, I thought, a mirror of the bright blue sky. I wanted my mind to be like that—empty, like a mirror. I wrote to Anna, about the lake.

The next day everyone talked about the canoe trip. I repeated my excuse about having been sick. I wondered why I hadn't gone. Maybe it was my own fault I didn't have friends. I had let myself be governed by my fears. After all, I would have survived it.

The canoe trip was on a Sunday. I had to wait until Wednesday to discuss it with Dr. Kurtz. It had been arranged that I would call my psychiatrist once a week from the privacy of the director's office. I had negotiated this condition with my parents. Mr. Nadler had been very accommodating.

I spoke into the black telephone, underneath a pair of antlers, against a wall with framed articles about the Nadlers and certificates testifying to their camp's excellence. Dr. Kurtz and I talked about fear. He said I should give myself credit for having gone so far as to sign up. I ought to look ahead, not behind. I should change what I could change and accept what I could not. He told me a wise man had said this. I felt frustrated after I hung up the phone and left Mr. Nadler's office. I thought of the things I hadn't said. It would be seven days until we talked again.

I slept with my arms beneath my blanket. The angel face in the next cot asked, "What are you doing, jerking off?" Then I slept with my arms on top of the blankets. I wasn't sure if this was what I should do—did it mean I was admitting he had been right? And I also thought that possibly I was *supposed* to be jerking off. I wasn't sure how his question had been meant. Maybe it hadn't been accusatory. He had told me on one of the first nights about his girlfriend's tits, and how she let him suck them, and he asked what base I had gotten to. After a few days he began to ignore me.

*   *   *

Sometimes at night, after the campfire, before lights-out, I would walk down a steep trail that led from behind the dining hall past the cabins toward the lake. Tree roots, like strong boys' limbs, crossed the path. I tried not to trip. I thought about Castaneda. Like him, I was gathering power. I walked carefully past boulders and ferns that merged in the darkness, which itself seemed to merge with silence. The path was damp. I felt at moments that the night was about to tell me something, but I knew that the darkness was all that was going to be revealed, and that I had to accept the simplicity of this, and its importance. I remembered what Anna had told me about Dante, how one had to descend before coming up. This experience, this steep downhill walk, had meaning. The trail was a metaphor. Conquering fear? Perhaps, I thought, I shouldn't think of it as a metaphor. I should experience it directly. Remembering don Juan, I thought, "This is a place of power." The trees were like tall old bearded men, watching. Something fluttered in the darkness. I stopped and felt a stone's coolness. I decided to allow myself the indulgence of my thoughts. Branches, like boys' arms, were in my way, but I slipped past them. Spruce needles brushed my face. The path was slippery. I could make out the velvet sky through the dense interlacing of the trees.

I came to the end of the trail. It opened out onto the meadow. The ground squished beneath my Keds. The lake was a dark eye, the only seeing thing on the face of the earth.

I returned reluctantly to the cabin. Entering, I was signaled to be quiet. The boy with the headband was perched on one of the rafters, his belt unfastened. There was suppressed laughter as the cabin's screen door opened and Houdino walked in. He seemed momentarily perplexed by the silence, and then by the piss that came streaming down on him.

In the morning the sun, filtering through the pine trees, caused patterns of shadow and light on the dirt outside the director's office. We waited for the mail. I looked for a moment at the T-shirted breasts of the girl next to me. I thought this was something I was supposed to do. The boys in my cabin always talked about her breasts. The light played on them as if they were gentle hills. "What are *you* looking at?" she asked, not gently. I wanted to disappear, to escape the glare of her mockery, to not be in that light. I did not know what to do with my hands, my eyes, or my thoughts. I felt perverted. I stood still.

Midway through the session, on visiting day, my parents came down from the Vineyard. They stayed at a motel near the Susquehanna. We ate lunch in the coffee shop. In the evening I would have to return to my cabin. I did not want to think about the way these hours were passing as I sat across from my mother in the coffee shop. It felt wrong that we should be talking about what to order when there was such a short time. I did not wish to think about this, but I couldn't help it. I wanted to appreciate the time; I didn't want to be so aware of its passing. A fly hovered near the milk container. I looked at my mother and I knew she felt as I did. I couldn't prove it. I knew it. We would both cry when they had to leave.

Outside the large glass window, the river I had not canoed rushed by, dazzling in the light. Dad asked if Mr. Nadler was a good camp director. I talked with him about Watergate. He asked if I'd made friends, and if I'd heard from the teacher I liked so much.

Mom said she wanted to collect some pinecones and take them back home. I sipped my iced tea. Back in the motel room she was able to fix the zipper on my windbreaker, which had been stuck for weeks.

When their rented Ford disappeared down the dirt road, leaving me back at camp, I was moist with sadness. But I soon dried. In a way I regretted this, but I realized camp was more than half over. I had passed "the hump."

One night at campfire a girl sang "Daniel," the song about Elton John's brother, who had flown in the night to Spain. Her voice drifted off into the darkness, toward the mountains. I'd always loved this song. What were Daniel's scars, and why had they not healed? I'd long felt I was on the verge of discovering a clue hidden somewhere in the song.

The girl who sang had seemed no different from any of us. But now she voiced a hopeful sadness, which I sensed we all shared but which was normally hidden. I looked toward the distant lights of the Piggly

Wiggly. I knew this feeling we had would vanish in the next day's light. Why were things like this? Why tomorrow would it all be gone?

Another girl befriended me. She was from Michigan but had a friend who had a cousin who had gone to my school. Still, I didn't understand why she would like me when others did not. I didn't get the arbitrariness of it. *Learn to be there among them,* Chuang Tzu had said. The girl said that God was the ground of all being. She wore a necklace with a fish. She thought I was "interesting." Kevin, the counselor, said she had a crush on me, but I couldn't tell if he was joking.

There were still many days when I didn't feel centered. I knew that the fields were beautiful and that I thought too much. In the distance the mountains were always a pale blue-green. And then there were mountains beyond the mountains. Sometimes I regretted that I wasn't more homesick, that I had become used to camp, that it wasn't as terrible as I had anticipated. Ira didn't stay the whole seven weeks. I wondered, after he left with his mother on visiting day, whether I would see him again. I often thought about meeting people in the future, and what it would be like. The possibility surrounded each encounter like the haze that covered the meadow at dawn. How would these meetings unfold? Would there be apologies? Would I apologize to Ira? Did I have bad karma because I hadn't been better toward him? Would those who had teased me apologize when we met on the streets of the future? I rehearsed over and over again: "Didn't you go to Camp . . . ?"

I had adapted. *I was learning to just be there among them.* As I walked through the tall grass, I thought that I had been wrong about what camp would be like. I did not want to admit it. This was because of my ego. I tried to let it go. Past the trees, toward the sky. Thistles stuck to my socks and my legs. Yield and Overcome.

Mud Pies and Medusa

Marcus Mabry

David Frost: You were a Negro, you were poor, you were homosexual. Didn't you feel you had everything going against you?

James Baldwin: On the contrary, I thought I'd hit the jackpot.

One of the two sets of encyclopedias that sat in Grandmom's living room was prophetically named *The Book of Knowledge*. I was home alone with my grandmother on Sunday—again. Bored out of my mind. I checked to make sure she was upstairs or in the kitchen where she couldn't see me. Then I crept to the lopsided bookshelf where she kept the encyclopedias. I fingered the several volumes on the lower shelf, tapping their stiff spines until I found the one I always went to.

Greedily, nervously, I opened to the page I always opened to, my heart banging so loudly in my rib cage I could hear it. Under the entry of some French painter named Jean Géricault was a half-page glossy print of *The Raft of Medusa*. I wouldn't get the translator's cheeky play on words (*raft* instead of *wrath*) until I was twenty-eight and hanging out in a hotel in Zagreb, Croatia, waiting for the Bosnian war to start, or restart, watching unintelligible Croatian TV.

I swallowed hard and let out the breath I had been holding in fear that someone, somehow, might come up behind me and glimpse what I was devouring.

There on the page, so vivid I could see the brush strokes, was a luscious tableau. A dozen men hanging on to a wrecked raft tossed in rough seas. Some of the sailors were sitting, some were standing, some were splayed on the planks. Most of them were looking in the distance toward an imagined siren off canvas. Some with broad rippling shoulders held up their shredded shirts, waving desperately at her. Others crushed their bodies against their shipmates', clawing to reach the invisible woman. Still others just lay on top of other men, dead or spent. All the sailors, their sinewy bodies glistening with salt water, were ravaged by the wrath of Medusa. A few, their eyes desperate or dejected, stared out at me, their bodies covered with sweat, yearning. Their hair was matted and wet, the sail above them threadbare and frayed.

For me, the sailors were alive. Seething and real. The French say, *"L'appétit vient en mangeant."* The longer I savored my secret fantasies, rendered in oil and canvas, the hungrier I got. I wanted to eat the page. I wanted to will myself into the eerily luminous landscape. When I could consume no more I ran up the rickety stairs of my grandmother's old house to find relief in our dilapidated bathroom with its peeling linoleum and broken pipes.

The wretched men were young and beautiful. But they were doomed. Even then I understood that their predicament mirrored mine. What adolescent male wouldn't? They were cursed by lust and so was I. Dangerous unseen forces tempted me, too, from off the dull canvas of my little life. I longed to touch the sailors like they hungered for Medusa. They fed my desire at the same time that they were being destroyed by their own.

It never occurred to me that the actual painting hung somewhere in *this world* on a museum wall. Could I see this thing of beauty, these half-naked men, bigger than the half-inch images that I slurped off the page? My God! That reality was unimaginable to me then. I could no more imagine seeing the painting for real than I could name the sickening shame inside me—and the feelings that brought it on.

I couldn't even call it "desire" then. I knew it was big and swirling and monstrous and overflowing and scary and exciting and hot and blistering and red, but I didn't know it was *desire* to touch Géricault's heavenly bodies. It was just a constant unsteadiness, an inexplicable feeling like some major portion of a puzzle was missing. It wasn't even concrete or consistent enough to be "bad."

*   *   *

My American Dream never included being a fag, a pussy, a punk. Little black boys, especially, are supposed to be tough. Toughness is supposed to inure us to the world's spite. Mindful of the demands that my community made on me—be a strong black man, marry a strong black woman, build a strong black family—I tried hard not to acknowledge who I was growing up. In the years that followed, I would fall over self-hatred, a string of male prostitutes, and a mountain of lies before I was able to accept myself. Not until I set off for Paris to be a foreign correspondent at twenty-five, thousands of miles from America, the black "community," and my family, would I leave the closet. Paris would inspire my declaration of independence, *my* emancipation proclamation. But, as a boy, horrified and horny, I couldn't know there would be a happy ending.

Until puberty I had antidotes to Satan's spells; girls looked at me in school and I became friends with them. I had a girlfriend every year from first grade on—actually two in first grade. We didn't do anything but play together and tell people we were boyfriend and girlfriend. Still, they provided a cover for my other inadequacies; they removed suspicion from my other pastimes and from my own mind. But with the burst of hormones at puberty my sick urges became undeniable, which is precisely why denial really kicked in just then.

All the early-warning signs had been there. One particularly incriminating photo hid inside our family album, popping out at the most embarrassing times like a roach on the living room wall. In it my brother Charles, my cousin Charles, and I are standing in front of the Big Tree in Grandmom's backyard. My cousin has his feet planted apart, his arms down in a karate pose. My brother has both arms bent in a biceps-flexing profile. I'm prissily propped against the tree trunk, one knee bent, both hands on one thigh, my head coquettishly tilted down, my eyes raised. Charles and Charles look tough. I look like a younger, darker version of Princess Diana. I could be excused, I guess. I was only about eight years old. But the picture haunted me as I grew up, reminding me, even after I had learned to control myself, what shameful things I was capable of.

When I was eleven, Mom finally told me it was wrong to hold my hands "that way" and to make mud pies. Her instructions made a greater impression on my pubescent soul than a picture in a book. I swear I had put it all together somehow: mud pies, placing my hands one on top of the other, wanting to look at the men in the encyclopedia. I don't think I ever put it all together in my head, consciously, but I'm sure that I felt it was all connected in some way—and all very, very wrong.

Driving toward the Delaware River and the old Champale malt-liquor factory, just inside the Trenton city line, Mom and her friend Susan discussed the dilemma of mothers raising boys without a man around. I sat in the backseat.

"Whatever I can do," Mom was saying, "I can't teach them to be a man. I can't be a father to them."

"Girl, I know what you mean," replied Susan, a single mother with a son too. "I'm always scared that Mikey is gonna be gay."

I felt all eyes were on me. I avoided looking in the mirror, afraid I would catch my mother's glance and that we would be thinking the same thing. I didn't turn toward my brother sitting next to me either. I just felt relieved that they weren't using the F word: *faggot.* (Kids who hate themselves demand so little.)

When Mom told me "little boys don't do that," referring to the hand business, I stopped. In fact, I did more than that. From that day forward, I monitored my every gesture, every change of timbre in my voice, to make sure I didn't betray sissiness. I never got overly excited, afraid my voice would screech. I kept my wrists rigid, my face composed. There wasn't much I could do about the way I threw a baseball, not having a dad to show me how, but I walked perfectly erect, with ramrod posture. Children, like adults, have strange and conflicting notions of what it is to be a man.

The mud pies I used to make in my grandmother's backyard when I was home alone and bored—often. I'd mix dirt and water in an old tin pan Grandmom let us play with. If any other kids were around when I finished "baking" my pie, I dished it out and they made a show of devouring it. But Mom took me aside one perfect New Jersey summer day and told me little boys didn't make mud pies. I felt dirty. I didn't even ask why. Whether I felt her own shame in the admonition or whether I had an innate image of masculinity from watching *Kojak,*

S.W.A.T., and *Baretta*, it was as if I knew Mom was absolutely right. Of course little boys shouldn't make mud pies. A macho lasagna for your girlfriend after a fight or a rough day on the beat, maybe. But pie? Never. I stopped making the pies.

Mom could have repudiated all the girly things about me at once as I entered adolescence. But she didn't. I think she wanted to clean up my sissy habits before I became a man, but she didn't want to lead herself to uncomfortable conclusions or make me feel like a misfit. So she chose to get rid of my bad habits one by one. It was motherly survival training.

Her fears were well founded. Little black boys and girls have a particularly excruciating way of disciplining little gay boys and girls, making us understand very, very early that it is just . . . not . . . done, my brother, period. Not here, not now. Not us. Never.

The girls reacted to any perceived homolike action—say, snapping your fingers or walking with the slightest soupçon of a twist—in one of two ways. Either they laughed at you—not a baby snicker, but a huge, rounded guffaw that shook the treetops, ending with a shrieked, *"Daaaamnn"* and the stated or unstated "He a punk!"—or they hurled a silent and cutting stare, usually accompanied by a roll of the eyes and often but not always a roll of the neck, and the sucking of teeth. The second reaction could turn violent if the girl perceived that you had somehow embarrassed her in front of her friends. That was only the case if she was attracted to you or if you were more woman than she was.

Boys were potentially more dangerous. Although nobody ever hit me because I acted like a fag, I knew as soon as I relaxed my wrists terror could strike. The most common black male reaction in the face of queerness was to laugh. So Rodney, the only conspicuously queer boy in our 'hood, hammed it up. Naturally, I avoided him, convincing myself that I didn't identify with him. He swished, he shrieked, and he jumped rope. All his friends were girls. Old people just identified him as "that funny chile." But nobody seemed to mind him. In fact, everybody liked him.

It was one of our contradictions: the community and our families were deeply conservative, but they were large and endlessly varied, too. Despite the common homophobia of African-American culture—and my

mother's own admonishments—black people could be miraculously accepting. I wonder how many queer black children's lives were saved
because a mother, a father, an aunt, or a neighborhood elder protected
them like precious jewels, like Rodney, while middle-class white kids
committed suicide to the shock of an until-then indifferent community.

African reverence for that which is special and unusual (the flip side
of ignorance and fear) may have saved me from an early death while I
waded through the self-loathing that came with gradual self-awareness.
In her kitchen my grandmother kept a calendar hanging on a two-foot-
wide chimney column that rose from the floor to the ceiling, covered
with old wallpaper. I don't know when it started, but at some point I
began to decorate the column. I made a bulletin board like the ones
teachers put in school. I divided the column into two sections: one for
my grandmother's calendar and the name of the month (I cut
construction-paper letters) and one for decorations, newsletters, an-
nouncements, and school-lunch menus.

I changed the color scheme every month. In February I used a white
background and red letters and border. In December, red and green
letters and a white background. In January, white and blue. October,
orange and black. No one seemed to mind. Mom took me shopping for
supplies and bragged about my calendar. In fact, my grandmother and
my mother, even my brother and my uncles occasionally, took an interest
in "Markie's calendar."

"Hey, it's the third of the month and you haven't changed the calendar," they would say.

My family considered my decorating tendencies benign enough; sometimes I did say I wanted to be a teacher when I grew up. After all, it
wasn't like I was playing with dolls.

Still, I made it a point not to be seen near Rodney. I was smart in
school, and that already made me sexually suspect. I have no idea where
black folks got the notion that smart boys are gay. Maybe there was
some ancient African caste of homosexual intellectuals. Maybe it was just
that the really stupid brothers looked to fight you as soon as they had
an excuse, since they had no other way of demonstrating their worth,
while smart brothers avoided violence—ergo, punk. Or maybe some incredibly crafty white man had decided early on that if he could spread

among the African slaves the idea that to be smart was unmanly, then the Negroes would shun education like a bad hair weave and remain forever ignorant. Whatever the genesis, it worked. Doing well in school could get you tagged as a fruit.

My escape from my doomed existence was TV. I watched from four o'clock in the afternoon when I got home through to the eleven o'clock news, making sure I did my homework during the reruns before prime time. I didn't even break for dinner; I ate glued to the television. I knew the programming schedule by heart. After school, *Lost in Space, Gilligan's Island, The Monkees, The Brady Bunch.* Then, the meat of the matter, prime time: *Love Boat, Three's Company, M*A*S*H, Family, The Jeffersons, Good Times.*

Almost everybody on TV was handsome: Parker Stevenson, Kirk Cameron, and Jason Bateman. I forced myself to notice the women and the girls, but already there was a campiness growing within that made me like the girls for the wrong reasons. I loved *The Facts of Life*—I knew the theme song by heart. But it was their crazy adventures that interested me—not all that hair and hips. On the other hand, I could watch Mike Seaver go through hours of insipid dialogue, barely listening to what he had to say. Ditto for all the other heartthrobs whose photos prepubescent girls got to cut out of teen-zines and put on their walls. The centerfold pictures had little hearts or teddy bears embossed around the edges. Such gooey sentiment made me want to vomit, but the models were all too appealing.

Bewitched took on a special significance. It was my favorite show, and Samantha Stevens, the pretty blond witch (bad habits start early), was my favorite television character. I watched her twice a day. When I stayed home sick from school, I would watch her twice in the morning and twice in the afternoon. I don't remember ever playing *Bewitched*—like my uncles and my brother and I played *S.W.A.T.*—but I probably did. I did try to twitch my nose without touching it. Like me, most of my relatives decided that I had a thing for the witch.

Given how many of my waking hours were spent devouring images of cute boys, I have no idea how I could have ignored my motivation. Despite it all, I looked like a relatively well-adjusted American Negro youth growing up in the late seventies in New Jersey. I was determined to make the image real, eliminating anything that threatened it. So just before my twelfth birthday, I took that photograph of my brother Charles, my cousin Charles, and me standing in front of the Big Tree in Grandmom's backyard and ripped it to shreds. For years I had looked at it, a bit of my self-esteem fading each time. Later I actually felt the jab to my stomach each time Mom hauled down the album. One day I taped a piece of carpet lint over my hands in the picture. The next time Mom showed off "her boys," she reprimanded me for defacing the photo. She peeled off the tape, making everyone even more conscious of the incriminating pose I had tried to conceal. The next time she looked the picture was gone. I destroyed it and cursed myself for not doing it earlier. She never mentioned it again. Maybe she forgot it, or was she as relieved as I was?

I could destroy evidence and conceal gestures, but I couldn't change what I felt. Despite my best efforts, someday the artifice of "normality" had to fall away. It did, early one Sunday afternoon when I was twelve. My cousin was sixteen.

I put on my blue velour robe and padded down the rickety stairs. My cousin was watching an old black-and-white movie on our black-and-white TV set. He wore only his Ewing High School J.V. basketball shorts, black with waxy yellow lettering. I sat next to him on the couch, silent. He would occasionally sneak glances at me. The glances grew longer and longer.

I noticed his slightly parted thick lips. Uncomfortable, I stood up and went to the front door. I pretended to look out the window up Field Avenue. The street was empty.

My cousin got up from the couch and stood behind me. He lightly brushed the soft fabric of my robe. "Let's get gay," he fawned in a mock faggy tone. "Let's get gay." He rubbed his huge hands over the thin fabric that separated them from my behind. He pulled up the robe.

Exposed and naked, my erection to the wind, I wanted to melt into his arms, to be held by him, to desperately answer the questions my soul had been avoiding, but I also wanted to shield my eyes from what was happening.

We went back to the couch, and I felt someone's hands on my genitals for the first time. They were boiling—his hands and my genitals. I sat back and closed my eyes.

My ecstasy from his touch. My relief from loneliness. Momentarily overcoming fear and shame. Then, the fall. Each of the half-dozen times we did it over the next four years it would be that way. While we were in the act, it was good. His heavy brown body lying against mine, providing the warmth I never thought I would have. He was tender and sweet. But after I came, shame tumbled on top of me, the pleasure buried, suffocated. The disgraceful white goo the physical proof of my spiritual delinquency.

Only once did my cousin and I mention our misdeeds outside the sacred and profane boundaries of our time together on Sunday afternoons when everyone else was out of the house or, later, when I came home from boarding school. We were fighting over the TV or something equally important. He wanted to watch football. I wanted to watch *Bewitched*. I said, close to him, my lips tight, "I'm gonna tell my mother what we do."

"Nobody makes you do anything," he snarled.

I felt like a baby for whining that I would tattle. But, for me, the fact that I liked it—and I didn't really want it to stop—or I wanted it to continue at least as much as I wanted it to stop—sealed my damnation. I was going to hell. From then on I multiplied the shame of being gay by the shame of incest. They became one. And they both grew bigger, badder, blacker. It would take another child's lifetime, three thousand miles, an ocean, and the refuge of Europe for me to pick up where I left off.

Becky's Pagination

Rebecca Zinovic

People have always asked me how well I can see. It's a strange question, which I have never been able to answer. When I just shrug or throw up my hands, people invariably try to help me get the right answer by asking a series of more specific questions. Can you see that tree over there? (The big one? Yes.) Can you read the writing on that street sign? (What sign?) How many lines down can you read on the eye chart? (I once read "OPLG," but I think I cheated when the eye doctor got distracted with something in my encyclopedia-length medical record.) Why does your head bob up and down when you read a book? (Doesn't everybody's?) How many fingers am I holding up? (Hmmm . . .)

After many eye operations throughout my life to give me sight and later improve it (I was born blind with congenital cataracts), I have spent a lot of time wondering what it means to see. During childhood, I asked the question literally: When I saw the color red, did my red mean the same to Billy, Cheryl, Pam, or even my surgeon, Dr. Marks? Maybe what they saw was purple to me, but they just happened to call it red. But how could I ever be sure if my perceptions were correct? Beginning in junior high, when I faced the full brunt of not fitting in, I started to ask the question more abstractly: How did I see the world? How did my perceptions of the world compare with other people's? And what was the relationship between how I saw the world and how the world saw me? Sight, I was beginning to learn, is as much about the meeting of my inner and outer worlds as it is about eye charts and colors.

Why is this stupid wrinkled lady in white go-go boots showing me a coloring book in special ed? If it were kindergarten, I'd understand, but this is seventh grade. Shouldn't I be beyond coloring books by now? Her pasty hand pushes a copper-colored Crayola toward me, and it's as if she's offering me dog shit.

"Perhaps you'd like a different color?" she says, extending a dark pink crayon.

Magenta just might be my favorite color, but I keep eyeing it with suspicion.

"Well, maybe you don't understand how special this book really is, so let me show you. I'm not above coloring books."

The teacher, who is new, snatches one of the crayons and starts to color, recklessly at first, then more slowly and carefully. As she works, I notice something weird: No matter how big she colors, her crayon marks stay inside the lines of the drawing.

She smiles a fake smile and offers the magenta crayon again. Reluctantly but defiantly, I pick up a different color, snot-green. I have to understand this. I have to see for myself.

I start timidly and methodically, trying to stay in the thick black lines on the page. But soon I discover that I too can color outside the picture without the slightest hint of making a mistake. What is happening here? I pick up black and carelessly color a boot worn by a prince riding a stout horse with his princess. The boot is small. I've never been a great colorer. But somehow the boot comes out perfectly, as if it has been done by Brenda W., the prissiest girl in kindergarten.

I head for the crown of the princess and slash at it with the black crayon. I'm in mortal combat, but no matter how aggressively I color, I keep seeing this perfect black crown on a pretty little head. It just keeps coming back, black, but definitely still there, still perfect.

"Why is the crown black, honey?" the special-ed teacher asks.

"Why won't it color outside the lines?" I want to know.

"This is just one of many special tricks I have for you," she says triumphantly, and reaches down into a shiny gray plastic tote bag with Mickey Mouse on the side. To my horror, it is filled with toys. "You see, people like you are what we call 'legally blind,' and sometimes you'll find the simple things that other children can do are just harder for you. The coloring books are specially designed for people like you. We know how much you want to fit in."

I run my palm and extended fingers lightly over the pages of the coloring book. I feel a waxy substance I couldn't see on all the places outside the lines. Mortified, I snatch my hand away as if I were Helen Keller trying to read the waffle iron.

I've often tried to sort out what made me different at school. When did the feeling first set in and why? Surely it had something to do with my large-print books. By the late sixties when I was about to enter junior high, a few publishers came out with editions that looked exactly like big versions of the real books the other kids used. To this day, I wander the aisles of Costco fascinated by the giant boxes of name-brand detergents and cereals, strange and familiar at the same time. I can imagine now that my classmates felt this sense of awe when they saw my big replicas of their objects from daily life.

More often though, I remember the frustration of not being able to fit the books into my desk. They lived at the back of the classroom because they were too big and too heavy. And most publishers didn't even try to make them look right. They were made of thick paper, not thin, shiny, and compact like the real books. My pictures were strangely flat, with richer, darker colors but also kind of dull. Something tells me that if I ran across one of them today, I would find it beautiful. But at the time I lacked the perspective and the confidence to see the magic in my world.

And then there was this problem with Becky's *pagination*, a word that still has a curious adult ring in my ears, a ring of impending difference not unlike that conjured up by words such as *homosexual* or *lesbian*.

Basically, it meant that I was always turning to the wrong page because the numbers in my books weren't the same as everybody else's.

My school addressed this problem, along with that of Becky's *social adjustment* (I was mercilessly teased by my classmates for appearing cross-eyed and wearing thick glasses) by having me meet twice a week with a special-ed teacher. Even at the time the experience seemed to have a yellowing feel to it, just like my mother's dusty sociology textbooks from the 1940s and 1950s. The teachers were old-fashioned. Their names were old-fashioned. Their words were old-fashioned. Their clothes were old-fashioned. I feared that as a drip who still came to seventh grade in bobby socks when all the cool girls were waltzing into the seventies in their fishnet stockings (pants were still two years away), I too was old-fashioned. Guilt by association.

Once again I'm waiting for my special-ed teacher to bring her Mickey Mouse bag full of toys. But I'm wishing that Miss Tiptree, my very first special-ed teacher from elementary school until the middle of seventh grade, was coming instead. Miss Tiptree and I understood each other. Huddled at a table in the corner of the audio-visuals room, we read great stories about cats who got in trouble or about competent little girls who lived in boxcars far away from people who asked questions. She listened to all the little stories I made up and told me that I would be a famous writer one day. She said that someday all the kids at school who called me Ice Cube Eyes or Clarence the Cross-Eyed Lion from that awful Daktari *TV show would envy me. She said people who were different eventually find each other and the rest of the kids would fade away.*

If Miss Tiptree were coming to the special-ed room today, I'd tell her all about my new friend, Lydia Gersovitch, a famous woman anesthesiologist who created her own country, became its president, and is loved by everybody who lives there—except for the occasional enemy soldiers who kidnap her, take her to their secret dungeon, and start to torture her until she is rescued by the beautiful princess who recognizes her worth and helps her escape. She looks a lot like Lydia Thorpe, the woman doctor on The Interns. *I cut out her picture from the* TV Guide *and keep it in a special box in my room.*

*   *   *

What really went on between Helen Keller and Annie Sullivan? Uncon-
sciously, I may have been asking myself this taboo question my entire
life. The pictures always arrested me: two women with their fingers
dancing over each other's mouths, always together, always touching. Of
course this was okay, the official interpretation says, because it was the
only way for a blind deaf-mute to communicate. And besides, the official
word continues, we all know that poor little crippled girls never even
dream of sex. But even so, a strange hush still surrounds this intimacy
in what—along with Plato and Socrates—surely must be the most famous
teacher-student relationship in history. Miss Sullivan was Miss Keller's
lifelong *companion*, a word so purposely devoid of sexuality that it can't
help but beg the question. Tiptoeing along the lines of Victorian re-
spectability, the two women's public intimacy seemed both necessary
and embarrassing, yet always puzzling in the face of the crude sexual
nature of so many Helen Keller jokes.

As a university professor, I've been on both sides of the student-
teacher relationship. I know that at some intangible level teaching is
about seduction. Learning is about falling in love. It's about discovering
sexuality. It's a dynamic tension between attraction and revulsion as each
of us sorts out our individuality, our place in the world.

*My special-ed teacher is late today. She comes in all out of breath and
tells me she was at the zoo.*

I hate zoos.

*"Of course you'd be welcome to come with us someday, honey! Would
you like that?"*

I hate zoos.

"I went with a special group of poor little blind children."

I hate blind children, especially poor little ones.

"They let the children touch the animals."

I hate zoos. I hate lions. I hate blind children. I hate you.

*"Well, we certainly are quiet today. Don't worry, next time we go to
the zoo, I'll make sure you aren't left out."*

"I'm not blind," I say in a barely audible voice.

"Ah, but you can talk! I was starting to worry about you, honey."

I ignore her because I've been obsessing on a single phrase she used in her first visit. "What does it mean to be legally blind?" I ask.

She looks puzzled and reaches down to scratch her nylon stockings under the table. I sit there listening to the scratch, scratch, scratch as if it is amplified by a hidden loudspeaker.

"How can someone be legally blind?" I try again. "It seems stupid. Either you see or you don't. I can see. I'm not blind."

"Well, dear, it's just a technical name so you can get special help from the state. People like me come to help you because you are Legally Blind."

"I'm not blind." I don't need help. Especially yours.

"I know, dear, but you can get lots of special benefits. For example, the state entitles you to ten dollars a month as a subsidy."

"What's a subsidy?"

"It's money, dear."

"For what?"

"For being blind, legally, I mean."

"I'm not blind, legally or whatever. But what's the money for, I mean, what am I supposed to do with it? Why do they give me money for being somebody I'm not? Besides, it's not very much."

"Well, beggars certainly can't be choosers, now, can they, dear! I guess you could do whatever you wanted with the money."

"Could I buy candy and gum or pizza at the snack bar?"

"I don't see why not."

I hesitate, thinking.

"Can someone be illegally blind?" I wonder out loud at last.

It's coming out the wrong way, like I'm just trying to be difficult, but part of me really wants to know the answer. She just stares at me, getting madder and madder.

"But what if I really didn't want the money?" I continue. "Would I have to take it anyway?"

"Dear, it's money. You get it because you're handicapped. You get it because the state feels sorry for you."

Scratch, scratch, scratch.

"What about marijuana?" I venture. "Could I buy marijuana with the ten dollars I get because I'm blind? I think a lid costs about that much."

"Young lady, I've had about as much as I can stand of you today! Our time is up!"

I start to feel victorious because we still have at least another half hour left. Maybe I am driving her out.

Nervously, she starts to gather her things from the table and stuff them into the Mickey Mouse bag. But as she paws her way through all the clutter on the table, she seems to be looking for something.

I grip her cold Mont Blanc pen in my hand until it sweats. Where could it be?

Bright-colored papers and crayons and pieces of games are flying in every direction as she empties the entire contents of the bag onto the table.

I let the pen quietly slip to the floor and give it a gentle tap with the tip of my shoe so that it slides over to her side of the room.

"Don't just sit there!" she stammers. "My gold pen . . . a present . . . I don't think I could have misplaced it. Did I have it when I came in? Help me find it."

"I think it's over there by the file cabinet," I report.

My junior high years were shaped by strange names on a spectrum of good and evil. Lydia Gersovitch was Slavic like me. I made up her name because I thought it sounded intriguing, exotic, and sexy, though I wasn't exactly sure at that point what *sexy* entailed. She spoke perfect English with an accent, one of many facts that made her more interesting than most of the other people in junior high. I had high hopes that this smart, beautiful woman would rescue me from the doldrums of turning into a woman. I didn't realize until later that she was my Dream Me at the same time that she was my role model and the woman I hoped to marry.

On the opposite end of the name spectrum was Norma Frostbender. It was only a few years ago that I could bring myself to utter my special-ed teacher's name, a name so absurd that I couldn't possibly make it up. Her name hovered over me like a ghost. (Even today, I still can't go to Fassbinder movies without feeling that twinge of creepiness from junior high.) *Norma* was bad enough with its implicit missing *"l"* at the end. But in junior high, *Frostbender* was just too weird for words. It symbolized everything that was wrong with special ed. It was strange rather than exotic. It represented a woman who refused to know me. It was the very essence of humiliation.

Waiting for the school bus to go home, I tell my best friend Chuck (her real name is Adrianna, but everyone calls her Chuck because she looks and talks like Peppermint Patty) about how I hid the pen and how stupid Mrs. Go-Go Boots looked trying to find it. I tell her about getting money for being legally blind. We plot how to spend it. I have a lump in my throat.

"Mrs. Frostbender sure looks a lot like a rooster when she walks across campus in her white go-go boots," Chuck tries to reassure me. "Go-go boots, really! That old bag is just trying too hard!"

But I blush when Chuck says her name. Something about it embarrasses me, as if by pronouncing such a clunky name out loud, All-of-Junior-High will find out about the coloring book, the trips to the zoo, and the ten dollars. I tell Chuck we can't say it, and suggest we call her L.B. instead, for "legally blind."

Eager to use our new name, Chuck says, "I made a sighting of L.B. walking across the quad with Myra Jergensen yesterday."

"It figures she'd be with Myra Jergensen," I snort.

"Yeah. You should have seen her in gym class last week. Miss Anderson was doing roll call before we went out to the pool, and Myra Jergensen wasn't there. So Anderson sends Patricia Malloy to go look for her, and a few minutes later they come back, and guess what? Myra Jergensen's bathing suit was on the wrong way so that her boobs were practically hanging out!"

"Oh, gross!" I say in delight. "What did Anderson do?"

"She sent Miss America to her locker to put it on the right way."

I'm silent, from both disgust and fascination. Myra is in eighth grade, and sees about as badly as I do if not worse.

*   *   *

Myra Jergensen was more of a concept than a person for me. I don't remember ever actually meeting her, and I don't think I saw well enough to pick her out in the blur of people who filled the halls in passing period. Something tells me that she wasn't very bright—after all, what smart person would put a swimsuit on backward? But who knows, today she might be on the verge of discovering a cure for AIDS. She might be married, the sunny mother of a boy and girl, living in a tract home close enough so she can walk to the mall, since she probably can't drive. She might be one of the hottest bartenders at Clit Club.

She was someone I came to know only through others, but with whom I still share a frightening intimacy. I've sometimes wondered what we would say to each other if we met today. What did she do with her ten dollars? Did she ever go to the zoo? Did she love or hate L.B.? Whose pictures did she keep in the box hidden away in her dresser?

Miss Tiptree might be good friends with Miss Russell, the dean of girls. Maybe they go on double dates. Miss Russell drives a yellow car with a black roof, and I always look for it wherever I go, in the parking lots outside of shopping centers, at stoplights, racing by on the freeway, gliding silently through my neighborhood. I can't see well enough to know exactly who is driving a particular yellow car with a black roof when one goes by, so I always assume it's her and that she's going someplace important.

I am thrilled and devastated the day I am admitted to her inner sanctum. During math class I receive a call slip summoning me to see the dean of girls. Trembling, I sit down in Miss Russell's paneled office by the flagpole in the front of the school. Through the venetian blinds I can see that it is passing period outside, strangely chaotic compared with the adult hush of the office. Only then do I notice Miss Tiptree standing beside the desk. She seems really upset.

"Thank you for coming, Rebecca," Miss Russell says, pulling out a chair so that I can sit down. She is icy cold, and I feel myself blush. My hands are shaking. My palms are sweaty.

I stare from Miss Russell to Miss Tiptree and back. Miss Tiptree clears her throat, starts to speak, then, looking at Miss Russell, stops.

"Rebecca," Miss Russell says, looking me straight in the eye. I try hard

not to look away, which is excruciating. She really is scary, but also fascinating in her short hair and tailored suit. Through the coldness, I can't help but imagine that she might have been crying. "Rebecca," she begins again, "I'm afraid that this is Miss Tiptree's last week with us. Next week she's being reassigned to another district."

I stare at the two women in disbelief, then I burst into tears.

"But why?" I ask, my throat hoarse.

"Don't worry, Rebecca," Miss Russell says in a low voice with a touch of kindness in it. "They've already found a new special friend for you."

I look at Miss Tiptree in amazement, hoping that she will say it's a joke. But her face is all twisted up, and she takes off her glasses to wipe them on her skirt. "Good luck, B.Z." She tries to smile. She walks over and puts her arm around me, then gives me a tender hug. "Sara—Miss Russell—will take care of you. If you need anything from her, just ask." As Miss Tiptree utters these words, she looks inquiringly over at Miss Russell, who nods gravely.

I must have been well into my thirties when I first saw *The Children's Hour* with Audrey Hepburn and Shirley MacLaine. In the almost empty Sunday-afternoon movie theater, it wasn't the story of a girl betraying her teachers' alleged unnatural relationship that brought me back to Miss Tiptree and Miss Russell. It was something about *Miss* itself. It was a code word for eligibility in a world where two sets of rules worked simultaneously, almost at cross purposes. After a certain never specified, yet universally understood age, "Miss" went from being a sign of a girl's heterosexual availability to a sign of a woman's homosexuality. Ever since I was a young child I had been meticulously deciphering this code without a lesson, without even knowing it was code: Miss Krummenacher, my camp counselor; Miss Foster, my journalism teacher; Miss Levi, my friend Regina's aunt, all held a fascination for me, while anyone who was "Mrs." somehow just didn't count. And when Miss Foster got engaged, it felt like a betrayal. Sitting in the dusty theater, I realized that in junior high I implicitly understood the existence of a lesbian culture long before I even thought to ask what a lesbian was.

*   *   *

Over the summer Miss Tiptree sends me a postcard from a cruise ship in Alaska. It has a big white glacier on it. She says she misses me but that Alaska is an interesting place. She says that even though Alaska is very far away, she hopes that I might come visit her and her friends someday. The women all live in a big house in a small town, a town too small to find on a map. She thinks they will be happy there for a long time. She signs the card "Vic," with "Miss Victoria Tiptree" in parentheses. I add the card to my special box with Lydia Thorpe's picture in it.

I've always sensed that disability and bisexuality have been intimately connected for me, though it is only recently that I have begun to consider just how. My comings-out have been a game of emotional and intellectual leapfrog; first I sort out something about sexuality, then something about disability, which in turn illuminates something new about lesbians, and then back again to Helen and Teacher. Just as if I were still in junior high, my revelations are random and contradictory, filled as much with self-love as with self-loathing. Sometimes the two emotions are hard to tell apart.

For example, ever since I can remember, I have assumed that I would never marry, an assumption shared—but never openly stated—by people in my family. Relatives always asked my younger sister about her boyfriends, while I stood by silently, almost grateful that I would not be put on the spot. As I became more aware of my not fitting the heterosexual mold, I somehow understood, with some relief, that I might join the Miss Tiptrees and the Miss Russells of the world; since it wasn't yet socially acceptable to ask girls about female lovers, I shouldn't expect any inquiries regarding my private life anytime soon.

But then one day I had a shock. I was reading an essay by a man in the nineteenth century explaining why blind girls should never marry. "Who," he asked in all sincerity, "would keep house? Who would mind the children who romp through parlor or garden?" I stared at the strange page in front of me and wondered how a girl who had needed wax to stay in the lines of a special-ed coloring book in seventh grade could possibly cope with a household's dust and spiderwebs. Would I never marry because I loved women or because people thought of me as the poor little crippled girl?

*   *   *

A few years later as I prepare to graduate from high school, I'm seated on a large picnic blanket in the blazing afternoon sun. Vic, now back from Alaska, called me out of the blue, wanting to know if I would be interested in going to a Joan Baez concert at the university with her and some friends. There are about ten women, all of them like Vic, all with short hair, all of them sitting on blankets like me. All of them sway in time to the music. I think they're a bit weird.

"So tell me about your boyfriends," Vic ventures. I shift uncomfortably on the blanket and feel the women staring at me.

"Right now I guess I'm just worrying about getting into college," I say.

One day not too long ago, I asked my parents what they remembered about Miss Tiptree, Mrs. Frostbender, and me in junior high. They sat quietly, lost in thought at the kitchen table. "I don't remember much," my mother said at last. "I think you were really unhappy, and I didn't get the impression you liked Mrs. Frostbender very much." I waited. What about Miss Tiptree?

After what seemed an eternity, my father broke the silence. "I think you really enjoyed Miss Tiptree; you seemed to have a real rapport."

"Yes," my mother chimed in, "but there was something very strange."

I held my breath.

My mother cleared her throat nervously, and continued. "You see, Miss Tiptree was convinced that you wouldn't go to college, and I'm not completely sure she was in favor of special education in the first place. She told us you were of average, even below-average intelligence, and that we shouldn't expect much from you because of your vision impairment. I remember getting really mad at her, and she backed off. I even thought of complaining to the school board."

Vic just smiles when I tell her how much I hated Mrs. Frostbender. I tell her about the coloring books, the money, and even my contrary plans to buy marijuana with it. I can't quite bring myself to confess about hiding the pen. But I'm proud to announce that I didn't ever have to go to Mrs. Frostbender again after complaining to Miss Russell. In fact, I never went back into special ed.

"There's nothing wrong with your being independent—in fact it's a good thing," Miss Tiptree says. "If you're already this sure of who you are, I guess we both did our jobs, right?"

Now, at the age of forty, as I think back over my story, I might well ask myself who sees clearly at thirteen anyway? Like the blurry letters of the eye charts in my doctors' offices, the vague outlines of sexuality were coming into focus, but I had no idea what this meant or if it was permanent. And like the many lines on the charts that I couldn't see, my future remained a mystery so foreign that I barely knew how to ask the questions, let alone how to seek the answers, of what it would mean to be thirteen no more. Perhaps the answers lie in the indispensable companion question that I was always asking without realizing it: Who sees the thirteen-year-old clearly?

1976

Doug Jones

*I went back to Colorado for Thanksgiving 1997, the fourth trip back home
that year. My father was dying from a brain tumor diagnosed less than
a year earlier, and this would be the last time I saw him. I stayed both
with him at the house of his current wife and at the house of his ex-
girlfriend, who had lived with us during my high school years. It was
while there, going through an army-surplus trunk full of school papers,
artwork, and childhood bibelots left in her care, that I found my seventh-
grade journal.*

*It was written in a seventy-page "Friends of the Earth" spiral notebook,
and though the cover is missing I think it had a moody, sepia-toned shot
of the planet Earth taken from the moon. I began this journal for an
English class taught by Mr. Clark. He was young, groovy, good-looking,
athletic, a poet; and early on in the class he introduced us to the concept
of the Renaissance man, which he clearly hoped to embody. Mr. Clark's
modus operandi was seduction; he used his charisma, and I desperately
wanted his approval and hung on his every word. In the entries his
influence is clear, though as events overtook me the journal took on a life
of its own.*

Mr. Clark died six months before my father, also of a brain tumor.

Jan. 26, 1976

Today was not bad, except for P.E. I felt like puking about 5 times, and the coaches seemed unrelenting. I must be getting paranoid. I think we are going to [Lake] Powell over spring vacation—I need to rebuild my village.[1] I think I'll build a palace this time.

Dennis is supposed to do dishes and I doubt that the pig will do them. Mom got the groceries—she's going to Boulder Tues. and Dad's going to Mexico on the same day. We don't have to have a sitter—Yah!

Annie and I played "tennis" with styrofoam balls by hitting them with our hands to bounce them against the wall. It was fun.

In case you're wondering, in my family there are Mom, Dad, Dale, Dennis, me, Annie, in that order. We have a dog, Blue, 2 cats, Sam and Stony, a rabbit Shorty, a hamster Nutmeg or Nut. All this is important because I will write a lot about them since they are the most important things in my life.

> Honor lost, much lost, Money lost, little lost,
> Hope lost, all lost

Jan. 27, 1976

It is a good morning. I am riding my second bus—I hope the day fits the morning. Discussed fear in Clark—and being alone. It made me think of Dale and I at Powell—with those monstrous cliffs and the broiling sun and how he almost fell—and how Blue got heat exhaustion and we only had some beer to give him (that was all we could drink too—we hadn't brought anything else). About carving our names in the rock high in the cave and seeing the deer in that hot lonely canyon. And of the Indian fort I found and the corn cobs from the Indian ruins—about camping with no one there to crowd you out and the huge, bright moon and stars lighting it up like a stage—and my family and how much fun we had and will have—I think all these things are the most important things in my life. I wish I was an archeologist already. I suppose I am

[1] I built structures based on Anasazi Indian cliff dwellings at approximately 1"=1' scale in the rock formations of the Utah desert where we camped on vacations.

in a way. I hope it either snows more or all of it melts—first would be better.

Waste not, want not

Jan. 28, 1976

I have to prepare 2 topics for speech, yuk! I'm going to have tons of homework and we're going to dinner at our "watcher" (sitter's) house. I want to finish my book and I'll have to play my piano. Ah, Life's sad sorrows. I guess it's not that bad. I may just be lazy. This is all pretty boring to you I'm sure, but I don't have anything else to write.

Jan. 29, 1976

I read one of my favorite author's books. It was called *The Changeling* by Zilpha Keatley Snyder. It was really good and had a lot of feeling in it—as usual. I have plans for so many books and I can never write; here are some titles:

The Phoenix
(trilogy) St. Augustine
Journey of the Unicorn
War of the Wizronds

Jan. 30, 1976

We had a huge fight this morning (Dale, Dennis, me, Annie). I left my lunch on the bus; didn't do my homework (E.L.) [Environmental Living]—bad morning—but I finished my speech.

I have decided that this journal is not going to be boring anymore. You have helped me a great deal by the discussion we had today and by seeing *Deliverance*. It was like nothing I ever saw before, and it drained me of lots of *energy*. But I don't care. I never get things done and now I plan to do it. I have planned a story for a long time—about 3 children surviving in the desert—alone. Two 12-year-old boys and a girl about 11–12 months old. They are on a pack trip with horses—a group of about twenty people and a guide. They camp on a small plain between a canyon and a cliff, when the cliff caves in and buries or shoves off the rest of the camp. No maps to go by, they become lost—in a place so desolate and unpopulated that it hasn't been seen for hundreds of years—since the Indians. They find an Indian ruin and live there—nearly 10 years in a place so silent and awesome—and no one but the most hardworking, brainy, and fittest can possibly survive. I don't know if it will be worth my effort, but I think I can tell it right if I really try. So much for that tonight (I might be writing rather long extra credit stories in here—be expecting it).

Today we got the report cards—I dropped a little—from 6 A's to 5 A's—but I still get in the honor roll. I don't want to sound vain—I just hope (pray) I can get a scholarship—it would really help. I'm really getting written out so—I hope it was worth the ink and paper.

Jan. 31, 1976

The wind blew up a lonely canyon, and then a light flickered, and grew, and the council's fire began a new life. As the tinder and then the wood burned, the somber spirit of the trees was driven away, and was replaced by a brilliant flame spirit, the dancing spirit. And as the uneven new light crept into the corners of the courtyard and the blank squares of the small doorways, the people woke. Yawning and stretching, the people gathered around the warming, lively fire. Soon more came down ladders and jumped from balconies, rejoicing with the new spirit of the night. A drum beat, and the people moved. Slowly at first, then gaining momentum, they circled the fire, and then they began to leap, and the drums pounded in rhythm with their feet, and their excitement rose to a screaming crescendo, fighting a losing battle to live again, and then stopped. The sun's first rays picked out the color of the trees on the rim of the canyon, and the sandstone turned orange—its natural color again. And they were gone. Had they ever been there? Where was the brilliant fire, the dancing people, the beautiful city?

A noisy band of tourists looked over the scenic trail at the sad ruins of Square Tower House,[2] and it was dead again.

(I fulfill my promise)

Feb. 1, 1976

I went to see *Tommy*. It was OK. Dad got home from Mexico and brought me a beautiful belt. Mom is expected to get in about 12 (midnight). Yesterday I finally got some new books from the library. It's getting late, and I'd like to can it, but I might write a story—OH, FORGET IT.

Feb. 3, 1976

ZILCH

Feb. 4, 1976

Yesterday I should have written because we had a family fight. I got whacked on the head and kicked in the butt, but otherwise came out unscathed. After that (after I had finished my work) I finished a book and read another. Both were very good, though on completely different subjects . . .

This afternoon I stayed in town and had plenty of fun. When Mom came from work to pick me up, the car got high-centered [in the snow] in front of Rexall Drug (our "Hangout"). We finally got out and made it home. I watched the Olympics, and I put Compound W on my wart (one of several! Uh!). I have an Idea for my story in creative writing, but what happened was true. I can probably use it. I hope so.

[2]One of the cliff dwellings of the extinct Anasazi Indians preserved in Mesa Verde National Park, about an hour's drive from my home.

Feb. 5, 1976

I went out this morning to shake the snow off the branches of the trees, but one large one had already broken. As usual, Dennis and Annie had a little "Disagreement," and she went screaming off to the bus stop. I am in 1st period Science Mr. Bond, and I have to do my speech next period. Uh!

I didn't have to do it! Ha ha! This period is getting boring (oops) Mr. Robertson was staring at me! Gulp! I started writing my story in English. I think it's going to be all right. Mitch [my best friend] and I played [in the snow] again at noon and got soaking wet. Beautiful! I am now in the living room listening to the Beatles and writing all this monotonous stuff down—tough tit for you! I THINK (amazing) I SHALL WRITE SOMETHING ON NEXT PAGE→

The Faun

On a snowy winter's day, a baby was born. Not in a hospital, but high in the mountains in a sheltered cave near a beautiful frozen waterfall. And because he was born during a lovely sunset, his young parents named him Alisseran Crimson Albas. This may sound strange to you, but not for them, for his father was a lithe young faun, and his mother was a tree spirit, a beech spirit. The child was small and graceful with silver-gray skin, but already they could see the little hooves and horns forming. Soon thick shaggy hair would grow on his goat legs.

Then they heard a shot. Hunters! They fled, and left the crying baby to die in the cold. When the hunters came, they heard the child crying and found him lying on a stone table, squalling and kicking his tiny hooved feet. And they took him home.

The parents found their firstborn gone, and knew they must take "revenge." They went in search of the human's house. And they took the only other small child there, a girl of three named Laurie Anne, and left a golden locket with Alisseran's name on it.

And so he became a "changeling." As he grew older, his foster parents realized there was something wrong (how could they miss). They took him to a specialist when he was five. By then, he had silver grey hair on his goat legs, and definite horns. His skin, even in the winter, was golden brown. He liked to run and play in the trees, but whenever they dressed him, he screamed and tore them off—but he was never mad or sad long. He was laughing and running around the yard with a special pet—a goat.

But the specialist couldn't diagnose anything—one thing for sure was that he was not human. Therefore he could not go to school. That was some weight off their shoulders, for they couldn't hide *those* legs for long.

Feb. 9, 1976

I must interrupt. First of all, on Friday night Mom left. She ran off, for reasons somewhat unknown even now. We went skiing Saturday, but weren't too gloomy, but Sunday a heavy pall had covered us. She called Sunday and Dad got mad and hung up. He tried to trace the call but the company wouldn't. But she said she'd come home tonight and she did, but I am almost crying now, because I think she's going right back. It's sickening and hopeless, and completely stupid.

He hurriedly got some socks and put them on, then went to the porch and slipped on his boots. He opened the door and shuffled dejectedly along the sidewalk. He stared at his feet as they slipped along in the mud and puddles of water.

The sky was heavy with a storm and the wind went through his light shirt to his thin body. He snuffled and hunched his shoulders against the wind. He finally got to the snow bank, and trudged over it, and, unable to hold out any longer, he began to cry. For thousands of reasons. And he walked on, conscious of the snow down his bare toes sticking through the cotton of his socks and rubbing the smooth lining of his boots. He walked on, bawling and mumbling curses to himself, sobbing loudly to make up for his every grief of the three short days of horror.

At some places the snow reached his knees, dropping into the boots, but he knew now, as he walked down the hill, he was finished with crying for a while. He wiped away the tears that hadn't been dried by the wind. He sighed and now really noticed the coldness of the snow, and his feet hurt. And it began to rain. Cold heavy drops of fresh winter-spring rain. It was a dark and cold and lonely rain—and it made him realize that they would make it somehow, sometime—it would take time.

Feb. 10, 1976

I guess now it has [taken time]. I'm over my bitter feelings. After my first walk [the story above], I ended up taking another one and then another childish bawling session in bed. I'm really tiring of this "topic."

I missed my piano workshop, but it won't kill me. I forgot about hair day,[3] what with my serious problems. But I made a beautiful Valentine, which is unfortunately a combination one, to be given to mom and dad together. I guess it can wait till they get back together. It will hold more meaning then.

I could have broken [my friend] RONALD'S scrawny little neck today. On the bus, Eric, Ronnie, and I sit together. So we started this thing about pushing the outside person out of the seat and into the aisle. Ronnie has happened to sit on the outside for at least 5 days and we didn't push him off once. But, low and behold, today while I had tons of crap on my lap, and was innocently reading a book, I got pushed off, of course (paranoid!). I got so pissed off. After thoroughly cussing him out, he started whispering something to Eric.

He always tells us his "PETTY PITY STORIES," and someday I am going to Puke in his lap. He's a spoiled brat and has absolutely no respect for other people's property. STUPID S.O.B.!

I don't write these things to gain pity, it is just easier to write them down than to hold them in. GOO NIH![4]

Feb. 18, 1976

Whew! What a week. Friday night my Aunt Pam got here from Beaulah. She and my brothers went skiing Saturday, and that night mom left. I

[3] I have no idea what "hair day" was.
[4] Good night.

think these "Hives" started to develop that night also. The next morning
we left for Powell!! Yah! We had to sleep in a trailer in the trailer court,
but it wasn't bad, except for hives. The next day they were really itching
and spreading, and my feet started swelling up. Dad made a poultice of
baking soda, and it helped some. I stayed home Tues. morning, and
went to the doctor. So it develops that I have a blood disease like my
(sister). Well, that puts me here in Community Hospital. I had better
cool it cause my wrist is swollen and I can't write very well.[5]

Feb. 23, 1976
Yesterday was a great day. We went to Hovenweep.[6]

Feb. 24, 1976
(I left my notebook at school.) There were some really fascinating buildings. I think I'll be a ranger there when I grow up. Now I've got to
write that story I missed on the 19th, 20th. It is on the next page.

Feb. 25, 1976
Hello sir. By now I hope you can begin to see some of the bad times
that have beset our family since the beginning of this journal. Mom gone,
Sam gone, Stony exiled, and Me in the hospital. Maybe your bad luck!
(snicker, snicker). I truly hope I will do better next time, and if things
settle down (including my hand and pen!) I am sure I will improve. I
hope you like the story on the next page. It is actually me and a Jimmy
I know. Today I got behind his Façade, and we had some fun. This
story is a sort of fantasy—you'll find out soon enough (please try to

[5]My sister had suffered a strange, unpronounceable form of anemia a few years
earlier; the milder, male version I suffered had no treatment except bed rest.
[6]A national monument in the midst of beautifully desolate scrub land and pinto-
bean fields straddling the Colorado-Utah border, designated to protect a series
of pre-Columbian Indian ruins. The trip was clearly a pick-me-up arranged by
my father after a weeklong hospital stay, about which I wrote nothing else.

excuse my inexcusable penmanship) after writing an entire speech in neat little words, I'm in a sloppy mood.

Scott just didn't fit into the school. There were the Honkies or "cowboys," which he really despised, and the jocks, which he just plain wasn't. He was short and skinny, with wild brown blond hair. His eyes were his strangest feature. They were large and blue gray, and he liked to catch people, mostly teachers, in his piercing stare. They almost always looked away. He wasn't really big enough or strong enough to be much of an athlete, and he didn't have the willpower to really work at it. He just didn't care. . . .

And then there was Jimmy. He was different too, and he had begun to lure Scott more and more. He could be very nice, and then Snap! he would be irresponsible, childish, and in the "Action" with his friends. . . .

Today [in P.E.] they were going to play volleyball again. During line-up, he got depantsed by none other than Jimmy. Scott coolly pulled up his trunks and stood patiently in line while everybody laughed. Maybe that was why they disliked him. He always took the punishment without doing anything. He would finish what he was saying then wait for the coach to get there, when he could quietly escape from having his nose twisted, et cetera.

During exercises, he wished there was a group for the cultured, the Learned, the "smart" people, writers, artists, etc. but that was wishful thinking.

Of course, it turned out that Jimmy was on Scott's team. The game went pretty good for a while—at least he got to serve. He watched the ball fly back and forth over the net, and then he saw it. It swung in a high arc, over the net and came toward him. He got his arms in position, and he seemed to wait an eternity as the ball came toward him. Out of the corner of his eye he detected a movement, but he didn't care. The ball came flying toward him, and he yearned for it to hit his arms. But [it] never did, for Jimmy came speeding toward him. Scott seemed to fly, twisting and flying toward the floor. He looked like a crumpled rag doll, the blood slowly spreading out from his head onto the honey colored wood of the gym floor.

The students clustering around him, the thin and distant wail of the ambulance were all hazy and unreal, and then he blacked out completely.

He woke up between the warm and white sheets of the Hospital. He found later that he had been unconscious 3 days. The nurse came in and gave him a pain pill. She said dinner would be served in a while, if he was hungry. That he certainly was. After he had finished eating, the nurse came to get the tray. She said some boy had been asking to see him. She giggled and told him that the kid thought he was dead. Scott told her to send him up. He was bewildered by this. Who would want to see him?

"Man, I thought you were dead," said Jimmy as he shuffled into the room. He looked terrible. His hair was in a mess, and so were his clothes. Gray smudges were under his eyes.

"God, you look terrible!" said Scott, peering at the gaunt and tired face.

"I've been worried. I didn't want to kill you—you weren't like anybody else, and I just couldn't"—he choked and started to sob.

"Couldn't get under your thumb. I know. But come on, settle down. I may not look it, but I am alive," he soothed. "How 'bout it—Friends?"

"Friends," Jimmy returned, smiling for the first time in 3 days.[7]

Undated, 1976

Doug—Yes! I did like the story—good images & details as well as the action! Don't let up, now—there is still more to do—and, keep yourself healthy! Yes![8]

Mar. 6, 1976

I bought the most beautiful book in the world today. I also went to the library and checked out quite a few good ones. I also bought *A Wizard*

---

[7]My middle name is Scott, and as I mentioned to Mr. Clark before the beginning of the story, Jimmy was real. Really handsome, and he tormented me, and I was attracted to my tormentor. Jimmy may or may not have been different, but I do know that he shot himself to death (accidentally?) in high school.

[8]Mr. Clark's midterm comments.

of Earthsea and *The Farthest Shore.* I already had *The Tombs of Atuan.* They are a very good trilogy by Ursula K. Le Guin. I bought them with some money I got shoveling snow off the roof of the trailer house. Mom came to visit again. I really liked what we did in your class, but I really kind of regret that I had to write, because it was so peaceful just to watch the candles and listen to the music. It was very good music. . . .

Mar. 8, 1976

Sorry—nobody is going to keep me from being an Archeologist (Scientist!). I know your not, but in a way you kind of offended me. I really *want* (and am) to be different, I really *want* to be subjective! I can't satisfy everybody, but I *will* satisfy myself. That's about all I can do . . .

. . . OOOHHH THAT DENNIS! I'M GONNA CRUNCH HIM. BAA, you want a perfectionist, you can have my darling brother CRUNCH! CRUNCH! Boy, this journal sure helps about things like that. It's just like screaming or crying. Of course, you've got to cry sometime, but this is much better. It really has helped me, and will continue to do so even after I'm out of your class. I'm going to go back and continue "The Flight."[9] I am revising it to hand in for the contest.

Mar. 11, 1976

Last night I started a poem. Just thought I'd warn you.

Today's discussion was very interesting, but it made me so depressed. It might be painful to leave 1 child behind, like in the case of Rodney [a classmate], but how could she leave behind 4 kids! Whew! ("disgusting") subject! Well, I'm a gonna start my story now, ya'all. S'long. DEATH! HAH![10]

[9]A very long short story I wrote set during the eruption of Vesuvius. An orphaned young Roman nobleman, a.k.a. me, flees the disintegrating city of Herculaneum in the company of an escaped male slave and a baby girl.

[10]I'm not sure what "whew-disgusting" refers to; perhaps I'd farted; I wouldn't put it past myself to mention it, if only obliquely. I don't get the "DEATH!-HAH!" either. This is the only entry with a judgment of what had happened with my mother.

Mar. 14, 1976

Yesterday, Wow! We went skiing with Dad and [his girlfriend] Cindy and Annie. Annie got sick and I ended up skiing with Stony, his [Dad's] friend—one of a group of school kids from Ignacio—a lady called Sally, Cindy, and Stony's girlfriend, Marcy. I'll tell you that Stony is Black, and I really can't believe how people can be prejudiced. We named our cat after him. Then I met Mitch and we skied for a while. It really was fun, except for sunburn. Wow! Then we went out to Dinner at the Assay Office. I had Crepes Louis. DELICIOUS. . . .

Mar. 16, 1976

. . . I really am not creating anything by writing this crud, you know, but, aw, what the heck. Larson's a beast. I just stuck my tongue out at a film projector reel, and she said "Would you shut up!" What a Hag! Drat. They just turned off some good music. Boy, girls are Dumb! That is a very bigoted opinion, but sheesh! I can't help but think all of them (well, not all) are complete idiots. Mrs. Axtell is really a very nice lady, but nobody really admits it. If she gets mad at them and busts them, it is their own fault. They really deserve it! I like Shelly Tomberlain, because she's quiet and nice and, well I suppose different. . . . That Larson! What a Ding Dong! . . . There she goes again! She really makes me sick. I wish she would be my friend, but some people, you just can't get through to them. . . .

I'm watching *The Man of the Hour* (TV), who is Telly Savalas (or whatever). Boy, what asinine crud they put on TV. But then again, TV is crud. I love the sound of a fire in our old coal stove. A muffled but throaty roar. It clicks and flickers, warming the cool air of our leaky house. Furnaces are very unfriendly, like snobs.

GOD helps those who help themselves. That is one of the codes of my life. I do not believe God should be feared, I believe that he should be loved. And that is what I try to do.

Mar. 18, 1976

I am still so tired I could just fall down. If I make it through the day, I can make it through anything! If these stories are just worth one page, I think I just crump out.

A Dream of Freedom

It was an ugly day. Grayish black waves tossed in the harbor, and a soft, drizzly rain dripped off of the red brown tiles of the villa's roof. It ran in ringlets around down his body, sticking the soft wool of his tunic to his sun bronzed skin. The sun was a soft glowing ball in the rain soaked sky.

"Get in out of the rain," shrieked Myra, the Domina's maid. "Get into the quarters with the rest of the slaves. You know how the master hates slaves hanging about the garden."

Oh, he knew all right. But he wouldn't. He hated that man, his brutal wife, and screaming, taunting brats. He liked the rain. It was soft and cool and kind.

Tonight was the night. He was going to escape tonight after dark.

He stood in the garden, like a bronze statue, waiting for night to come. He finally decided it was time to flee, and he crawled through the cool, dripping plants of the garden, through the elegant dining pergola. As he crawled over the low stone railing and began to hurtle toward the ground, he felt a deep satisfaction, but not for long. Because he fell crookedly.

Aragon had been taken slave months ago. His handsome face had a blemishing scar from the war he had lost, but the burning spirit of freedom still burned in his eyes. The Romans and their scornful taunting and pagan gods—now he would never see Greece again.

Now he lay, waiting to die in a cold, dark dungeon, sitting by a drunk, stinking gladiator. His leg was shattered and mangled, and the spirit, his soul, was dead too.

The rain, where was the rain? He tried to hear it through the thick stone walls but couldn't. It was gone, as was his dream of freedom. And he laid down on the cold stone and died.

Undated, March 1976

Well done, Doug—please do a sketch for me of Mr. Clark—I'll give you the paper—do it in ink—yes.[11]

[11]Mr. Clark's closing comments.

A Close Escape

David Bergman

I had a lover for many years who believed he had had an idyllic childhood. His favorite memory—which he would recount whenever he felt
the urge—was of a game he played with his two younger brothers on
their farm in Maryland. He and his brothers would shit in their pants
and then roll down a steep hill at the back of the farm that ended in a
large pond. When they came to the pond, they would strip, jump into
water, and clean themselves and their clothes. It made no difference to
him that this story never proved as delightful to his listeners as it was
for him; in fact, the groans of disgust the story elicited served as proof
to him that by growing up, we had lost some vital connection to this
Edenic state of grace. He was determined never to grow up in this
manner, and in that resolve he succeeded more than he knew, which is
why we are no longer together.

But his story has haunted me. The picture it paints stands in such
marked contrast to my own childhood. I was raised in Queens at the
very edge of New York City in a neighborhood so faceless that people
moved from there to Levittown to be part of a community with character.
And instead of yearning to return to those days, I felt this enormous

sense of relief once they had passed. Even as a boy, I wanted out as fast as I could and found adolescence a release from what had seemed a life sentence of pain and confinement. Each pimple was a reprieve from the prison house of the child. The Sturm und Drang of my teenage years, no matter how painful, seemed even at the time to be worth the discomfort: I understood that all its upheaval was needed to excavate a happy space for myself. Now I can see that I was in some ways better off being an unhappy little boy. Still, I don't look back at childhood with the regret of my ex-lover, who sees his later life as an enormous disappointment. I remember those years before becoming a teenager with a sigh of relief—I'll never have to go through them again.

To be blunt, I had a perfectly miserable childhood. Not as we now think of miserable childhoods—tots locked into closets, their bodies savagely battered by their mothers' crack-smoking boyfriends—but in the fifties sense of miserable, imaginatively starved and emotionally repressed. I was, to use that quaint, faintly Victorian expression, "a sickly child." For long periods of time I was in bed because of a brain injury—I had fallen from a swing and slipped into a coma—and later I had terrible back pain, caused—I learned only after it had passed—from spinal compression, the disks in my spine too small to bear the weight of my overgrown vertebrae.

Yet as far back as I can remember I was aware that my illnesses were just a physical manifestation of some larger difference separating me from other children. I watched my brother and my cousins play their noisy, nasty games, and I didn't join in—not just because I wasn't allowed to—but because I didn't want to be noisy, nasty, and rough. I wanted and needed another kind of childhood, one I couldn't have defined although I kept getting glimpses of it.

Recently a novel I read triggered a memory—what I knew even then was the happiest day of my childhood. It was a bright, cool summer morning. My mother drove me to a nearby park where she had read a marionette theater was performing "Sleeping Beauty." I was very clean in a white shirt and blue pants, and I sat up straight in a tiny chair. I loved the Victorian stage, and the old-fashioned puppets. I loved the way the characters floated through the air with their delicate, stiff movements. At the end of the performance, the curtain above the stage opened, and the puppeteers—a husband and wife and a young assistant—took bows. I couldn't imagine anything more wonderful than being a puppeteer, hovering above the marionettes, pulling the strings that animated so magical a world. Afterward my mother and I walked down to a little stream, and I watched some swans majestically sweep aside a wave of golden dragonflies. I remember thinking even then, *This is the childhood I was meant to have, this is the enchantment that has always been missing.* I begged my mother to bring me back again, but she never did. How could she have known how important it was to me, that forty years later I can still hear the clatter of the puppets' feet on the flimsy stage and the swish of the red plush curtains snapping shut forever? Clearly I was not like other little boys, and I used being sick—or my parents used it, or most likely, we conspired together to use it—to explain why I was different.

So it wasn't only being sickly that made my life miserable—in fact, it may have been responsible for some of the moments of tranquility and freedom I enjoyed—it was more the uncharming, unenchanting world that I was forced to attend.

And nothing was less charming, less enchanting, than P.S. 156, the neighborhood elementary school. It was exactly like hundreds of other grade schools in New York—a U-shaped, red-brick building with stone lintels above the doors, carved with the city's seal. The school was fenced in with heavy wrought iron in front and ten-foot-high chain link in back. The basketball hoops had long ago lost their baskets, but the handball courts—that austere arena of urban life—were then in perfect condition, the concrete walls free of graffiti.

What made P.S. 156 so inhospitable was its obsession with "excellence," which in those dim days of the second Eisenhower administration was an excuse not only for translating conformity into an imperative, but also elevating rigidity into a virtue. To maintain its reputation, the principal instituted a strictly regimented curriculum in which students were kept with those of similar aptitude. No attempt was made to hide the rating system. Class 3-1 was the highest, 3-2 came next, all the way down to 3-6 or 3-7, a murky depth of kids—mostly boys—with whom we were never allowed to associate. I was at the bottom of the top class, and as such always in jeopardy of sinking to the lower depths.

Because of this ruthless sorting practice, the same thirty children were kept together for six years. The only other class we were allowed to have contact with was the one just below us. The jealousies, the cliquishness, the competition that might have dissipated in a more flexible school structure were instead increased by the system's strict hierarchies of achievement. Indeed, in that Cold-War atmosphere, we were encouraged to cultivate the fear of, as well as contempt for, those poor masses whose education went on around us. In *Remembering Denny*, Calvin Trillin's memoir of a college golden boy who happened to be gay and ended his life in suicide, Trillin quotes a friend who speaks of the " 'poisonous template' of the fifties." You didn't have to go to Yale to feel the pressure of the template around you or its poison.

I'm not guessing that I stood at the bottom of the class. Only two students were beneath me, Judy Taucher and Benny Freund. Judy was somewhat of a scandal in the classroom. One day in the fifth grade for "News and Views"—our weekly current-events class—she brought in an article from the *National Enquirer* with the headline MOTHER EATS BABY WITH RICE. Before Mrs. Friedman could stop her, she had shown the class the picture of a baby in a stew pot with some of its stomach sliced away. Her face bright red with anger, Mrs. Friedman ripped the article out of Judy's hands.

"Did your mother know you were bringing *this* to school?" she asked Judy.

Judy, who was very small and pretty and the only girl to have pierced ears, nodded.

"Your mother allows you to read the *National Enquirer?*" Mrs. Friedman asked, not trying to disguise her astonishment and contempt. Her mother might as well have allowed her to read the *Daily Worker*. Judy was told to sit down, and we were ordered to put our heads on our desks. Then Mrs. Friedman left the room to show the offending article to the principal, who called Judy's mother to school to explain how she could let her child, who was in the top fifth-grade class, read the *National Enquirer*.

How carefully each of us was monitored, our academic performances providing vital information not just about ourselves, but about our parents, too. The Cold War and the shadow of McCarthyism stretched across our lives, teaching us to be alert for both the dangerous enemy without and the still more dangerous enemy within. Several times each month we practiced lowering the blackout shades that still hung in the high windows of the classrooms and hiding under our desks just in case Long Island was bombed. Each year our parents had to tell the school whether we were to be sent home or remain in school if there was a nuclear attack. I imagined myself finally released from school, hurrying home to take cover in our basement fallout shelter, and just as I am about to turn the corner, my block is ionized by a direct hit.

Such fears placed no one above suspicion. If we did poorly in a subject, our failure might stem not from being slow, or having forgotten to study or pay attention; it could be from a more serious transgression— questioning the very standards and values that judged success. And where would a schoolchild learn to question American standards and values? Nowhere but from parents. Since I wasn't the best of students, I'm afraid my mother had a lot to answer for, including what became known as my "bleeding-eye paintings." Instead of doing those conventional scenes of cars or airplanes, which all the other boys in the third or fourth grade had done, I produced a series of abstractions of concentric circles slashed by thick, dribbling blood-red lines. My inspiration was my mother's best friend, Janice, a painter whose exhibition of large and violent expressionist paintings I had recently seen.

My teacher was horrified. The paintings indicated some sort of regression to the scribble of toddlers (a regression their tests had failed to predict). A nine- or ten-year-old was supposed to have "advanced" to representation. Worse than regression was the possibility that these paintings might be showing contempt for the canons of naïve realism, a rejection that at the time smacked of subversion. My mother sidestepped both regression and subversion as explanations. These pictures, she argued, *were* representational—I had cut my eye on a thornbush and it had bled—and although schematic, the paintings were my attempts at depicting the accident. My mother's explanation filled my teacher with relief. I had not regressed or rebelled, I had merely painted poorly.

What would have happened if one, just one, of my elementary school teachers had taken a particular interest in me? I don't know. None of them did. The better teachers left me alone to find my own way. The worse tried to make me toe the line. I hated them. I hated most of my teachers in grade school, but my anger did not win them over or make them pay me any more attention. I don't blame them. I was not an especially nice or winning child. Morose, withdrawn, resistant, I kept my teachers at arm's length even though what I craved was the smallest bit of encouragement to express myself and to find that glimmer of enchantment I had witnessed at the puppet theater in the park.

Actually my life began to change even before I entered junior high school. Sometime in the sixth grade my spinal disks caught up with my vertebrae, and the back pain that had wailed through my body was reduced to a low grumble. For the first time in years I felt free to move around. Then the following summer I made my first real friend, Laurence Traiman.

I had known Laurence since the first grade, when for a short time we were in the same class. But he was soon moved to Class 1-2, and he remained throughout elementary school in that second tier. In the summer when we were twelve, we found ourselves together at Boy Scout camp in the bunk where the scoutmaster threw all us odd kids. What made us odd varied—sometimes it was being poor or Catholic—but none of us questioned that we were indeed odd.

Laurence was a wiry boy with a mop of curly blond hair. His hands flowed through the air when he talked, and he talked constantly—of movies and disasters and his beloved *Titanic,* which united his twin obsessions of wreckage and cinema. His knowledge of old films was as encyclopedic as it was indiscriminate. He loved great epic pictures, except those starring Victor Mature. We delighted in Irene Dunne comedies, Ida Lupino *noir* melodramas, and Busby Berkeley musicals. His mother was a violinist, and Laurence had a particular passion for film scores. When we weren't watching old movies on television—I would be called almost every night and instructed to turn on the TV to watch one memorable scene or another—we would study the music. My job was to listen and laugh. Laurence was proud of how giddy he could make me. He'd time his jokes so that I would be drinking during the punch lines. Then he'd watch in mock horror as I sprayed the room.

My interest was mostly in the theater. Nearly every Saturday, armed with twofers, we would take the bus and subway from our neighborhood at the edge of Queens into the heart of Manhattan and see a matinee. The trip took an hour and a half, and the tickets would cost us a dollar or two at most if we sat in the second balcony. Often we were the only two people under fifty in the upper reaches of the theater, surrounded by old women with bags from Schrafft's. We saw everything. And if there was no play to see, we would head for the movie revival houses. We fell in love with Greta Garbo that year during a festival at the New Yorker, literally a rattrap of a theater. Sometimes if we had bought popcorn or candy, a rodent would scamper up to us during the thinly attended matinees. We learned to starve for Garbo.

Our other amusements were reading plays to each other. We'd split up the characters and act out all the parts. Edward Albee's *The Zoo Story* had just appeared in paperback, and we performed the play over and over—hypnotized by the long monologue about the "colored queen." It felt very daring to say those words aloud. Secretly at home I mooned over Albee's handsome, Waspy face. Laurence's sisters, both older, would buy copies of *After Dark,* the pre-gay gay magazine, which featured pictures of nearly nude male dancers. We pretended to be interested in the theater and movie articles.

Kennedy had assumed office that winter. There was much talk of a New Frontier. That spring I had won an essay contest for junior high-schoolers on the subject of the Peace Corps. I had my hair cut in the Kennedy style, a large pompadour up front and tapered toward the back, while my brother still sported his very Eisenhowerish flattop. Our second year in Boy Scout camp, Laurence and I would sit by the lake as the morning light filtered through the trees and made the dew rise from the grass as if purged of ghosts. I felt then as if I were able to make a new start on life, cleansed of the dirty, tattered skins of my childhood. I had the sense that I could leave the past behind. I didn't know if I felt the requisite "vigor" that the Kennedys were trying to inject into American life, but I felt a strange new strength. All of a sudden, it seemed quite possible that everything could change.

And things did change. Laurence's genial personality attracted people, and so I found myself for the first time in a circle of friends. At lunch, in good weather, we would gather at the edge of the school yard and talk. I'm not certain how many of us grew up to be gay, but we had no illusion about being, if not sissies, at least very queer birds. One of the group was the most effeminate boy in the seventh grade, a nasty, thin lady-in-waiting, an only child conceived late in his parents' lives. He made fun of the rough and beautiful boys he was, no doubt, enthralled by. "That one," he'd hiss, "doesn't just have dirt under his fingernails, his fingernails *are* dirt. I saw his hands in gym. Pitch black." By the eighth grade he had left with his elderly parents for the desert of Arizona. There was a round, jolly fellow, who was the best French student in the eighth grade. He had found in French an escape from that weightlessness of early adolescence, when things seem especially pointless, chaotic, and wholly ungrounded. The basement of his house was covered with travel posters of France and a huge diagram of irregular verbs. We'd throw darts at the chart and then conjugate the verb we had hit. He, of course, won all the rounds.

And then there was Hal, as sweet and mild a boy as I have ever met, who attached himself to us like a fragile puppy. All I remember of what Hal looked like is that he had the creamiest skin and chestnut hair that fell in his face and against long lashes. I developed a terrible crush on him and fantasized about kissing his full, bow-shaped lips. Before we graduated, he, too, had moved away.

There must have been a lot of sexual tension between all of us, but sex was never mentioned, and we barely touched. Touching was the privilege of those other boys, who wrestled, raced against one another's bodies, or threw their arms across one another's shoulders. Our hands might fly whenever we talked, but they always came to rest safely at our sides. Yet there was no going back to what we were. Homophobes like to justify repression by arguing that the intensity of adolescent same-sex friendship could lead the unsuspecting teenager into homosexuality. If all I had felt for other boys was the love I felt for Laurence, I would never have become gay. I would have been like so many other men I see, whose closest relationships are with other men for whom they have no sexual desire. But for Hal I felt something very different and intense, if far less lasting, than I felt for Laurence—a romantic yearning. I wanted to feel what Hal felt; I wanted to sense his pleasure at my pleasure, to enter into the life that was just beyond my grasp. When my father drove me to school in the morning on his way to his car pool, we would pass the block where Hal lived, and I would think of him eating his breakfast, getting ready for the bus. Inside me I carried a fantasy life of Hal. For Laurence I felt the enjoyment of association, which after thirty years we still share.

Our little group didn't attract much attention—it was a large junior high school, with more than two thousand students. But I was harassed intermittently by a big black kid, Harris, who played trombone in the school band. I played the sax. The band room was in the school basement, in a relatively unfrequented area beneath the auditorium where sound would not travel and disturb the other classes. Outside of practice one afternoon, Harris tried to shake me down for a quarter. He grabbed my arm, spun me around, and tried to force an arm behind me in a hammerlock. (I was addicted to watching wrestling on TV and knew the names for all the moves.) A bunch of Harris's friends stood in a chorus line behind him as the other students in the band looked on. I remember dropping my books—were they in my other hand?—and somehow wiggling out of his grip. We stood face-to-face. Years of resentment gathered force, and with a swiftness that astonished me, I punched him squarely in the jaw with all my might. It was a classic right hook. His head jerked back. He looked stunned and then crumpled against the wall, momentarily knocked unconscious. As his buddies tried to hold him up, I retrieved my books and walked up the staircase. I was never hassled again. "He's crazy, man," I heard one of Harris's buddies say of me in a tone that didn't quite hide his newfound respect. Craziness, I learned that year, can protect you.

Such respect was all that I needed or felt was possible. I didn't crave Harris's affection. But in the sixties there was a general confusion between love and respect. We couldn't imagine one without the other. We were enjoined to love people of different races. To love our enemies. And yet between parents and children—where there should have been love at least—there was a growing sense of fear, a gap of affection. It was around the time I was in the eighth grade—my brother, who was four years ahead of me in school, had not yet gone away to college—that we had a fight with our mother that was a sign of both our age and the times. I don't remember what occasioned this fight, but these battles were always fought over our mother's increasingly arbitrary and irrational need to assert control. At the end of the fight my mother, more hysterical than usual, declared, "I never expected love from my children, but I demand respect!" My brother and I were silenced by this unexpected admission, just as thirty years later we were frozen in our seats by her announcement that she hoped to be reincarnated as a bird "so I can shit on everybody." I remember feeling how strange—how *unnatural*—such a declaration was. Love was what one should get without asking; respect was what one needed to earn. I could love my mother, even as I found it hard to respect her authority. But now I can see how much more disturbing, how much more chilling that declaration was, for its subtext—which my brother and I must have felt even if we couldn't have put it into words: *Don't expect love from me; all you might get is respect.* The grudging respect I got from Harris, this respect without affection, this cold, defiant acknowledgment of power—was, I felt, the best that I might receive. Today when the unctuous, condescending, and hypocritical Christian right declares that it loves the homosexual but hates the sin, I remember Harris and how much more honest and valuable was our mutual unloving respect.

And perhaps Harris's friend was right: I was a little crazy. I was feeling a sort of desperate urgency I had never felt before. In the past I had accepted my unhappiness with whimpering passivity, but I didn't feel passive anymore. I felt a kind of unrelenting manic restlessness. I was not alone. Puberty has this effect, but it seems to me that the energy I felt coiled within me was not just racing hormones, or else the country also was suffering from some sort of physiological imbalance. The Cuban missile crisis was symptomatic of this feverish, uncertain need to assert oneself. It was a theatrical cliffhanger that jolted me. Life could end at any minute, so I had to start living.

If my relationship with my parents had entered that difficult stage that most teenagers move into, it was offset by a new relationship with the other adults around me. I entered Ida Traiman's life at a difficult moment: Laurence's older sisters, Jessica and Vivian, were engaged in open and extended warfare with her. Laurence, younger and more accepting, simply kept his distance. Mrs. Traiman was on the verge of losing her family when I stepped in, delighted to be with her, talk about my life and feelings with her, and listen to her stories and jokes. Many afternoons Mrs. Traiman and I would sit at the kitchen table drinking coffee while Laurence walked their two enormous poodles.

Mrs. Traiman was not a pretty woman—gaunt, nervous, badly pockmarked from adolescent acne—and she had none of the vanity of even plain mothers who felt that they should make an attempt to be attractive. She accepted her ugliness as one of the jokes that life plays on everyone—cruel, unfathomable, and unalterable—just as she accepted as one of those funny twists of fate that she had married a man of surprisingly dapper handsomeness. Later she accepted as yet another cosmic prank losing an eye to cancer, which meant that she had to memorize all her music because she found it impossible to read the score and watch her fingering at the same time. I knew no other mothers with her brand of gallows humor, and nothing, I suppose, is more likely to win the heart of the thirteen-year-old than a mother who could bray with laughter as she recounted the family funerals she was forever attending.

She had an understanding of pain that my own mother—who was forever complaining of one malady or another—seemed utterly to lack. I know that Mrs. Traiman understood that I was in pain, and she tried, not to shield me from it because that would have been impossible, but to put the pain in perspective. It was this understanding—tacit, persistent, and unconditional—that was her gift to me. Her understanding is one of the central tales of my thirteenth year. It is a tale also about how events that seem on the verge of separating us can drive people more firmly together.

One of the things we talked about was music. Before she got married, Mrs. Traiman had played in an orchestra in New York. After her marriage, she gave up a musical career but played every week with an amateur string quartet. She practiced every day, locking up the poodles in the basement because they howled at the sound of violins. "They're my worst critics," she once told me. Her children refused to learn to play any musical instruments, so she was happy to find that I had been taking piano lessons for several years. At some point she gave me a book of Mozart violin sonatas and told me to practice an easy piano part so that we could play duets. I worked on the music for weeks, but it was beyond my capabilities. We played once together. She was enormously patient, unbothered by my constant mistakes. We went over and over the first three bars until I got them nearly right. After an hour or so, she said we should stop but continue next week. I was too humiliated to try. I felt that I had disgraced myself and exasperated her, but I also felt guilty about giving up, especially since she seemed so keen on working with me. I made some excuse the next week, and then the week after that. Soon she must have realized that despite all her kindness, I, too, had forsaken her, that some harmony that she searched for with all the people in her life was to be denied once again. "Someday, you'll be ready to play with me," she said when I offered to return the book.

But our brief work on the Mozart sonata brought us closer together than anything we ever did. One of my excuses for not playing the piece better was that my mother forbade me to practice when she was in the house.

"That's ridiculous," Mrs. Traiman said.

When I insisted that it was true—it was—Mrs. Traiman wanted an explanation. "I think it's because I play better than she does, and she's jealous," I said.

"You've got such a swelled head!" She laughed and got up, disgusted by my egotism. I was hurt. Here she refused to believe a truth that was painful to admit, yet she accused me of arrogance for admitting it.

Mrs. Traiman and my mother had very little to do with each other. There was no animosity between them, but they had little in common except the fact that their sons were best friends. Yet occasions brought them together, and sometimes they would speak on the phone.

Weeks after we tried the Mozart sonata, Mrs. Traiman called me in. "I have to apologize to you," she said in an unusually serious voice. "I was wrong. Your mother *is* jealous of your playing. It wasn't your illusion."

"You didn't tell her what I said!"

"No, I wouldn't do that. We were just talking about your playing, and I could sense it from what she said." Then she pulled me to her and hugged me, a rare thing, and then we started laughing. But we both knew she had dipped into a body of pain that required a different compass to navigate. She never gave me advice. What advice could she give?

Play poorly; stop playing; get your mother a piano teacher? She knew that nothing could be done about such resentment. In high school, when I stormed out of my house in anger, afraid I might commit violence, and showed up shaking at the Traimans' door, she never said anything, except "I'll call your parents so they'll know you're here." Then she left me alone with Laurence, who found these battles all too familiar from his own family. What she said to my parents, I will never know, but somehow they worked out whether I should return that night or stay with the Traimans until everyone had cooled off.

School changed. My teachers finally began to take an interest in me, and I found in them what I needed. My seventh-grade English teacher, Miss Vaughn, had bright hennaed hair, and in the last days of the term, when it was too hot to do anything else, she read us the entire text of Long-fellow's *Evangeline*, in a low, sultry voice. June in New York can be semitropical. I remember that year was particularly hot and humid. Miss Vaughn had the windows in the room pulled open, the blinds pulled down, the lights shut off. Perhaps I was a little dizzy from the heat, but I was entranced from the very first lines she read:

This is the forest primeval. The murmuring pines and the hemlocks,
Bearded with moss, and in garments green, indistinct in the twilight,
Stand like Druids of eld, with voices sad and prophetic . . .
Loud from its rocky caverns, the deep-voiced neighboring ocean
Speaks, and its accent disconsolate answers the wail of the forest.

Yes, I had heard those "accents disconsolate" even in my own heart—my soul resonated with "the deep-voiced neighboring ocean."

Miss Vaughn assigned us to write poems for a school contest. Even before hearing those lines from *Evangeline,* I wrote about sitting on rocks in the woods, and the poem won. The prize was a volume of poetry, *Cleopatra and Other Poems,* written by the chair of the English depart-ment, James Cliftonne Morris. His inscription: "Now let us open up and create! I should read of you in years to come."

No teacher before had encouraged me to create. No teacher had instructed me to "open up." These weren't the sorts of things teachers said to the children of the fifties. But this was a new era.

On the back of the dustjacket of *Cleopatra* is a photo of Mr. Morris—a studio portrait—showing a man much younger than I am now. At the time I thought of Mr. Morris as old (I don't remember any young teachers). He is seated on a ledge of shag carpeting with a classical column faintly visible in the background. His hair—a nappy pompadour—is already receding. He looks a lot like Langston Hughes—his round, happy face is crossed by a stylish mustache, his slightly wasp-waisted sports jacket is accented by a bright white handkerchief whose points rise from his breast pocket like a miniature alpine landscape. From the biography on the flap I learned that he was born in Talladega, Alabama, and eventually made his way to Columbia (like Langston Hughes), where he earned his B.S. and M.A. degrees. After nearly three years in the army— most of them in Europe—he married his childhood sweetheart. Of course, what the note could not have stated was how legendary a teacher he had already become in Junior High School 59. He taught both the very worst and the very best students, and for each he brought the material alive.

This could not have been easy for anyone, but it must have been especially difficult for him. For Mr. Morris had a severe stutter. And to make matters worse, he had a deep Southern black accent. The first week I was in his class, I barely understood a word he said, and then all of a sudden, I was able to screen out the stammer and get the hang of his Southern speech mannerisms. What was left was music, a rich, soulful, passionate music. In his eighth-grade class, we read *Macbeth* and *Romeo and Juliet*. We'd read a speech and then he'd paraphrase. Since a third or more of the students in my class were Jewish, he'd translate the speeches into an idiom we'd be familiar with. Of the nurse in *Romeo and Juliet,* he pointed out, "S-s-she's such a y-y-y-yenta. 'Oy yooou k-k-k-kids give me such a k-k-k-klop in k-k-k-kup!' " It was a performance even the least imaginative of us couldn't help but be delighted by.

He gave me private writing lessons after school. I was to keep on producing sonnets until I got one right. He was a demon on redundancy. Robert Frost was my model; Mr. Morris punned that I was "F-f-f-frost-

bitten." I wrote yet another poem about a forest. I described it as "silent
and still." He took out his big red pen and crossed out *silent*. "Th-th-
th-these a-a-a-adjectives, they're too c-close."

"What about 'quiet and still'?" I suggested, not getting the point.

"N-n-n-o. You think a-b-b-bout it," he said sternly, for as gentle as
he could be, everyone sooner or later saw how swiftly and how fero-
ciously his anger could be aroused. But he never quarreled with what I
had to say. The "bleeding-eye" controversies were far behind me. No
longer did I have to defend what I was doing artistically. In my last year
at junior high I wrote my term paper on the theater of the absurd and
off-off-Broadway. Mr. Morris didn't think it strange that I should find
in the world only the significance I gave to it. He seemed to share the
same burden of hollowed-out meaning. He wrote in one of his poems:

A song may be a blackened hate,
the Lazarus at the rich man's gate,
a muttered curse, a cry, a bruise,
a man alone moaning the blues.

I can admire now what I couldn't have seen then, the reversed stress in
"moaning the blues." The rhythm changes course just before it ends.
The music is slurred like a blues singer sliding down from a top note.
Only after graduate school did I read Langston Hughes and Countee
Cullen and then with a shock of recognition, for I had heard this particular music before, indirectly, in the little pink volume I had won in
seventh grade, and in those after-school workshops with Mr. Morris.

Finally, after many tries, I finished a sonnet that satisfied him, and he
urged me to send it to a citywide contest for junior high school students.
When it won, he came to the awards luncheon. He had met my parents
before, when they had come up to school for the usual parent-teacher
conference. Now he rushed over, filled with more than his usual ebul-
lience. As he bubbled on, my folks stood stiff and smiling, and when he
was finished they said, "Thank you, thank you," and shook his hand.
But when he walked away, they asked for a translation. "He said you
should be proud of me."

"We are, we are," they said, and took their seats.

How odd, I thought, that he should be telling them to be proud. Maybe he sensed that they didn't know what to feel about having a poet as a son. (My mother had made it plain that she had no intentions of reading my poetry.) But I had no doubts about his feelings, his pride. If at the marionette theater I had been overcome by someone else's enchantment, Mr. Morris had led me to discover how I could find a sort of enchantment in myself. He had shown me, "Here inside you are the words that will cast a spell." He gave me the sense for the first time that I might actually become a writer.

In the spring of seventh grade I was bar mitzvahed. It was not as bar mitzvahs are supposed to be—joyous introductions to manhood—but rather a reversion to the grim past. I had never felt at home in synagogue, and the synagogue we attended was across the street from P.S. 156, almost an extension of the dreaded elementary school. My brother looked upon his bar mitzvah as something to which he was entitled, his moment to shine. His was a noisy, crowded affair, and at the luncheon afterward, a long dais was set up for his school friends. There were many fights trying to keep the guests to a reasonable number. My bar mitzvah, by contrast, was small. I had few friends, and besides, I wanted the entire thing to be quiet, modest, and dignified. Not that I wanted to be bar mitzvahed, it was something expected of me, and like all familial expectations, it allowed no opportunity for success, only for humiliation and failure. I think that is why I wanted to become not just a writer but a poet. No one expects anything of poetry, so whatever I did, I did for myself. And in writing for myself I could feel—even if I was ignored— a sense of accomplishment.

I was not bar mitzvahed alone. I shared the occasion with Rick Kuklemann, who had been in my class all through elementary school. He was an unusually fat boy, and my mother—the daughter of a tailor— admired how Mrs. Kuklemann always got his pants to hang right. "It's hard to get creases to fall straight on a boy that fat," my mother noted with her usual damning praise. My voice had changed by this time. At thirteen I had an unusually deep voice even for a man. Rick's hadn't changed yet. The difference gave the service a particularly comic element. First we would hear Rick's reedy pitch pipe of a voice, then my basso profundo. But Rick and I did what we had to do: We performed in the letter-perfect way in which we had been trained. I experienced this strange separation between me and everything else happening around me. After this, I thought to myself, I will never have to go to shul again. And although I have attended services, even partaken in one or two for my niece and nephew, I have remained estranged from anything that goes on in a synagogue.

Toward the end of the luncheon that followed the service, Laurence and I fled outside to take a breath of air. It was March. Spring was arriving in the spotty, furtive way that it comes in New York, a day of burning followed by six of freezing. The Saturday was bright, but the blades of cold wind had not been entirely dulled. We looked out from the steps of the synagogue at the school. The crocuses in the iron-gated front yard of P.S. 156—pathetic blotches of yellow and purple—rattled from side to side. In the yard out back we could hear the squeal of girls, the *cachong* of a basketball ricocheting off the backboard, and the *pong, pong, pong* as it bounced on the pavement. Laurence looked at me and I at him, and we burst out laughing. It had been such a close escape, but we had made it through, and we never had to look back at it again. After a while we went inside, where I collected from relatives more envelopes with cards holding checks, bonds, and stock certificates, which later I used to pay for my first year in graduate school, where I met the lover whose childhood had been so perfect.

Waiting for Blastoff

Bia Lowe

for Denny, Anne, and Valentina

The new uniforms of upper school were just the tip of the iceberg, a glint of some lurking and sinister peril. Replete with pleated skirts and shaved legs, the transit into high school, into the seventh grade, was an obvious rite of passage, a refinement of girls into ladies. It boded a new and imposing culture, and we lived in fear of making a false move.

The sailor-style uniforms probably were intended to sidestep the tyranny that might have cowed the less fashion-savvy. Yet even the smallest nuance, say, the thickness of one's knee socks, separated the cool from the hopelessly maladroit. A plaid barrette was out, a solid in. Two-tone saddle shoes were better than solids, unless they were clean bucks. Midknee skirts meant you were wholesome, an inch higher screamed depravity, but a half-inch lower banished you to geekdom. The list goes on.

We were the rookies, learning the ropes, desperate to assimilate. Some of my classmates, like arrivals at Ellis Island, brimmed with hope of fitting into the new surroundings and making a success of it, but I wasn't one of them. To me, adolescence was alchemy in reverse, gold about to degrade into lead.

There are moments in one's life, lucid, nearly clairvoyant, when one peers into the depth of the future and knows the present moment is doomed, therefore exquisite. Seventh grade was rife with such moments when, gaping into the abyss of high school, I pined for the childhood crumbling beneath my feet.

But this cynicism (or lucidity) was not mine alone. It was part of the zeitgeist. Though mid-twentieth-century America wowed us with simon-ized optimism, and astronauts were routinely rocketed into space, the apocalypse burbled just beneath the surface. The A-bomb and all of its sci-fi monsters hulked behind the curtains of every sitcom family room. A new book by a woman named Rachel Carson foretold of a polluted Earth and the extinction of species. The fallout of Freud's bomb contin-ued its contamination of Victorian etiquette among the sexes. And the evil Russians, who promised to bury us, who beat us into space by launching *Sputnik,* plunged America into an era of foreign espionage and domestic paranoia. Where was progress taking us? The future was a difficult and fearful realm to project into. I should have been able to picture myself like a paper doll: six more years pasted into that sailor getup, then four years in the garb of a coed, followed by a lifetime in a housewife's frock—but I couldn't.

My pal Denny was an essential figure of my childhood. From day one Denny and I were at each other's houses, integrated into each other's family. Her sisters dated my brothers, we went to the same school, in the same grade. She was brainy, introverted, wore glasses, and walked on her tiptoes. I was the opposite, preferring the anarchic playground to anything requiring stillness and concentration. In spite of our differ-ences, or perhaps because of them, we were instantly companionable, fastest of friends.

Throughout lower school the strengths of our personalities melded— she eventually gained confidence in her body, I in my wits. And for a time our closeness was able to withstand even the stresses of upper school.

On weekends at my parents' country home we'd climb an oak in the late afternoon, hoisting up mason jars, ice, and bottles of Squirt. We'd drape ourselves along the corrugated limbs, talk about the universe, and watch the light turn golden, then blue. We'd pretend our Squirts were cocktails as we clinked the ice in our glasses. Later, after dinner, we'd bundle ourselves in our jackets, step out into the autumn night, our necks craning to find Telstar inching across the Milky Way.

Denny's house was an adventure. It was large, alien, and full of old furniture. Denny had a governess, an old English woman with a creaky girdle named Mrs. Askew. Though our pronunciation of her name was routinely corrected ("ask you"), we persisted with the inflection we felt best described the workings of her mind.

Sometimes after walking from upper school, Denny would invite me over to her house to play her guitar. First stop, once there, was a visit to her mother, Pru, who could be found lounging on the chaise in her dressing room tanked to the gills. She had long silver hair, wore mint-green dressing gowns with marabou lapels and cuffs. In her smoky voice she'd amuse us with tales about her last soirée, calling us "darlings" and patting our heads. Soon we'd be itching to reach the refuge of Denny's bedroom and her guitar, to work on ways to harmonize to "If I Had a Hammer."

Once, at an overnight at Denny's, she slipped into bed with me, suggesting we play "lovers." She rolled on top of me and ground her pubic bone into mine, and I remember being inspired by her sheer persistence if nothing else. Though we both worked diligently at the fantasy of grown-up abandon, neither of us seemed particularly aroused. I was also dimly aware that if she hadn't yet broached this activity with a boy, it wouldn't be long before she did. Denny was transforming, like her sisters before her, into a beauty.

It seemed we squirmed and rolled together for hours until Mrs. Askew materialized in a wedge of blinding light. Before closing the door and restoring darkness to Denny's room, Mrs. Askew said only that she was checking to see if we were asleep, but I wasn't entirely convinced. Hadn't she spied Denny's butt roiling beneath the covers? Denny, who had long since stopped caring one iota for anything Mrs. Askew thought, and who, more important, had never had one doubt about her own sexuality, merely sighed and muttered, "So what if she did? Big deal." Denny sighed again, this time sleepily, and it was clear our simulation of adult sex was over. We lay side by side, placid as a pair of shoes. We were, I think, both grateful to surrender to our sexual disinterest in each other. The quandary of our pubescent bodies included an absence of chemistry just as surely as it contained passions. "Yeah. Big deal," I echoed, unconvinced. And so, with our pajama tops knotted up to our armpits, and our bruised mons of venii, we fell asleep.

What about me had Mrs. Askew witnessed? What in my sphere of pre-pubescence held me in thrall, besides the members of my own family? A horse's warm breath on my palm, the architecture inside a geode, the prospect of travel in a rocket ship. I was still a child, my libido in a wide, polymorphous orbit. The world was my oyster. Neither hetero nor homo, my orientations had not yet emerged from my universe, like stars culled from cosmic gases. Nevertheless, an anxiety burbled inside me about what I sensed was my anomie. Why was I different? Why was assimilation so daunting?

This inability to focus, this absence of orientation was not the perversity that would eventually get me into trouble in upper school. It was, rather, my desire to remain a tomboy, my refusal to forfeit what I considered to be my authentic nature for a feminine affectation. I wasn't ready to assimilate into the demure world of womanhood. Perhaps I never would. The currency of tomboyishness no longer held any value in this new regime and would, in a year's time, become a pox.

Gradually Denny and I saw less of each other at school. Her socks may have been a hair too thick, but her sex appeal and good grades qualified her for the clique of popular girls. I think she couldn't understand why I was so damned stubborn about what I called my "nonconformity." Though we now traveled in distinct and antagonistic circles, we never harbored scorn for each other. We kept good faith on the other's behalf, just as we had loved our childhood in the trees.

As the cool girls gravitated toward one another, the creeps, too, coalesced, debris drawn together by increased mass. Anne and I kept company at that time, each indignant on the other's behalf, defenders of the downtrodden and dejected.

Sometimes, after school, we'd walk home together and Anne would ask me over to her house. At Anne's the *Playboy* magazines weren't hidden; they were stacked in a pile in an attic bookcase. Once inside the attic, among the squeaky floorboards and her family's collection of odds and ends, Anne closed the door, made a beeline for the bookcase. She threw a pile of *Playboys* onto a small guest bed and then threw herself, as though making a shallow dive, onto the chenille bedspread. Her gesture invited me to do the same. We lay head to head, bellies down—oxfords and bobby socks dangling above us—and might have appeared like teenyboppers cooing at photos of their heartthrobs in teen magazines.

Of course we examined the centerfolds with a prurient, if masochistic fascination. The women in the photos were inhuman, androids from another galaxy, without blemishes, without apparent modesty or shame. Their display of flesh seemed simply receptive, self-involved, singularly devoid of responsiveness. Bodies were as curvilinear and as tan as a pile of Twinkies, the glut of processed flesh highlighted by taffy fingernails, nipples peaked like meringues, eyes opaque as Necco wafers, hairdos of spun sugar.

I was not (a big sigh) like the females in those soft-focus photos, and even though my breasts had started to swell, I knew I'd never have the kind of body that ballooned and splayed on the pages of *Playboy*. For one thing, I wanted to be a viewer, to touch, to taste, to be the cook, the guest, the gourmet; but not at this table, not among these platters and platters of soft white cake. Anne too seemed caught in a quandary between repulsion and participation, understanding hunger—even as her young body must have—but not sharing the appetite. She must have wondered secretly, as did I, is this loving?

Ultimately, though, it was the cartoons that riveted us with their particular brand of sadism. We'd study them and feel the shame of our incomprehension, then struggle to laugh hoarsely, even cruelly, never to become the joke's brunt ourselves. The ability to find humor in these smarmy gags seemed the key to power—power over the genitals, over lust, over intimacy and identification, and especially, power over the female body. To look at these pages without fear or apprehension was to practice being tough, to study insouciance, dissociation. I concluded I was different, not quite a woman, that perhaps it was I who was not of this earth. At times I imagined myself to be a case study, the mirrors in my home to be two-way, family members and school mates to show a scientific interest in my alien behavior. And I sensed in Anne, my cohort among the outcasts, a shared strangeness.

When I was able to fantasize sexually, I saw simply a chase. I envisioned myself running through a forest, pursued by an extraterrestrial whose sexual prowess and psychic knowledge of me—once I was wrestled to the ground, if ever—would be like nothing known on earth. Sexual desire at twelve was, simply, anticipation of something unknown, something with which I was not yet able to be entrusted, like a promise to myself from a future me. I put it in a drawer to save for later; I placed it in a time capsule and shot it into the sky. O that I could have made love to that child I was; that she could have been soothed with stories of heroic women or shown a human touch.

Within a year we rookies of upper school would begin to turn on one another with vigilante fury, to brandish the punishments we each so feared. Deflecting shame, we would become masters at the art of name-calling. *Phony, conceited, spaz, lezzy* were just some of the curses we'd sling to keep one another in check. We were learning to recite the mantra of our gender: Don't trust your path, don't stray too far, don't aim too high. This is how, even in that age of rocket ships and astronauts, a glass ceiling congealed to daunt our aspirations.

Queer, inasmuch as it described sexual behavior, was still an abstraction to me, much as any notion of having sex with a boy. During lunch hour at school I'd make my pilgrimage to the Big Dictionary in the school library and look up *intercourse, vagina, penis, homosexual,* hoping a definition might clarify the adult and incomprehensible world. And no matter what I read in that giant tome, no matter how compulsively I scanned and rescanned it, I was unable to understand human sexuality, least of all my own. I was vexed by the mystery between my legs, by the sphinx I was becoming, by a preternatural creature dashing through a forest, hoping to be pursued by an entity as strange as herself.

*   *   *

Eventually, of course, I became a homosexual but not entirely happy ever after. Didn't I become my own country, draw my borders, and begin to construct the fiction that is my history? Didn't I fabricate an identity out of the cloth of indignation? Of course I'll wear the word *queer,* and I'll wear it resolutely; but O for the seventh-grader poised at the exquisite moment, for the child without recourse to a lifetime supply of plot, alibi, just cause. O for the kid and her pal scouring the starstrewn night! For the uncharted, limitless future! For a world without such strident curfews, without such ruthless boundaries and uniforms.

In June of the seventh grade I went to my brother's high school graduation ceremony. The young men's voices rose in a solemn rendition of "You'll Never Walk Alone." I imagined walking through a cruel storm, the Valley of the Shadow of Death, a dark labyrinth through which, if one were to lose hope, one could become forever lost. It sounded like a funeral dirge. Walk on, those voices urged, walk on, with hope in your heart. I cried, in part for the swelling of the boy's voices, which was a thing of beauty, but also because I could see the approaching thunderheads within the specter of the next school year and could imagine no end to them. Eighth grade was to be the worst year of my life, and there would be no recourse, no stopping the inevitable.

Within that oncoming squall Kennedy would be gunned down, children in a Sunday school in Alabama would be blown up, and I would begin the small mortifications of adolescence. Childhood was over. What I was trying most to avoid, but what seemed a certainty, would happen: I would be called a *queer,* and I would take that spit wad and redeem myself in the social construction of myself as a lesbian. Of course that victory would be bittersweet. An identity will never describe the protean nature of sexuality, not mine anyway.

By the time I was thirteen I would learn to seal myself off from the abuses of my peers. I would buy a guitar and sing my own songs of alienation and star-crossed love. I would be bolstered by the bookish tasks of latency, the way geeks often are. I'd discover, with the inherent optimism of algebra, how an unknown quantity might find resolution. I'd read how the minstrel cicada first spends its tender years underground. I would read how singing Orpheus carried the imagination through the depths like a torch, until finally he emerged, blinking, only to lose his love in a moment of self-doubt.

But it would be decades before I would learn to rewrite my own bitterness, to hold my head up high and attempt to forgive; decades before I would study the lives of women or deconstruct the psychology of oppression. The century would be nearly over before I would learn that in 1963, while I slipped like Orpheus into the depths of the eighth grade, a woman cosmonaut, Valentina Tereshkova, orbited Earth.

This hero must have peered out over the blue arc of her home, far from uniforms, rhetoric, gender, so far even from duty, approval, or ego; she must have felt a hunger so pure; must have known what it is to be human, the way the dead know—those who gaze down at our lives, shake their discarnate heads, and scoff at our time-bound definitions.

Fashions of 1971

Wayne Koestenbaum

Appliqué

What was I wearing in 1971?

A blue-piped white jersey with the word LOVE in plastic appliqué. Its cotton, not ordinary, had a pressed, pampered quality, akin to velvet. With the jersey I wore blue pants that bordered on velveteen.

"Femme," said a history classmate, male, to the LOVE shirt, or to its wearer, and so the item was exiled to the drawer.

I don't mention the LOVE shirt in order to garner sympathy.

I had a fondness for clothes that required my affection to bolster them. No one else would wear the LOVE shirt, therefore I secretly prized it. The sleeves puckered, drew close around the arms, like a peasant blouse around new breasts. I knew many pairs of recently developed breasts. They surrounded me. I had an attitude toward them. Now I wish I could define that attitude. It was a mist. It didn't incorporate nipples. Breasts were slopes without personality or give. At best they were wealth. At worst they were neutral architectural features—pilasters.

Apache

Apache scarves took the nation by storm, and so I bought three, at Penney's, with a gold ring to fasten them. These were not my wisest purchases, but they were my most visionary, even if I wore them, each, only once. Odd, that I can't remember my mother saying, "Why aren't you wearing your apache scarves? We spent good money on them." Either she didn't notice, or she understood the sense in keeping them in the drawer.

I wish I could remember their colors. Were they solids, stripes, checks? I respect them; today, I wear a faux leopard-spotted scarf, knotted squarely, to look Neapolitan from a distance, as I once wished, with the apache scarves, to look morose within the dust bowl of the sun-blessed suburbs.

Also at Penney's I bought my Boy Scout scarf. Scout uniforms are the most feminine pieces I've ever owned: They take part in the world of the fetish, and echo nurse outfits and the boy-emulating garb of den mothers, who dignified scouting by their proffered cupcakes and wifely hospitalities. I sing the easy chairs and carpets and TV sets of den mothers. I sing their calves, nylons, and mules. I don't sing den mothers very loudly, however. Their outfits form a counterpoint that tastes like Fritos—the chip factory, which we toured. We also toured the police station. I rode in the backseat of a patrol car while the cop did his duty.

Bell-Bottoms

Bell-bottom year was 1970. At Macy's or Emporium I purchased a striped specimen, a fancy pair of pants for a boy with cabaret aspirations, who saw "mod" and "Parnassian" as fraternal twins. I might have been the only boy wearing bell-bottoms. Ours was a nonexperimental neighborhood.

Bell-bottoms enlarge—identify—the groin. They frame it. Groins need affirmation. This point doesn't suffer from repetition.

I was afraid of LSD in the school doughnuts.

Fringe

I didn't wear fringe, but Nancy did. I knew two Nancys. One wanted to be president; the other wore a brown suede fringed jacket. The second, fringe Nancy, was nice, though also "hard"; among hard chicks, she was the kindest. I imagined that we had a secret understanding, and I included her on my list of Nineteen Girls—schoolgirls I considered friends and acquisitions. Nancy of the fringe earned a place among my nineteen because she was short and pretty. I saw her at the Westgate Mall's record shop. I was flipping through LPs. She said something clever about Alice Cooper. I danced with Nancy at a Friday-night gala and kissed her at the one "makeout" party I attended. She had a Polish last name? The details fade.

The first Nancy had long straight hair and a regal, perjured nose. Her mother once brought a special cake, in a bakery box, to a school event. She was in a hurry. I admired her meringue-pale hair, and the scarf (or hairnet?) she wore over it, to protect it from turmoil. I liked rushed women, their minds on higher pursuits. This mother doted on Frank Sinatra. I don't blame her. She lived on a court, which was a special kind of street, with unique responsibilities and privileges. She respected Boston. She told me so. I knew quality women.

Jockstraps

In P.E. (the word had a friendship with *pee*) I wore a jockstrap under red shorts, and an unattractive, thick, reversible red sweatshirt, white on the verso. The jock—uncomfortable, unaesthetic—had no meaning: I couldn't grasp its relation to rupture prevention. I bought the jock at Penney's, probably with my mother. It came in a box. I didn't associate the jock with sexuality; it was merely hygiene supply, like Ban Roll-On. Deodorant itself seemed a purposeless, elongated form of lipstick, in the visual family of Eskimo Pies. I didn't stink, but I'd reached the deo age. I still had what Myra Breckinridge scornfully called a "boy's equipment," but it was time to pile my package into a Bike mesh.

If P.E. was a place of possible humiliation, it was also a strip joint. In the locker room I discovered boy bodies; I woke to disparities between levels of physical development. Some boys, like me, were at the beginning of the bumpy road to love; others, like an idol named Joe, were far along. Joe was my top nude, Frank my runner-up.

Another P.E. fashion item: tube socks. I hated them. They had no heels. (Just now, I almost compared tube socks to castration, but then I took back the comparison.)

My only concern was not to get hard, which meant brief showers and no looking around. I'd save looking for later, once I was dressed. I don't remember seeing boys with hard-ons in P.E. Isn't that strange? Not even a semi-boner. I hope I'm repressing a juicy memory.

Coach's Wife

In 1971 I saw my second-favorite gym coach naked. He was in his twenties. I saw him walk out of the teacher shower. He didn't alter his conduct when in the nude: I was just a boy visiting coach headquarters to hand him a signed health excuse, exempting me from sport. He toweled himself off. I thought, *Well, there it is, the teacher's prick, and all the accompanying garnishes.* Seeing his package, I thought, *Coach is accustomed to locker-room nudity from his college days.* Additionally I realized, *This is the kind of body one sees in college.* Here was the first remarkable thing I learned about college.

Let it be known that I was mildly disappointed in his anatomy: *So this is all?*

I also thought, *Coach towels himself off, just like this, in his wife's presence. Right now, standing in front of me, he's casually drawing the white towel over his adult body, and this is the same performance his wife watches in their master bedroom.* I imagined Coach's wife as a cheerful, presentable woman, good at sports, who took for granted her husband's frequent nudity and was proud of his body in a noncommittal, smug way. Not for a second did I imagine her body, though I pictured her cotton garments. I dressed her in comfortable, springlike fashions that permitted easy transition between work and play.

Literary Criticism

My favorite coach—short, sadistic—had a polished chest, the most masculine I'd ever seen. He reminds me of a literary critic I know. This is not praise.

The mean coach put us through the paces of a ritual called dress-and-run. It might more accurately have been called undress-and-run. He shouted, "Dress and run!" and we stripped off street clothes, donned gym gear, ran a lap, and then lined up for roll call, jock check, and jumping jacks.

The mean coach had a mustache that resembled a clone accoutrement. He had a seductive way of looking slantwise at me and absenting me from the death penalty.

I asked him to sign my yearbook. He wrote something about chicken shit. He was obsessed with fowl.

Pietà

The math teacher with a crew cut wore short-sleeve dress shirts and said he wanted to kill the guy who smashed the *Pietà*. (This was 1972?) His wife, the music teacher, who played violin and looked like the soprano Mirella Freni, favored loose, impressionistic fabrics that were paisley in effect: swirling, incoherent. Her hair was spun sugar.

Theirs was a marriage of convenience: *my* convenience. It was convenient to picture her soft bun in the same imaginary frame as his buzz cut. I liked cross-wiring, in fantasy, her pearlized-seeming features and his machete-sharp absence of beauty. I imagined that he was content with his naval or martial masculinity, its geometry; I imagined, too, that he found a culvert, within his maleness, for his blurry wife, a nutmeat, to dwell.

Elles Parlent

The shiny polyester dress of the buxom lunchroom attendant spoke dress shields and girdle.

The plaid A-line skirt of the history teacher spoke Northern Ireland.

The bun of the typing teacher spoke roses.

The crew cut of the dean spoke Nixon's cheeks.

My mother's home-sewn pants suit and my father's store-bought leisure suit spoke two-car family.

I bent my eighth-grade French textbook in half; I broke its red spine. The teacher, a dry woman in flat shoes, didn't speak French. Her specialty was Spanish.

Ecology

My wrestling partner, fellow lightweight, a boy with "skaggy" chin-length hair, called me out—dared me to fight him, tomorrow after school. I agreed to the duel.

His skinny arms were nothing to fear, and yet I stayed home from school the next day and had a masturbation marathon instead.

We'd planned to rendezvous by the locked, parked bikes, near the ecological simulacrum of a habitat, created by the science teacher to show us how to respect the planet.

I preferred teacher to student bodies, with a few exceptions. The science teacher, for example: He had no body—just a droning carapace for preservationist sentiments.

Slip of the Tongue

An inch of Becky's slip showed below her dress. She was number one on my list of Nineteen Girls. I asked her to go steady, and she said no, which was okay, because the main reason I'd asked was to pass the time: I'd thought, *How to decide which girl to ask to go steady? Why, I'll choose Becky, because her slip showed beneath her dress when she stood up in English. Also, she wears light pink lip gloss. I want many opportunities to see the slip and the gloss.*

Chap Stick

In 1971 I applied Chap Stick to the locks of hair that hung down, nonce sideburns, on my cheeks: I wanted the hairs to stay put, to adhere, and I didn't know about pomade.

One of the few Jews in my junior high was a slight, talkative boy who wore untucked beige safari shirts. He was friends with the "faggy" teacher, or his parents were. My friends and I joked about this teacher's probable membership in the Mattachine Society—Saturday outings to San Francisco. He wore a Hawaiian shirt to the school dance, which he helped chaperone.

One fine day, through his open classroom window I tossed a water-filled balloon. Unfortunately he came around the corner and saw me throw it. His eyes said, *Tsk, tsk.*

Questions dominated my nights. Was his flashy blond hairpiece real? Was his penis artificial? Was his recipe for Waldorf salad a success? Was his interest in algebra feigned? What had been his college minor? Did he live in a bungalow? A ranch? Was he born in Denmark, or did his coloring come from drugstore arts of the tube and jar? Had he ever admired the history teacher's breasts? Had he envied the art teacher's legs? Would he agree that my penis was a petri dish?

Straight Hair

The best of the Nineteen Girls wore miniskirts or hot pants—sometimes with cream-colored nylons.

Mark the embarrassed proud face of a girl sporting short skirt or hot pants (maybe knee socks?) in 1971: En route to her locker, she holds binder and books. She smells like cigarettes, because she has dawdled in the girls' bathroom. Her long, straight hair is parted in the middle; she wears judicious makeup and chews gum. When she poses for a yearbook picture—boys and girls in homeroom lined up—she presses together her exposed knees, and her thighs don't touch.

I wanted to impress the girls, and so I took care with my clothes. I removed my curl by wearing a knit beanie cap overnight; when I woke, the hair was plastered down straight. I wanted girls to notice me; I wanted boys to leave me alone. I wished to see boys naked, of course, but otherwise desired nothing from them. I longed to be a hit with my Nineteen Girls. To be popular among girls was nirvana; boys' approval meant nil. Seeing boys strip, however, fed the spirit.

By 1971 I'd seen hard-core porn photos: men and women. Their congress looked like dog stuff. I couldn't make sense of the combined organs, the mess. The man's balls were incoherent: furrowed with experience, and far too close to the buttocks.

Uncut

The Mormon redhead's uncut penis in the locker room startled me. He was standing in the collective shower. His organ was long, its head sheathed by a droopy cowl. Above his penis was a pink tablet of hair, unimpressive. Though not a close friend, he was certainly polite to me in the corridors.

With him in first grade I'd pushed Play-Doh through the Play-Doh Factory to make scatalogical objects.

In 1971, the Carpenters' "We've Only Just Begun" stirred me. I fantasized about getting in touch with Karen Carpenter to ask her to sing in a benefit for our youth orchestra, so we could raise money for a proposed tour of Costa Rica.

Frames

I wore black plastic frames, clear at the bottom, dark at the top (originals of the frames I wear today). I combed my bangs to meet the frame's top, so no forehead showed. I always tucked in my shirt and wore a belt. I was a neat number.

I wore horizontally striped jerseys, as did my foxy piano teacher.

She told my mother, "Stripes make my boobs look big!"

I wish I could say my mind was in the gutter, or in someone's groin, but my mind was nowhere. Perhaps my mind was in the backyard. I hear my mother—memory—say something to my father about lawn fertilizer. I see—memory—sacks of fertilizer in the garage. Every year, our lawn failed. Eventually, we gave up on grass and settled for ground cover.

Still Life with Boys

Lisa Cohen

Boy. Boy dances with me to the sound of Earth, Wind and Fire. We hardly move. The reasons why: It's slow, so that's the point; also, one drink has made me ill, which means controlling nausea is a big part of this dance. And his mysteriously gentle attentions—what are the reasons why? Then I run home (it's right nearby) to be sick and think about his corduroys. And to think about the way he runs his pick through his hair, even while we dance, and to consider the differences between him at school and him at night. Crouched in the bathroom, I draw upset conclusions about the forces of description. I think: *People talk out loud—your name and an adjective or two—and then you're stuck.* There are no reasons why.

Boy. This boy is tall and he walks languidly. His jeans are loose and flowing; his shirt's unbuttoned halfway down his chest. We walk around a graveyard one whole afternoon, which should be fun, or dangerous, but is not. Mostly I listen to his gossip and goad him into telling more. (He says our teacher's fucking students with impunity.) At my front gate,

I vaguely promise him another date, then go inside and find my mother, who's been watching us. She says: That boy's a bit *swishy*, don't you just think? I cannot speak. I'm stunned again by something so slippery I think I'll never find a way to understand it or respond. It's her conspiratorial tone, and her confidence that I'll agree. She's watching me. It's the power of the word, and my fear of being named that way. She won't let up. She says: I think he's a bit *swishy*, don't you? It is my desperate but vague sense that this, and everything, is wrong. Don't you? I try to block her out. But she says: Don't you? Don't you? And the watch I wear, she's told me more than once, is awfully *mannish*.

I didn't always feel this way. I used to have a label gun—orange, and the sticky tapes it printed out were red—and used it frantically. A lamp, the phone, my father's typewriter when I visited him, even the ceiling—I anointed them all with identification. But there was a girl down the street (behind a big fence, in private school, and exotic like all Wasp's) whose name was Gay. How could this be? I spied on her through the fence, upset by all their money and her name. I played with her younger sister once or twice, and thrilled when she casually said something like: "When Gay comes home we're going to . . ." Then shivered again when, illicitly listening from the other side, I heard their mother calling her to dinner, loudly, with no shame: "Ga-aaaay, dinnertime, honey!"

Boy. Boy flamboyant wishes he were Elton John. Or maybe he's in love. Boy wears glossy, thick white plastic glasses, and high-waisted, pale beige pants that billow down to red platforms. His mother shops with him for everything. We're twelve, thirteen, and I'm amazed at how this works: How he can tell her what he wants, why she doesn't hesitate to outfit him this way. Boy is a miracle, I think: Perfectly confident and so contemporary. When we graduate from eighth grade we all sing "Your Song," and he makes sure we get it right.

Boy drives a Mustang; he's hot shit. His little butt fits right into greasy Levi's, the jeans are slightly flared, and his walk has great extravagance:

long strides and always bouncing on his toes. Yes, he's glamorous in a filthy, carlike way, and the Mustang is a conversation, sex, and all we do: just drive around. It's black with low-slung seats, convertible, and has the smell of boy and speed. I'm trying to find some feeling—for a boy and for myself—and want to be enticed by his harsh beauty and his car. But secretly I scorn him too, because the car is automatic, and shifting gears is now my most inflamed idea of fun.

I listened to some girls talk about boys. They said: "He's foxy! What a fox!" But I longed for women's beauty, and dreamed of getting lost in obscure auras of intelligence and skin. I rode around the city on my bicycle, staring at cars and memorizing license plates from other states. I idolized the cars my teachers drove and wanted to run off to work as a chauffeur for some kind woman, far away: I'd love her car, and she would care for me. At home, my sister and I waited for the sound my mother's car made, and—too attuned—we always knew when she was coming down the street.

Boy's wavy dark blond hair hangs in his eyes, and he has a gentle voice. I watch him walking in the hallway before school; he's with his girlfriend and she's beautiful. I watch them kiss. It's clear that they are meant to be entwined; they almost look like siblings actually. I shouldn't stare— I'm sure that she would not be moved by my appreciation of her face. Instead I scrutinize her friendship with another girl; I look at other pairs of girls talking intensely, fighting, making up. I wish they'd see the passion this implies. But I don't speak.

Boy's tiny, almost dainty, but he likes to think he's tough; he's got the anxious bluster of the small. We're in some plays together, and I go to his bar mitzvah in the suburbs one spring day. I'm slightly older than this boy, but still unsure here—I've never been to one before; Judaism is a secret sect to which I don't belong. After Hebrew, gifts of money, dried-out food, and a tacky band, boy takes me to the backseat of a car. It can't be his, because he's just thirteen. We don't take off our clothes, but I still explode—that's that—in one brief, Bicentennial minute. Then we go back and everyone is mad at the boy for disappearing from his own bar mitzvah party. *Oy.*

At the time, I wasn't sure whether I was living in the thirties (the movies I watched), the fifties (my mother's heyday), or the seventies. I read plays by Noël Coward and Philip Barry: Witty and gay. I read Tea and Sympathy*: "Years from now . . . when you talk about this . . . and you will . . . be kind." I found* The Boys in the Band *and wrote about it for my English class. My thesis was: They hate their lives.*

Boy walks me home, then leads me to my own backyard. It's clear he's on a date. Everything about him strains against his crisp, clean casing (pale blue slacks, white polo shirt), and I find him comical, extreme. I also think he's bullying. In the backyard, he presses up against me, gets my lips wet, more. Now all my mortifications blur together. I feel his body and at the same time see my strangely static life—years frozen in solidarity with my mother—I see it all lit up, exposed to this boy's view. But the fact is, none of this is visible, even to me. My mother's closeness and coercive style are ordinary now. I just know that there's a window over us, her room. Her light goes on and then goes off again. And I know boy has to go. It's a spring night in the midseventies, and I've just been to dinner at his house. His father is an anthropologist, but I'm the one who needs to learn how other people live.

Boy. Boy comes to rehearsal in a short black cape and announces he's decided on his stage name. He's slight, and gestures hugely for the simplest things; he cannot speak without projecting. During breaks he demonstrates his magic tricks and star impersonations; when we perform, he brings his complicated and enormous makeup kit. Part Edward Everett Horton, part Vincent Price, and part Al Jolson, his mad theatricality is almost frightening—and makes me cringe about my own obsessions with the stage and screen. But he's so obvious I also envy him. I'll never fully capture Katherine Hepburn's snooty mannerisms, but this boy's already a full-blown, resplendent queen.

*   *   *

One night I took a friend to the flat roof outside my bedroom window. The sky was dark and full of stars; her hair was brilliant black and wild; the roof was soft black tar. My mother's room was underneath. I spread out some old towels; she lay down. I sat up paralyzed: feverish with the closeness of her mouth and hair and laugh, and too afraid to move.

Boy finds me at my summer job in Harvard Square, then takes me for a swim one afternoon. How did we get out to the country? We do not have a car. Boy's friends are all the cool, pot-smoking, jazz-musician boys, but he is pigeon-toed and odd. Boy needs me, I find out, because he thinks I'll understand why he's been having sex with his best friend. Of course they've only done it once; well, twice. All I know, as we walk around the woods near his aunt's house, is that I want him to tell me more. I wish that I'd been there. But most of all, I wish he were a girl. Instead, later at the pond, he strips in front of me, wants me to watch while he swims nakedly, and asks me to undress as well.

Boy listens when I tell him I like girls. And one especially. Why do I talk to him? Because the pressure of not speaking is too much. And now I'm almost seventeen. Because I know I'll have to kiss him otherwise. Boy says he understands and tells me to declare my love to her. But now I realize that I've made a huge mistake. He's too excited; he'll repeat what I've just said. Why did I say her name? Why did I say her name?

Eventually, I read the local homo newspaper, with pleasure and disdain, and then got rid of it so well, I thought (in a bag, in a bag, in another bag, then in the garbage can by our front gate). Later I learned my mother searched through there voraciously.

Boy. Boy takes me for a sail out in the dirty city harbor one spring day. Hours later, when I come home—after the encounter on his sofa he required (when I said no, he said: Oh, I'll keep on my underwear), after the pancakes he whipped up at 3:00 A.M.—I find my mother isn't furious. No inquisition, accusation, tears, or anything. I'm trying not to think. In general, cynicism is my anesthesia—cheaper than drugs, and a good way to feel adult. But this time it doesn't work—or works too well—because I'm not too numb to see that he is not a boy at all (he's twenty-eight), that he's a friend of hers, and that she must have hoped he'd be a cure.

Lost in Translation

Michael Lowenthal

I'm glad to hear you have a close friend at home. Everybody should be so lucky. The fact that he is a he and not a she is nothing to worry about. That will come later.

—*A summer camp counselor, writing to me in 1982, shortly before I turned thirteen*

I still think of him as Patricio: this wide-jawed redhead with the hypnotic grin, toiling to say his own name in eighth-grade Spanish. His Anglo-Saxon features seemed to hinder him, physically, from pronouncing it. "Pat*rrrr*icio," Señora Maldonado growled, modeling the correct way to roll the R's. "*La lengua. La lengua.* Use the tongue!" But no matter how stridently the teacher coached, Pat couldn't introduce himself.

"Pat-dicio," he'd spit earnestly, then shrug and flash his front-teeth gap, and even Señora had to forgive him.

Was it this breach in Pat's hypercompetence that let me plunge parachuteless into love? As Pat Chapman, he was the wrestling-team stud: cocksure, suave, untouchable; but as Patricio, stuttering his way through an alien vocabulary, he was thrillingly waifish and exposed.

Try to see him as I did the first day of school: on the room's left side, over by the windows, so the afternoon sun sparked his cinnamon-sugar hair. It was kind of parted in the middle, kind of not, disheveled and perfect and winging over his right ear as though he'd just woken from a nap. He squinted in the glare, providing my first glimpse of the dimples that flickered at his nose's bridge when he was frustrated or laughing or—instantly, I imagined it—having sex.

Pat and I didn't speak, not for two or three weeks. But we couldn't help noticing each other, because his accent was worst in the class and mine was best. (My family had lived in Peru till I was three, and though by eighth grade I remembered little more Spanish than "*sí*" and "*no,*" the music of it lingered in my brain.)

Señora Maldonado was a crusader for *español*. The most glamorous teacher at Westland Middle School, impeccable in her designer skirts and stiletto heels, she viewed any failure at fluency as denigration of her heritage. With an Argentine propensity for drama, she latched on to Pat and me as examples. She would use Pat to illustrate the most heinous language butchery, then beckon me to correct him, proving that someone besides a native speaker could properly inflect the Latin vowels.

"*Patricio,*" she demanded, pacing before the blackboard like a supermodel, "*repite por favor: 'A mí me gusta el béisbol.'* "

Patricio tried, but his attempt to express an affinity for baseball sounded like a drunken trucker hounding a waitress in a honky-tonk.

"*¡No! Escúchame bien,* listen close." And then Señora, hands on her high, elegant hips, repeated the sentence at *Sesame Street* pace: "*A mí me gus-ta el béis-bol.*"

Pat scrunched his nose in wrinkly concentration, the indentations at the bridge as dark as scars. He tried again, but the language eluded him.

"*Ay ya yay,*" Señora lamented. "*Chicos,* what are we going to do? *Pobrecito Patricio tiene la lengua gorda.* But maybe Miguel can say it right. Would you, please, Miguel?"

I feared offending Pat with my proficiency, but I couldn't defy a teacher's request. I spoke the words in deftly accented Spanish, a balance of impatient crispness and lush exuberance.

"*Perfecto,*" Señora cheered. "*¡Perfectísimo!*"

But I hardly registered her praise. I was still fixed on what she'd said about Patricio: that he possessed "*la lengua gorda.*" I knew it meant tongue-tied, indistinct of speech. But the literal translation was that he had a "fat tongue."

*   *   *

I was twelve at the beginning of eighth grade—a year young, by virtue of my having skipped ahead in elementary school. Sometimes I like to blame that gap for my inability to fit in properly, but I suspect another year wouldn't have made a difference. I just wasn't good at being a kid.

I tried. I eavesdropped on the cool guys' conversations, panning for nuggets about the latest trends. But the fickle logic of adolescence confounded me. I couldn't have told you why the Knack was awesome and the Village People worthy of scorn; why Pumas were cool shoes and Stan Smiths for geeks. I had no opinions of my own, only the fervid drive to be normal.

But no—I'm forgetting politics, my sole indulgence. It was the first year of Reaganomics, and growing up in suburban Washington, D.C., the opportunities for dissent were manifold: the nuclear freeze, Central America, handgun control. Once a week I trooped to the high school for meetings of the Student Union to Promote Awareness. Led by Sundance, a Guatemalan poncho-clad, incense-smelling senior, we discussed oppression and painted protest banners.

In my classmates' eyes, I must have been a freak. Did I see this? Did I realize the extent to which spending weekends marching on the Pentagon, when other kids skateboarded or stared at cartoons, imperiled my campaign for normalcy? Perhaps it was a subconscious experiment. Already sensing my sexual difference, and the ostracism it would likely spark, was I testing my aptitude for exclusion?

The big rally that fall was Solidarity Day. Sundance shepherded us to the Mall, which swarmed with disaffected teamsters and machinists. The atmosphere was heady. I got near enough to Pete Seeger to count the frets on his banjo neck. I marched next to Bella Abzug. The triumph, though, was finding a T-shirt for my infamous collection (BREAD NOT BOMBS; A MAN OF QUALITY IS NOT THREATENED BY A WOMAN SEEKING EQUALITY). The new acquisition was a green shirt shouting DEFEND ATLANTA'S CHILDREN, NOT EL SALVADOR'S JUNTA.

Yes, I thought. A stroke of genius! Twenty-three black kids had been killed by a madman in Atlanta. Why were we propping up a murderous regime in El Salvador instead of stopping the slaughter in our own backyard?

Monday was unseasonably cool for Washington—windbreaker

weather—but I wore just the T-shirt anyway, the gooseflesh on my arms a badge of pride. At the bus stop, though, kids stared quizzically. By school time, the perplexity turned to ridicule.

Jon Secrest challenged me as we awaited the bell for Spanish. "Junta?" he said, pronouncing the word with a hard J that bestowed a seedy, suggestive tone. "What the hell's a junta?"

"Not '*djun*-ta,' " I corrected him. " '*Hoon*-ta.' It's a military government."

"Well, I still don't get it. What does Atlanta have to do with El Salvador?"

I began to defend myself, but other kids joined in the jeering. I heard snickered "Atlantas" and "El Salvadors." I withered, spotlit by their derision.

And then, in sauntered Patricio: all smile and squint lines and casual backhand wipe of nose—boyness embodied. He stopped in front of me, glanced at my shirt, seemed to sniff the air like a danger-sensing dog. "Hey, man," he said, "I dig your shirt."

Even in my dreams, I'd never dared hope for such ennoblement. In those first lonely weeks of school I'd prayed for Pat to acknowledge me, maybe utter a quick hello. But this! He had swooped me from the fiery pit, untied me from the railroad tracks.

Pat sat down, and for the rest of class I stared at him, wondering how I'd earned his protection. When Señora Maldonado asked him to conjugate *poder* and *querer,* and he flubbed the irregular verbs for the hundredth time, I attempted a reciprocal rescue. "*Queero,*" he guessed, and I mouthed, "*quiero,*" but he never thought to look in my direction.

After class I tailed him to his locker. "Hey," I said. "Thanks. Thanks a lot."

For a second, Pat's brow creased in the same pattern as when Señora stumped him. Then he looked at my chest. "Oh," he said. "No problem."

I spun the numbers on the neighboring locker's dial. "No offense," I said, "but with the trouble you have in Spanish and all, I was kind of surprised you even know what a junta is."

"A what?"

I was about to repeat the word when I realized, in a heart-draining epiphany, that Pat had no clue what my T-shirt meant. He couldn't pronounce *junta*, let alone argue why El Salvador's was unworthy of defense. But with a single beat's lag, my heart swelled again when I understood that Pat, walking into class, had simply perceived the injustice of my taunting and, out of the great mystery of human comradeship, had shielded me with his aura. This meant far more than if he'd merely agreed with my politics. We had a bond now. We had a sixth sense. He cared for me.

The progression of our relationship over the next few months was as inexplicable as Pat's initial overture. I tried not to be too eager, but I spent so much time with Pat in my fantasies that seeing him in person, I often forgot that we weren't, in fact, best friends. Every day or two I concocted an excuse to approach him. I'd found an Erasermate on the floor; had he lost one? My O.P. shorts had worn a hole; did he know the cheapest place to buy a pair? Pat usually greeted my buddyness with a muddled "Wait, I know I know you from somewhere" look. I should have been angry or disheartened, but I was only grateful to be granted an audience.

And then, just when I thought all hope was lost, that our brief connection had been a fluke, he would astonish me with a show of thoughtfulness. In October, when Anwar Sadat was assassinated, Pat brought me *The Washington Post*. "I know you're into politics," he said. I'd already read the paper at home, but I studied it again now, every word, unable to keep from smiling despite the account of sniped bullets and shattering skulls.

A week later, on a Friday afternoon, Pat chased after me when Spanish class let out. "Miguel," he called. "Wait up, Miguel." And after a pause during which he seemed to search the air for invisible subtitles, he wished me a good weekend in not-too-badly savaged Spanish: *"Tienes el bieno fin de semana."*

"Tú también," I managed, *"tú también."*

For a minute, the Westland hallway was like the emerald corridor to Oz, its Pine-Sol scent consecrated incense. Pat wanted me, too; this was his code. But then I thought of all the times when he ignored me. Was Pat sending signals or wasn't he?

What was certain was that I'd never felt this way. I'd been attracted to other guys, had even fooled around with a few. But that had been all skin and breath and horniness. This was deeper. My toes would curl when he said my name. I got teary at the thought of his hairline. When I imagined something as innocent as holding Pat's hand in a movie theater, the very folds of my brain seemed to unfurl and snap back in a new arrangement.

How to explain this aberrant passion? In Spanish, there were rule-flouting nouns and verbs, but these exceptions were all listed in our textbook. "Don't question," Señora told us, "memorize." But I had no such primer for sexuality. I couldn't trust the broken grammar of my feelings.

Before Thanksgiving, our entire class was bused to the Smith Center, a nature retreat in western Maryland, for a long weekend of hands-on science. I was nervous about spending three full days with my classmates, from whom I normally hid my nonschool life. They would see me get dressed. They would hear my bathroom noises. Who knew what secrets they might surmise?

But my fears were balanced by the ticklish prospect of so much time in Pat's proximity—seeing *him* get dressed, listening when *he* relieved himself. Maybe I could decode his cryptogram.

College-student interns split us into groups to study the local habitat. We poured plaster casts of possum tracks, plucked sassafras leaves and sucked their root-beer stems. Dinner was army-style in a giant mess hall, in which we then watched movies on a sheet hung from the rafters. The entertainment aimed to sedate us for bed, but the main selection— the original *M*A*S*H*, with its buxom Major Houlihan—only stirred the riley hormones that inflamed us.

Back in the boys' bunkhouse the air was galvanic with arousal, as though sex was a gas being pumped in from hidden vents. I'd tasted this ether before, at summer camp, where my cabinmates and I staged jerk-off shows. It was familiar, too, from the night of Adam Glickman's bar mitzvah, when I snuggled into Gil Miller's sleeping bag and left my sticky offering between his legs. I wanted it again now. I wanted Pat, below whose upper bunk I'd claimed my spot.

Jon Secrest instigated a debate about the desirability of big tits versus small. Then Keith Sommers took a poll as to whether pussies smelled more like tuna fish or burrito filling, but no one would admit to first-hand experience.

I don't remember who brought up the Smurfs, the tiny blue gnomes that were the latest cartoon craze. Did they have tiny gnome-sized genitals, someone inquired? If they had pubic hair, was it blue?

Above me, the bunk creaked, and Pat leaned his head over the rail. "Forget the Smurfs," he said. "You know what really grosses me out?" Silence shrouded the room. "Red pubic hair. Have you ever seen red pubic hair? It's nasty."

Giggles of assent and mock retching sounds ensued. A teacher knocked on the door and warned us to settle down. In minutes phlegmy snoring could be heard.

I lay wide awake in my bunk, confounded by Pat's remark. Pat himself had red hair, lustrous strands that made Señora call him *pelirrojo*. Surely, then, his own pubic hair must be red. Was his statement evidence of self-loathing, betokening deeper doubts—like my own—about sexuality? Or was it possible that his pubes were indeed different from the hair on his head? Perhaps he had a freakish genetic condition. Perhaps he was blond there, or brown, or Smurf-blue.

Back at school, I craved to know all of him. I became a spy, pestering mutual acquaintances with questions. I didn't learn much, but the bits of story bloomed yeastlike in my imagination: Pat was adopted; he had an older sister, adopted too; he liked cats; he wore boxer shorts.

And then I learned the devastating fact of Pat's attachment to Marisa Hughes, a girl known for her brunette hair and her bouncy, precocious breasts. She and Pat had been going steady for a year, I heard. The rumor was, they "did it" with regularity.

I was crushed, and envious, and forlorn, and aroused. I would masturbate to the image of them having sex, then get so upset that I couldn't finish, then finish anyway with myself in Marisa's place.

Spanish remained my guarantee of seeing Pat, at once a comfort and a punishment. He still sat on the left, underneath the windows, mullion shadows striping his face like prison bars. Señora Maldonado continued her crusade of Latinizing suburbanites. We were beginners and thus condemned to the declarative: *I am, I go, I say, I do*. But Señora hinted at tricks we might later learn. "It's really the subjunctive," she said once when asked to translate a certain phrase, but then, dismissing the thought, offered a more simplistic version.

The word *subjunctive* goaded my curiosity. I asked Señora after class what it meant, and gratified by my extra-credit interest, she revealed the tense of contingency, of *what if?* In Spanish, she explained, verbs assumed different forms when referring to fantasy. She taught me key words—*quisiera, pudiera, tuviera*—plaintive, vowelly cries for help.

For weeks, while the rest of class struggled with basic vocabulary, I conducted an advanced self-study course. I penned line after line in my three-ring binder, Spanish renditions of my private subjunctive dreams: If I were to tell Pat, to kiss him, if he were mine. If only I could spend time with him . . .

After Christmas break, as if my incantations had cast a spell, a miracle: Pat invited me home.

Maybe he wanted help studying for finals. Maybe Señora had suggested tutoring. The truth is, I don't remember. And though it would be easy enough to invent a scenario, I'd rather convey the episode as it seems to me—a disjunctive island of memory—because Pat and my feelings for him so defied accountability.

My recollection starts midstep in the yard of Pat's house. The building was small and off-kilter on its lot, as though it had been wide-load trucked there and the driver, in a rush to get to his next job, never bothered to situate it properly. Untrimmed shrubbery crowded in. The neighbors must have thought it an eyesore.

When I walked inside, I tingled with a tourist's edgy thrill; Pat's house was the shocking, exotic antithesis of my own. The furniture was darker and dustier. They had trinkets on the walls, carpeting. The rules were different. Anything could happen here.

Pat's room was up some stairs, tucked into an unfinished loft. Actually, the loft itself was the room. There was no door, no clearly marked boundary, just a bed plunked amid spackled drywall and bare two-by-fours. Pat said his father had been promising to finish it for years. The renegade arrangement struck me as enviably grown-up, like Greg's attic pad in late *Brady Bunch* episodes. But it also made me feel sorry for Pat, a metaphor for his adopted-child existence and what I imagined as his inability ever to be truly at home. This was what I wanted to believe: that Pat—like me—felt out of place, in need of kinship.

Pat elbowed a heap of dirty laundry from the bed, kicked off his shoes, and lay down. I lay down next to him, in the skinny space he left, and finally, for the first time, we really talked. School stuff at first, petty gossip: who had been caught smoking in the bathroom. Eventually we steered toward the personal. Pat mentioned a fight with his sister, and I told him I fought with mine, too. Recently I'd flung a skewer at her, puncturing an artery. "Sick," he said, but I could tell I'd gained guy-points.

Pat asked about my folks' divorce, what it was like to have to visit my own father. He said he wondered sometimes if his parents, too, should split. Things had been strained lately, and they scapegoated him, nagging him to cool things with Marisa.

"So, do you guys . . ." I asked, unable to help myself.

"Me and Marisa?" he said, blushing until his forehead blurred with his rusty hair. "I shouldn't say anything." And as disappointed as I was not to hear the details, I was gladdened by Pat's ability to keep a secret.

For dinner we fried cans of corned-beef hash, which we ate in front of the TV. During a commercial break, I called my mother and told her not to worry, that I was at a friend's and I'd probably stay the night. She asked if adults were present, and I promised her that they were. But I hadn't met Pat's parents. Perhaps they'd gone away for the weekend. Perhaps they worked the late shift.

It was Friday, and so we could have gone out, but instead we watched sitcoms until midnight and then retired to Pat's loft. The fact that nothing monumental passed is what, for me, made it monumental. This was his routine. And now I was part of it.

As we prepared for bed, I hoped I might finally answer the riddle of Pat's pubic hair. I'd dreamed of seeing him naked or at least in his underwear so I could glimpse his inner-thigh tinsel curls. Pat ducked behind the sheet of drywall that separated his "bedroom" from the toilet. I heard the gurgle and then staccato spurt of his peeing, followed by a curious pause. I sat on the bed's edge, picturing double plays and squeeze bunts to forestall a hard-on. When he reemerged he was shirtless but wearing baggy white karate pants tied at the waist. His pubes were still a mystery.

"You can take the bed," he said, and burrowed into the dirty clothes on his floor.

Not having pajamas of my own, I slipped under the covers wearing my pants. *"Buenas noches,"* I whispered, but Pat replied with ragged snores. I nuzzled the pillow—his pillow—and numbed myself with the anesthetic of his scent.

Saturday we woke up and wolfed huge bowls of Count Chocula. We lounged in front of the TV again, then napped the way only boys can after sleeping ten hours straight. Eventually we walked into town. We killed time. We did "stuff." I was so lost in telling myself to memorize every step and breath we took that I didn't notice much of anything.

Pat didn't ask if I wanted to stay with him another night, and I didn't ask if I could. I just did.

His parents still hadn't shown, and beneath the flood tide of Pat's bravado, I began to gauge the undertow of loneliness. Again I slept in my clothes, desperate to expose myself but too fearful to make the first move. Instead I just watched him sprawled puppylike below me: all limb-twitching and stomach growls and circling to gain position. I yearned to scratch the scruff of his neck.

Sunday brought the same blissful aimlessness. We didn't need the crutch of "activity." Being together was our only purpose. We were effortless soul mates, *compañeros.*

When night came, I sank into an unspoken melancholy. We dined on corned-beef hash again, but already the ritual sagged with nostalgia, an attempt to preserve something I knew must disappear.

I was lacing my shoes to leave when Pat's hand landed on my shoulder. "It's late already," he said. "Just stay here again?"

"But what about school?"

"We'll go together," he said. "We can take my bus."

And the teetering earth was righted on its axis.

We stayed up till two in the morning, talking and listening to records by bands I pretended to know. I confessed to feeling different from the other guys at school. Friendships were important to me, I said. *His* friendship. Did he understand?

Of course he did, Pat assured me. He was different, too. And as he yawned his way to sleep, he mumbled something cryptic about there being a "special school for people like us."

My brain buzzed as if with electroshock. A special school? People like us? I dreamed of sitting in a huge classroom full of Pats: chisel-jawed redheads with winning smiles. We'd study love poems in all the world's languages!

I nearly admitted then how I'd snooped on him. I sucked a breath. "I love you," I almost said.

Monday we rode to school together. I was a mess in my four-day-rumpled clothes, but I relished the stares I drew, proud of each wrinkle and stain. That afternoon we didn't get to talk in Spanish; Señora Maldonado sprang a pop quiz on us. I caught Pat's attention, though, when he handed in his answer sheet, and he knighted me with his secret smile. We had a brotherhood. Our bond was irrevocable.

Or was it? That question plagued me in the following weeks and months, as I waited futilely for a second honeymoon. Pat wasn't cold. When we passed each other in the halls, he punched my shoulder and called me Miguelito. We ate lunch together two or three times a week. But on weekends Pat was busy. His father needed help with the yard-work; Marisa booked his Saturday nights. "Maybe Sunday," he said a couple of times, then didn't call.

I went crazy wondering. From close up had Pat found me lacking? Had I murmured something in my sleep that turned him off? Or maybe his distancing betrayed "fear of intimacy"—a diagnosis I'd heard Dr. Ruth offer on the radio. It was on this last possibility that I fixed my hopes. I, too, was scared by our closeness, and by how much closer still I longed to be.

Previously, when I'd wanted sex from a guy, I devised ways to snooker him into complicity. Discussing masturbation might prompt a demonstration. Mentions of penis size could inspire show-and-tells. But I didn't want just sex from Pat, I wanted love.

"Pat," I imagined saying, "I . . ." But the thought always dangled unfulfilled. I *want*? I *wonder*? I *am*?

Finally, I decided to consult a friend. Dave had been a counselor at my progressive Quaker summer camp. In the off-season, he kept the books for a college in Massachusetts, and the two jobs reflected his balance of sensitivity and pragmatism. But if I didn't to this day have Dave's response tucked in my file drawer of mementos, I would hardly believe I'd had the guts to write him. Though I didn't yet have any precise concept of "gay," I'd read the desktop graffiti about Mr. Davis, our wisp of a geography teacher, and his rumored proclivity for gerbils. I knew a fag was something I shouldn't be.

My letter to Dave described Pat and my undistractable love. I recounted our rapturous weekend and Pat's actions since. I asked if he thought I was sick or crazy.

Dave was the model of levelheaded support. He paid particular attention to Pat's comment about the school for "special people." "Have you ever asked him what he meant by that?" Dave inquired. "Does he mean that the school is for bright people like you? Or that it is for politically involved people like you? There are lots of harmless interpretations. If it still worries you, ask him about it. I'm sure you can think of a tactful way to bring it up."

Of course! The special-school comment would be my ruse—but not even, because I truly wasn't sure what Pat had meant. Dave had rescued me. Now I had a plan.

Spring shed its grace on Washington. The city flushed pinkly buoyant, cherry blossoms scattered everywhere as if in the wake of a giant wedding processional. Even the pollinated air smelled optimistic.

Easter break was in two weeks. Despite my new hopefulness, I decided to postpone talking to Pat until just before the holiday. That way, if things backfired, I wouldn't see him for a while. I marked the date on my calendar and counted down.

But when the day arrived, world politics intervened. Argentine troops invaded the Falkland Islands, overtaking a squadron of British marines. Señora Maldonado canceled her lesson plan and expounded on imperialism's evils. She insisted we say "Islas Malvinas" instead of "Falkland Islands." No one had ever heard of the Falklands, but Señora, dead serious, lectured bombastically the entire hour. At the bell, Pat sprinted out so fast I couldn't corner him.

During the vacation, I read Dave's letter over and over until the thrice-folded page grew soft as a rabbit's foot. I vowed to approach Pat when school resumed. By then, though, there were ten thousand Argentine troops in the Malvinas, with the British navy sailing south at full alert. Spanish class was no place for personal troubles.

Because of my activist's reputation, I was expected to take a stance on the conflict. Loyal to Señora Maldonado, at first I supported the Argentines. But Jon Secrest called me on the hypocrisy. "Defend Atlanta's children," he mocked, "not Argentina's junta." It was true. Argentina's government was not much better than the one in El Salvador.

I wasn't the only bewildered leftist. Sundance convened an emergency session of the Student Union to Promote Awareness. Some students called for picketing the British embassy; others threatened to quit if we sided with Argentina. Everything that had once been clear became a blur.

As General Galtieri and Prime Minister Thatcher traded ultimatums, I finally issued one to myself: I must talk to Pat by the beginning of the month.

I waited until the final hour, the night of May 1—a week and a day before I turned thirteen. I locked myself in the spare bedroom in our basement. I took a yellow legal pad, in a last-ditch hope that a brilliant script would occur to me, and a Rubik's Cube to provide Zen-like distraction. As I worked up the courage to lift the phone, I twisted the cube, trying to match reds with reds, blues with blues, greens with greens. The manufacturer boasted of forty-three quintillion possible configurations but, of course, only one correct outcome.

In a blind, breathless rush I dialed his number. He answered. Yes, he was alone; he could talk; what was up?

Alone, I scribbled on the legal pad, then added: *TALK!*

"Crazy stuff in the Falklands, huh?" I offered as a starter.

"Las Malvinas," Pat corrected me. *"¡Por favor!"* I noted that his accent had improved.

"You're right," I said. "Don't report me to *la señora.*"

He promised not to, and then we fell silent. Static on the line, breath, trepidation. Having two languages to draw upon didn't ease my task.

"So, um, Pat?" I finally asked, as if during the pause maybe someone had usurped his place on the other end.

He confirmed his presence with a "yeah."

"What I was wondering was . . . well, you know how when I slept over that time, you mentioned a special school?"

"Um," he hedged. "Wait. What exactly did I say?"

I wrote *special?* on my paper, then underlined it twice. "A special school. For people like us?"

"I guess I'm not sure I know what 'people like us' means."

"Right," I said. "I mean, me neither. That's what I wanted to ask about. I wondered how you think we're, you know, similar."

Pat didn't respond right away. I could picture him in his messy loft, his brow creased in seductive puzzlement. I cranked the Rubik's Cube and locked four yellows into line.

"I don't know," he said. "Don't you think we're similar?"

"Yeah," I said, brightening. "But, see, I feel like I'm kind of different from most other people. People besides you."

"What about those hippie freaks you hang out with?"

"They're not really freaks," I said.

"Don't get me wrong, I think it's cool. But you've got to admit, they're kind of freaky."

"Okay, does that make *me* freaky, then?" I said. "Because I do these things. Well, I don't *do* them. They're more like feelings I have? And I'm wondering if maybe you have them, too."

There. The setup. Point of no return.

And so when Pat asked the inevitable "What kind of feelings?" I had no choice but to own up to my love. Actually, I didn't say "love." Probably I mumbled "like," or "like a lot." But I told him almost everything, far too much.

"So," I asked, "am I, like, a freak?"

Now the interminable wait. I doodled mindlessly on the notepad, my palms greasy with leaking sweat.

And when finally Pat coughed and began to talk, the music I heard, the sweet resurrecting aria, was: "No, of course you're not a freak."

How long did the moment last—that crystalline moment of beatitude? A split second? Two seconds? Three? I would have sworn it was time enough for a roomful of monkeys, typing randomly on their roomful of Underwoods, to compose the complete love sonnets of Shakespeare.

But then Pat said, "I'm flattered, I really am. I like you a lot as a friend. But I don't, you know. I mean it's not the way . . . Do you know what I mean?"

I lost my wind. No, I didn't know what he meant. Aside from the jokes about Mr. Davis, I'd never heard gayness talked about—and in that vacuum I'd assumed the issue was governed by clear extremes. Either you were the joke-teller or the object of the joke; a hater of gays, or gay yourself.

I almost wished Pat would scream "faggot" and slam the phone. I wished he would never speak to me again. Then I could hate him right back for his intolerance. But he hadn't rejected gayness; he'd rejected *me*.

Pat tried to fill the conversation's gap with small talk, but I couldn't bring myself to answer him. I spun the Rubik's Cube careless of pattern, letting entropy do its dirty work. When finally he said good-bye, he'd see me Monday, I hung up, mute and bewildered. On my lap lay the yellow legal pad, my stenography as illegible as monkey scrawl.

The next day, Sunday, a British submarine sank the Argentine cruiser *General Belgrano*. News footage showed the ship engulfed in flames and smoke. Because of the oil that slicked from the ravaged steel carcass, even the sea itself appeared to burn. Three hundred sixty-eight Argentines drowned in the South Atlantic.

In school on Monday, kids chattered about the gory TV reports. But they also gossiped about Adam Glickman's having gone to third base with some girl at a pool party. They traded crib notes for that afternoon's

English test. How could they all be so blasé? Didn't they know the world was a danger zone?

I stumbled through the halls, stupefied by tragedy. At lunch someone asked what was wrong, but I couldn't explain that I'd glimpsed my future and it petrified me. I shrugged and blamed my teariness on allergies.

And then came the ineluctable: Spanish class. I considered skipping, then saw there was no point; I couldn't skip the entire rest of the year. I claimed a chair in the very back of the room.

I had promised myself I wouldn't look, but of course I did. Pat was in his usual spot, torturously radiant. He wore a SEX WAX T-shirt, O.P. shorts, Pumas with no socks. When he turned my way I shifted my gaze to the front.

Señora Maldonado was slumped over her desk. Hair had pulled free from her bun and skewed like a defunct engine's wires around her face. Melted mascara darkened the puffiness below her eyes.

"I'm sure you've heard," she began, barely audible. She rested a trembling hand on her heart. "Forgive me," she said, "today I don't think I can . . ." but the rest vanished in her shaking sobs.

I had never seen a teacher cry. It was horrible to watch, like witnessing a parent's humiliation, further evidence of the world turned upside down. Señora Maldonado wept openly, far beyond the point of shame, and I wanted to rise and comfort her.

"My brothers!" she cried. "*Perdidos*—everyone lost."

I looked then at stoic Patricio, who stared out the window, away from me. Backlit by the May sun, he appeared to emit an armorlike force field, golden-red as the highlights in his hair. With his pencil he tapped a rhythm on his desk—maybe the drumbeat of the Knack's newest single? I could hear it, but I couldn't guess the tune.

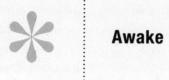

Awake

Jim Gladstone

Doug Spanner was my friend, too. Not just my brother Lewis's. I was in seventh grade, they were in sixth. Mainly, Doug played ball and roughhoused with Lew and the other guys in their class, but the summer before, right after the Spanners moved into the neighborhood, Doug and I were in the community-center play together. *Tom Sawyer*. He was Tom and I was Huck. That's when I got to know him. Doug's mom taught us the dances and said, "Please call me Carol" instead of Mrs. Spanner. Doug and his mom were both cool.

It seemed to me that Tom Sawyer was the perfect part for Doug. In real life he was just like Tom. Even though he'd just arrived, he was awfully popular. All the guys liked him. And he got into trouble like Tom Sawyer, too.

After school started that fall, Doug would set off cherry bombs in the cafeteria. He would lift packs of Tic Tacs and Bubble Yum from Bell's Pharmacy. He would even sneak a peek in the girls' restroom.

The low ceilings at Albert Riggs Middle School were just big rectangles of acoustic tile balanced on a metal grid. Miss Carpenter once got overexcited during a map talk about India and thrust her pointer skyward, dislodging one of the tiles, which came slapping to the floor like an overstarched flying carpet.

In the few minutes between the end of morning classes and the bell that permitted us to run downstairs to the cafeteria, some of us seventh-grade guys would head to the boys' room. Doug always came along, too. We figured he could hang with us older guys if he wanted. One of us—usually me—would play lookout, lurking by the door to make sure no teachers were headed our way. The others would boost Doug up on top of the white porcelain urinal. He could have climbed it himself, but Doug didn't want to get any residue from the ammonia-smelling toilet cake on his black Adidas.

Doug would reach high with both hands, knock a tile out of place, grab the grid, and pull up toward the ceiling, his feet clambering, then pushing off the urinal's chrome handle. His muscular "Oof!" and the roar of flushing water sent a surge of adrenaline through me. I would glimpse away from my lookout crack in the bathroom door to see only patch-kneed jeans and sneakers dangling down from a neat, rectangular hole in the ceiling. And just where the rest of him became engulfed in the shadows above us, I could see a pale band of belly as Doug's bright red T-shirt tugged out from his belted Toughskins.

"I'm closer, I'm closer," he'd say, narrating his own motion in an enticing stage whisper as he arched himself over the dividing wall toward the girls' room ceiling. "I'm closer . . . I'm closer . . . I'm touching it."

My mind clouded with a vision of dextrous pink fingers gingerly setting down on top of a thin foam tile and resting there, dangerously, only five feet above the braided hair of a tinkling neighborhood girl.

The swoon would be broken by Doug's grand finale. He'd pound a fist on the tile, sending it tumbling down on our victim's head. As the girl broke into a scream, he'd whoop a Minnie Pearl "Howww-deee!" and we'd all buckle over laughing as he proudly descended from on high with another punctuating flush of the urinal.

We'd swagger out of the boys' room, choking back giggles and tossing off daredevil pleasantries to any adults who passed our way:

"Lovely day, isn't it, Vice Principal Lawrence?"

"I suppose so, Mr. Spanner. Shouldn't you be down at lunch by now?"

"I sure am looking forward to art this afternoon, Miss Wolfert."

"So am I, James! We'll be working with modeling clay!"

Doug pulled me aside on the stairs as the other guys charged their way to the lunch line.

"Guess what I saw, Jimmy Boy."

It felt good to lean in toward his whisper, taken into his confidence.

"What?"

"Maybe I shouldn't tell."

"Aw, c'mon. You know I can keep a secret."

"Wellll . . ." He worked at suspense, "What I saw is . . . Mallow's hairy pussy!"

"No way!"

Melanie Mallow was, as our teachers would have put it, the most "mature" girl in the sixth grade. Heck, in the whole school. Which is to say, she had returned from summer vacation sporting tremendous boobs. As big as Miss Wolfert, the art teacher's.

For years Miss Wolfert had been nicknamed "Booby Wolfert" by the students, a moniker I feel certain she was well aware of and used to her advantage in maintaining order over a bevy of smart-alecky yet easily intimidated boys on the cusp of pubescence.

Even the likes of Doug Spanner had a hard time doing more than getting mealymouthed and settling down when Booby Wolfert cha-cha'd their way, tossed back her hairdo, thrust forward her frontage, and asked, in a bedevilingly sultry whisper, "Now, baby, do we have a problem here?"

When Melanie Mallow brought her new breasts to school that fall, we all became incredibly squirmy and uncomfortable. Here, personified, was the treacherous mountain pass we would all soon traverse. At this age, even most of the other girls were aghast. The only way to contain our fear was to give it a name. Well, a nickname. "Booby" being taken, we opted for "Cups." As in Melanie's Mallo-Cups.

In the fall we boys and girls had taken separate sessions of health education down in the school's multipurpose room (cafeteria/gym/auditorium/place-to-watch-slide-shows-of-fallopian-tubes). But with all the line drawings you could show us, and all the seeds and eggs you could tell us about, none of it was adequate preparation for the premature glandular reality of our own schoolmate's burgeoning bounty. And now, if Doug spoke the truth, her hirsute hidden treasure.

"I swear!" Doug crowed to me. "I sure did see it! The bearded clam itself. Leave it to beaver."

"How?"

"She *showed* it to me." He punched a fist against his own chest.

"Get out of here!"

"No kidding, Jimbo-rama. Before I sent the tile flying today, I lifted up the corner and peeked down into the stall."

"Geez, Douggie, she coulda screamed. She coulda had Mr. Lawrence paddling your butt in a minute."

"First off, she could hardly tell who it was just by my eyeball. Second off, I could have ripped out of the guys' room in a sec. And third off, old Mallo-Cups wasn't exactly chasing me away. She was sitting there, but it didn't sound like she was peeing or anything yet. She hears the tile lift and looks up toward the ceiling. Then she sees me. I'm frozen scared, but then she smiles. Then she waves. And then—you're not gonna believe this!—she rubs her tongue all over her teeth like the Pearl Drops lady on TV, bends back, and arches up toward the ceiling." I didn't exactly believe this part, but the excitement in Doug's boastful voice was infectious. "It was right there. I coulda reached down and touched it. Mark's brother was right, by the way: It smelled like a tuna sandwich. Speaking of which"—Doug winked at me—"I'll race you to the cafeteria!"

As he would so many more times, Doug Spanner bolted off, leaving me behind. But as he shot that dashing wink, I sensed that I could recognize him by just his eyeball anytime. He was a memorable kind of guy.

Doug and Lew and I all played on the same Little League team that year. My dad and Mr. Spanner ("Call me Bruce, guys!") were the coaches, Doug and Lew the stars, and me, most of the time, the bench-warmer. One night, after a particularly massive trouncing of the Ardmore

Orioles, the five of us went to Pizza Town USA for a postgame cele-
bration. I wanted to say something to the moms when we came home
after, because I knew that the fathers were muttering and staring at
Diane, the waitress. Doug was looking too, and elbowing a pretty-much-
oblivious Lew, who occasionally stage-whispered something along the
lines of "Jell-O Mama!" just to prove he was in sync with the prevailing
sentiments. The jukebox played "Disco Lady," Johnny Ray singing
about moving it in and moving it out, shaking it round and about.

Lewis asked Dad if Doug could sleep over that night, and Dad gave
the okay. I swallowed nervously. After too much TV and much pro-
longing of our designated bedtime, my parents marched us upstairs, sent
me off to my room and set up the cot for Doug in Lew's room.

"Nighty night, Jimmy Boy!" Doug joked as they shut the door.

Alone in the dark, I felt a pang of jealousy over Lew's friendship with
Doug. But then it was supplanted by a haunting calm. A sense of in-
evitability. Exactly what was inevitable I didn't know. What I did know
was that all I could do was wait. Something of great import was about
to happen.

I slipped into bed and, as soon as I was under the covers, decided
to remove the Fruit of the Loom briefs I normally slept in. I flung them
across the dark room and lay naked. I felt the pale blue sheet, slightly
damp, against my back. The weight of the room pressed me flat against
the mattress. The red digits of the clock radio burned 1:17. I heard
them creep out of Lew's bedroom and into the hall. They tuned their
voices down to mere breath, speaking to each other in word-shaped
exhalations. I swallowed hard on my own anxious laughter.

"I will lie still," I repeated to myself. I watched a film of emotion-
charged images projected on the burnt-orange screen of my closed eye-
lids: my father shaving, Mrs. Spanner dancing onstage. At the same time,
though, I heard my own Tom Sawyer dance partner tiptoeing across my
bedroom carpet, where he was surely observed by my odd couple female
sentries—side-by-side posters of the roller-coaster flesh of sitcom starlet
Loni Anderson and the butter-knife figure of supermodel Cheryl Tiegs.

"Lewis," Doug whispered, just feet from my bed. "Shine the light."

As I shut my eyes, the narrow beam of my brother's penlight swept
over my covers, then flushed my face. It was a physical presence, this

beam along my body. My groin pulled tight when it crossed the blanket there. The soft hairs above my upper lip were set dancing just before the beam touched my eyes and turned burnt orange to warm marmalade.

For these seconds, trying to lie still, every sense was heightened. Everything I knew in the universe seemed to be hurtling at me or out of me. Lying still, I wanted to jump out of myself. Blood rushed to my groin, and I squinted tighter as I grew hard. I was unembarrassed, strangely powerful as I exerted some magnetic force over Doug.

"All right," he whispered to my brother. "We're almost there."

I felt the light now, crossing my waist again. I sensed Doug's pink fingers reaching toward their goal. I believe I could actually feel him pinching the sides of my top sheet before he raised it up, like a tent. I swallowed as the light touched, then rested on my bare erection. They might be better at baseball, but there was satisfaction in knowing they were still sixth-graders; that I still had some kind of edge. Fearfully, I allowed myself to indulge the narrowest possible opening of my eyes.

They were staring at me now, seeing the curls of new hair, the thickness. I wished that they wished they could be like me: the Pubic Samson. At the same time, I felt pinned down and helpless, Gulliver, perused by Lilliputians.

"Geez. This is too weird," complained Lewis, suddenly forgetting to whisper.

"Shush! Keep the light still."

For an hour, or a minute, we were transfixed.

"Let's go already," Lew whined.

"Yeah, uh . . . all right," Doug muttered, half-consciously.

Doug Spanner let go of the top sheet. It dropped to my body, sending a breeze across my skin. They were gone. I kept my eyes closed and my mouth shut.

Then I heard Doug's laugh. His feet pounding back down the hall to my brother's room. Doug bounced, raucous, on Lewis's bed. He released a holler of welcome.

"Howww-deee!"

Nancy Booth, Wherever You Are

Rebecca Brown

Every year when I was a kid I went to summer camp. A few times, around the years of my parents' divorce, it was church camp, but most of the time it was Girl Scout camp, which I preferred. At church camp there were boys and girls, and boy and girl counselors too. The counselors were earnest football guys and sincere, toothy gals. At church camp the boys got to do the neat capers like chopping wood and building fires and digging holes. At church camp the girls had to do girl capers: set the table, cook, wash up. For activities after Bible class, the boys got to hike and fish and learn to use a compass in case they ever got lost in the woods. Girls got to do bead work and découpage and make pot holders. At church camp we slept in cabins, six or eight kids and one counselor to make sure we didn't tell ghost stories, which were against the Lord, or sneak out to visit the boys, which was temptation.

At Girl Scout camp, though, where there were no boys, girls got to do all the chores, including the cool, possibly dangerous ones. You got to hike and sail and ride horseback. You got to stay up late in your bunk, which, whether it was in a huge, four-bedder platform tent, a Conestoga wagon replica, or a cabin, was counselor-free, though they were comfortably within shouting distance in case you got afraid. You could scare each other to death with stories about ghosts or people who'd escaped from insane asylums or maniacs, or read with your flashlight under the covers or lie awake in your bed and think of your handsome counselor.

I'd been in Girl Scouts forever: Brownies in primary school, then Juniors; then in junior high, Cadettes; and finally, embarrassingly, in high school, Seniors, though only for a year, because only the homeliest, nerdiest girls stayed in after that. I stayed in that long because of camp.

I liked the hiking and horseback riding and sleeping under the stars. I liked the being away from home and wearing shorts and a T-shirt and sailor cap and swimming in a river or lake or pool every day and cooking beans and hot-dog stew above an open fire. But also, I realize in retrospect, I liked the women.

Most of the counselors were sweet, fair, long-haired girls who liked leading campfire songs and doing crafts and working with little kids. They were reliable young women, college girls home for the summer who would go on to teach grade school or work in the helping professions and have babies of their own. They were sporty girls who didn't wear makeup or ridiculous clothes, who liked the out-of-doors.

At camp we didn't know them by their real names, but by "camp names." These names were to make them distinct from us, with our Beckys and Kathys and Dees, and suggest their friendly authority over us while not sounding as formal or school-like as Miss Spencer or Mrs. Williams or Miss Pike. Counselors' camp names were meant to be fun or friendly or site-specific. They were usually names like Bandana or Dandi, as in dandelion, or Cricket.

But there were always a few counselors whose names were different. They didn't go gaga over the cute little Brownies and would never, as far as anyone could imagine, have babies of their own. They were women who liked living away from home in a single-sex environment. They were tanned, surly women whose hair was always short and who would never, ever, ever wear a dress. They did not have fun camp names like Cricket, but no-nonsense names like Gunwale or Cracker or Dock. They were tight-lipped, wrinkled women, and they were not just regular unit counselors, but special staff, the heads of sailing and riding and swimming, women more comfortable in the boathouse or stable or pool, with their equipment, the hardware of their work, than with the children. They wore flexy watches and the sleeves of their T-shirts rolled. They were women without families for whom Girl Scout camp was just a way to kill time in the summer, women whose real lives were lived as gym teachers or juvenile-detention officers or in the Reserves. Occasionally, they smelled like cigarettes.

There was a pair of them at horse-riding camp, Davy and Lou. They were the only ones I'd ever known of with names like that, names that could be human, male, not cartoon names like Dusty or Spinner or Spoon. And none of us tried to guess their names, if they were Rachel or Cindy or Marion. We knew their names were always their names; they were always Davy and Lou.

Both of them were quiet and tough, though Davy was tougher and quieter. They each had brown hair, Lou's curly, Davy's straight, but each so short you could barely see it coming out of the back of the wide-brimmed cowboy hats they always wore. They never cut up or rode like ruffians. They always rode sternly and quietly, as serious as John Wayne: back ramrod-straight, one hand cupped loosely around the reins, the other resting calmly on the thigh. They didn't sleep in a cabin or tent like everyone else but shared the trailer they drove there every year from wherever it was they lived. I didn't know where they came from but I wondered.

I wondered a lot about Davy and Lou. I wondered about their lives outside of camp. I couldn't imagine them living in a neighborhood like mine. The apartment complex where I lived with my mom was full of other overtired, working single moms and their millions of screaming kids and occasional boyfriends. I couldn't imagine Davy and Lou living there, or them with regular jobs, like teachers or nurses or secretaries. I couldn't imagine them politely saying "yessir" to their boss. I couldn't imagine how Davy and Lou would live in a world of men.

Their competence with horses, their terseness with girls, their difference from anyone I'd ever met before, the way they looked, both frightened and excited me. I felt confused. I wanted and I did not want them to notice me. I wanted and I did not want to know about wherever it was they came from. I knew I wasn't like the sweet, long-haired coun-

selors who were going to have kids of their own, but I also knew I could
never be as tough and brave and different as Davy and Lou.

The last year I went to summer camp I felt old. There were only a few
other fourteen-year-olds there because the other girls that age had become too cool to go to camp. But a few other girls from my troop and
I went. We were decent, hardworking kids who knew that going to camp
was a way of getting out of our summer jobs—for our moms or dads or
baby-sitting or a paper route—for a couple of weeks. We knew to take
advantage of being a kid as long as we could.

    We'd been friends for years, and talked to each other about every-
thing—our parents' fights and losses of jobs, our pregnant cousins and
horrid younger siblings, our complexions and weight and crushes on
guys, our tryouts for plays, our thoughts about God and where we
wanted to go when we got out of the boring Texas town in which we
lived. We tried to act ironic, and we swore to each other that we would
never, once we got to high school, refer to the fact that we had been at
Girl Scout camp together the previous summer.

    The camp was divided into units, each with about twenty campers
and two or three staff. The staff who slept in your unit were your regular
counselors who you did most things with, like hikes and meals and
capers and flag. But each unit also housed a special counselor or two
from the pool or dock or kitchen or office. There were four units: Pi-
oneer for Brownies, Tanglewood for Juniors, Lakewood for Cadettes,
and Brazos, the unit my friends and I were in, for the older Cadettes
and the very few Seniors like ourselves. The cabins in Brazos were
further apart than the tents or cabins in the younger kids' units, so you
didn't hear absolutely everything going on in the cabin next door. The
front of every cabin in the Brazos unit had a covered porch with a bench.

    At the end of every day there was an all-camp campfire and all the
campers and unit counselors were there. Sometimes the special staff
came too. The only ones who were never there were Davy and Lou.

    At most all-camp events you had to sit with your unit and your unit
staff, but at the nightly campfire you could sit anywhere. We all sat
around the campfire to do skits or stories or folklore or stars and finally,

right before we went to bed, sing. I think this was partly to make the little ones sleepy, the way lullabies do, but it didn't me. The songs were songs the Girl Scouts had sung forever. Some, like the ones by Joan Baez and Bob Dylan and other folksingers, were fine by me and my would-be sophisticate cabin mates, but others we considered extremely stupid. Some of the good songs were "Dona," "Blowing' in the Wind," "Michael, Row the Boat Ashore," and "Kumbaya." Dumb songs were "The Girl Scout Round," "The Smile Song," and "Today."

"Today" we considered the sappiest. It was so sappy that our cabin began to cut it up. We started singing it very loudly, then extremely overdramatically. We pretended to cry and wail. We put our arms around each other and swayed back and forth like we were being saved against a revival.

After campfire we all filed back to our units and got ready for bed. At lights-out you were supposed to go to sleep, but my friends and I considered it a point of honor to stay up at least a little late to gossip and giggle or whisper dirty jokes to one another. After my cabin mates got to sleep, I snuck out of bed and went out onto the porch. I liked how cool and quiet it was. I sat on the porch and looked out at the night and thought about things, or I turned on my pocket flashlight and read a book.

One night, a few days into the session, I was sitting on the porch and saw a flashlight on the path in the woods coming back to the unit. I thought if I went back inside the cabin whoever it was would hear me, so I decided to just stay there and hope they didn't see me in the dark. I was up way after I should have been in bed.

The flashlight bobbed closer, and I could hear this person walking. When she reached the clearing of the unit she turned off her flashlight and I saw it was Scuff. Scuff was the swimming counselor. She wasn't like the one the summer before who yelled at you when you couldn't do something, then told you afterward it was to "make you work." She was nice. When kids were scared she talked to them, not down to them or in baby talk the way some of the gushy, cheerleader-type counselors did. She talked to them quietly, she listened. And though her hair was as short as theirs, she wasn't terse like Davy and Lou. She hung around by herself a lot or with everybody equally. Sometimes she made jokes that no one else got, and she'd just shrug and smile to herself. I could tell she was smart.

When Scuff got out of the trees she turned off her flashlight and looked up at the sky. There was a terrific moon. When she started walking again, I saw her see me.

"Hey," she called out to me quietly.

"Hey," I called back. She walked over to the porch and said, "Mind if I pull up a chair?"

I said, "Go ahead," and she sat down next to me.

She told me she was coming back from the pool. She'd gone swimming. You weren't supposed to swim alone, but she didn't say there'd been anyone else. You also weren't supposed to swim at night. She didn't ask me what I was doing up after lights-out or tell me to get to bed. She said, "So, what are you up to?" and I said, "Nothing." I was sitting there with my book. She asked me what I was reading. I don't remember what it was, but I had just started reading my brother's science fiction books, Ray Bradbury and Ursula Le Guin and James Tiptree, Jr. She asked what kinds of books I liked, and I told her. She didn't talk to me like a counselor to a camper or an adult to a kid, but like one person to another. We talked for a long time. I remember her profile, a line of her face that caught the light of the moon. I remember the movement of her mouth and hands.

After a while we stopped talking. It was cool and quiet, and we listened to the night. It sounded close and very far away.

Then after a while she said it was getting late and she'd better get some sleep. She stood up to leave, and I said I'd better get some too. I didn't watch her leave. I stepped back into the cabin where my friends were sleeping. These girls had been my friends for years, good friends I'd done a million things with, study hall and book reports, first cigarettes and beer. We'd covered for each other to our parents. But this time, for the first time, I felt apart from them. I felt different from them suddenly. I felt I had a secret, though I did not know what it was.

I crawled into bed. I lay on my back and looked up at the ceiling I couldn't see. I looked at the window and out at the dark. I didn't sleep.

The next day I didn't know how to act. I didn't know if I should pretend I didn't know Scuff had been swimming and that she knew I'd been up after lights-out. I kept thinking of what she'd said to me, of everything. I said her name to myself, over and over in my head. I felt like everyone could read my mind and knew that I was thinking of her. Part of me wanted to tell everyone, but also I didn't want to tell, I wanted them just to know without my telling, as if I wouldn't tell because I was so cool about it. But I also wanted no one to know. I was afraid I'd get in trouble about being up after lights-out, but there were other reasons too. I felt excited and confused. I was afraid.

I tried to tell myself it wasn't a big deal. Maybe she was just being nice, which was her job after all. Maybe she would talk to anyone she ran into, not just me. Maybe she thought nothing of talking to me.

I was eager and nervous to see her at swim. The assistant swimming counselor was getting us into our lesson groups, and everyone was running around. Scuff was at the deep end, but she walked down to us and stopped me and said, "Hey, nice talk last night."

"Yeah." I shrugged like it was no big deal. But I was thrilled.

I tried to swim my best that day, but I swam terribly.

The rest of the day dragged by. I wanted it to be night, after lights-out.

At campfire that night I couldn't keep myself from looking to see if Scuff was going to be there or not. I tried to be subtle, but after a while my friend I was sitting next to whispered, "What are you looking for?" I shook my head as if to say nothing.

The last song of the night was "Today," and my friends and I cut up again. We put our arms around each other's shoulders and swayed together that sappy way. Some of the other girls laughed, but a couple of fussy counselors shook their heads. I was feeling superior with my friends when I saw Scuff at the edge of the campfire. Suddenly I felt stupid, like my friends and I were so juvenile. I wanted to quit, but I couldn't stop swaying between them. I hoped Scuff wouldn't see me, but she did. She must have thought we were funny too. She was looking at us and smiling.

That night after lights-out and after my cabin mates were asleep, I got my book and my pocket flashlight and went out onto the porch and tried to read. I looked at the words and turned the pages but didn't take in much.

It wasn't that late when I saw her light, but it seemed like I had waited my whole life. I saw the white beam bobbing on the trees. I watched until she got to the clearing, then I looked down at my book. I kept my pocket flashlight on my book and listened to her walk, but I didn't look up. I only looked up when she said, "Hey." She was standing a few feet in front of me.

"Hey," I said back. "You wanna pull up a chair?" She laughed and said sure. She sat down next to me on the bench, and we turned out our lights and talked.

She said we'd been funny when we were cutting up about "Today." I felt relieved she didn't think we were being stupid. Then she asked me about the music I liked, and I told her. This was when sixties music was about to turn into seventies music. My brother was in a band at college and my sister was a hippie, and I had listened to their records for years. I told her who I liked and we talked about music.

We were quiet for a while, then she asked me, out of nowhere, if I could be anyone in history who would I be. I was recovering from a recent bout of Christian fundamentalism and said, halfheartedly, "C. S. Lewis?" When she asked me why, I shrugged. "I wouldn't really want to be him, I just can't think of anyone." She said she'd read him years ago but didn't anymore.

"I know who I'd like to be." She paused, then said, "Gertrude Stein."

She asked me if I'd heard of her, and I said I hadn't. She told me she was a writer, the one who had said "A rose is a rose is a rose" and that she'd had all these amazing writer and painter friends and a salon where all of them came. She never married but lived this incredible life with her roommate, another woman, in Paris. She told me to make sure to remember her name.

After this we met on the porch every night and talked about all kinds of things, about books and politics and ideas. I felt she saw me as I was, a smart-enough kid who could get along all right, but also a different-enough kid who would, if not immediately then sometime in the future, be grateful for what she gave me.

She didn't tell me everything. She didn't tell too much. She didn't want to frighten me, just to tell enough to let me know that there were other, different, still mysterious, ways that I could live.

She told me that after the summer was over she was moving up north to live in a self-supporting community of women.

The last night of camp was the big all-camp campfire. Everyone showed up for the campfire, including the special staff and kitchen folks, even Davy and Lou. They gave out the patches to whoever had completed their junior-lifesaving course or basic or advanced sailing or canoeing. Davy and Lou gave ribbons to the winners of the gymkhana. All the units got to present a skit or song, and some of the counselors did too. The campfire went on very late, and because of that, but more because it was the last, and they, like all of us, were watching dying embers and falling stars and singing quiet songs, a lot of the little girls—some of the same ones who had wept miserably the first few, very homesick, days of the session—tonight, because they didn't want the two weeks to end, cried. They clutched one another's hands and sobbed on one another's shirts. My friends and I did not, of course. We were above all that. When the sad songs started, we snickered and sang off-key. At "Today" we draped our arms around one another and wailed. By then, some of the other girls in our unit had begun to ham along with my cabin mates and me.

When we started on the second verse of the song Scuff left where she was standing with the waterfront staff and walked over to us. She reached her left hand out to me. When I took it she pulled me up, and as everyone started singing the third verse, while she held my left hand in her own, she put my right hand on her shoulder and began to waltz. I knew some of this from gym, where every year since fifth grade we had one day a week of square dance. I knew one person was supposed to lead—it was supposed to be the guy—and one person followed, who was supposed to be the woman. Scuff pulled me beside her carefully until I got her rhythm, then she dipped me, then hoisted me over her. When she lowered me we galloped like horses until she pressed the side of her face to mine, I could feel her body beside me, and thrust our arms in front of us for a tango. She slid her sneakers along the ground like it was a polished ballroom floor. Outside the circle of her warm, milky breath and my uneven gasps, I heard the whole camp sing and laugh and my cabin mates whoop and clap. We did a square-dance do-si-do, then linked our elbows and spun. She took my hands in both of hers and twirled me around. I got dizzy. When I started to fall she caught me and held me up. I laughed and panted and caught my breath. I was glad the song was coming to an end. She held my shoulders to steady me. When the song was over everyone clapped and shouted En-core! I knew I couldn't dance anymore and hoped she could read my eyes, my tentative body. She shook my hand and bowed the way you do at the end of a dance. My head still spun, so I only nodded a little. She kept her stable arm around me as she walked me back to my friends. She sat me down, and before she left she squeezed the tops of my shoulders with her hands.

I didn't wait out on the porch that night.

The next morning after breakfast we packed our gear, the stuff we had brought and the stuff we had made and collected at summer camp, and waited for our parents or whoever to come pick us up. There weren't lessons that day, so I couldn't count on seeing Scuff at the pool. I packed quickly, then wandered around the unit to look for her, but she found me first. I heard someone behind me say, "Wild party last night." I turned and it was her.

"Yeah." I laughed but then didn't know what to say. I stuck out a piece of paper and said, "Can I have your address?"

"Sure," she said. I was glad she didn't hesitate. "You got a pencil?" I pulled one from my pocket and handed it to her. She tore the paper and handed half to me. "Give me yours too," she said. She wrote her address while I waited. When she handed me the pencil, I wrote my name and address, and we gave each other our scraps of paper.

She'd written her real name, not her camp name. It was Nancy Booth. I couldn't bring myself to call her that out loud, but I hoped someday I might.

She tapped the address and said, "That's my parents', but it'll be good for a while and they should forward stuff after I move."

I tapped mine and said, "That's my parents' too, well, my mom's, but I'll probably be living there a while." I said it like a joke because we both knew I was just starting high school and would be living at my mom's for years. It was a stupid joke, but she laughed.

I wrote her long, confused, and very earnest letters. She wrote back. Her letters were smart and funny and generous and also, I realized later, very careful to not lead me on. Of course she knew I had a crush on her, a colossal one, but she did not make fun of or take advantage of that. She could have.

In her letters she talked about ideas and books and, after her address changed, about the community of women she lived with in Chicago. They were writers and artists and musicians who grew a lot of their own food and did their own plumbing and house repairs and mostly supported themselves as a printing collective. Some of the things she said about them reminded me of the friends of Gertrude Stein.

That fall when I went back to school, to high school for the first time, I tried to check out a book of Gertrude Stein's at the library, but there weren't any. I went to the downtown public library and found some there. I kept going back there for more about Stein and then for other books I learned about from her.

We wrote for years, through several changes of address for her, through my entire time in high school. Sometimes I wouldn't hear from her for ages, then I'd get a long letter about a trip she'd taken to Berkeley, Colorado, or New Mexico. Sometimes she'd say she was moving and would send me her new address when she had it.

I don't know which was the last letter I got from her because I had no idea it would be, but after a while her letters stopped. I tried more than once to get in touch with her via her parents' address. Though these letters were never returned to me, neither were they answered.

Sometimes, still, I think of her. I think of her kindness, her example, what she gave to me. Sometimes I wish I could get in touch. I wish I could know what had happened to her. I want to know her life is good. I want to let her know that I survived. I want to tell her that a tomboy she met years ago, a girl, like any girl, with her own set of pains and fears and mysteries, was helped by her. I want to tell her I survived and I am grateful.

Nancy Booth, wherever you are, thank you.

The Change of Life

Ralph Sassone

Many days that summer, my mother entered my bedroom without knocking. She would plant herself on my blue shag carpet and say, "Quit reading a sec. Look at me." But I would linger over my Hesse and Carson McCullers and movie reviews, afraid that one day I'd glance up from my student desk and hardly recognize her anymore. She was still quite pretty—big dark eyes, high cheekbones, an Italian's shiny black hair—but a Nixon-esque sweat pebbled her upper lip and forehead. She had not been herself for months.

My workaholic father referred to my mother's "change of life" furtively, murmuring this phrase the way he did the fearsome word *cancer*, as though he could mute it into nothingness. Although her condition had all but driven him out of the house, I didn't have his options. All day long I loitered in our big colonial with my mother and my books, withdrawing into them the way a small child retreats into riddling fables, terrified of what would come next but rapt by the dark journey.

"Do me a favor. Cross your legs," my mother said to me one afternoon in late June. When I braided my ankles primly, she frowned. "No, not that way—at the *knee*."

I swallowed and looked away. Lately, if it wasn't our knees she wanted to compare, it was the whites around our eyes ("Open wider! Like you've seen a ghost!") or our propensity for shakes ("Squeeze your thumb and forefinger together—hard!") or how winded we would get after a few deep breaths, how much we could curl in our toes, how much we could crush a pink rubber Spalding with our bare hands and for how long.

Although she at first said, "Do me a favor—don't tell anybody about this," by now this went without saying. Everyone else had escaped the house and I was too unpopular for confidants. Our loyalty was absolute by default.

"Go ahead," my mother said now. "Do it."

I crossed my legs, noticing how they sprouted the first forestubble of hair. I even let my top leg swing flirtatiously.

"Hold it there—don't move," my mother said. She jabbed me under the knee with a light karate chop, and my leg shot up reflexively. Her strong jaw clenched, and she sat beside me on the bed, crossing her own legs. Then she sighed. "I think there's something wrong here."

"Why?"

"*My* leg barely moves when I do that. My reflexes—they're shot! You do it to me."

I crouched near my mother's knee. It was dimpled and white from lack of sun exposure. I started to karate-chop it lightly. Tentatively. Yet nothing happened. I couldn't locate the border between the nerve endings and the little hood of fat covering her kneecap. Nothing there but anxious dormancy. My mother flushed crimson and twitched. I jabbed harder and harder until her leg swung once, just a little. I jabbed again and got the same torpid response.

"You see? Nothing's wrong, Mom." I sat beside her again and re-crossed my legs. I jabbed myself well under the knee, aiming for my inert zone intentionally, mimicking her leg's weak response and hoping she'd be fooled. "You see?"

She nodded absently and darted her eyes around my room: at the movie reviews fanned on my bed, at the Laura Nyro album on my record stack, at the old black Flower Power decal on my closet door. Worry tightened her mouth. Perhaps she knew the truth and perhaps not; perhaps she didn't want to know the truth. As she headed out of my room she left the door half-open behind her.

"You see?" I croaked into the hallway after her. My voice quavered and cracked when I raised it. "You see?" I called. "Everything's fine."

As a reward for putting up with her, my mother sometimes drove me to the town library in the afternoons. She figured I loved the library, since I always had my head in a book. It was housed in a squat, U-shaped brick building on the edge of town—its interior two wide beige rooms with gray indoor/outdoor carpeting and a hush as palpable as the anxiety that spoored through our house like dust. In the library I would hunt for inappropriate books like *Slaughterhouse Five* and *Helter Skelter* while my mother fidgeted in the corner "magazine nook," snapping the pages of *Better Homes & Gardens* until a fresh panic surge made her announce we had to leave.

"Can't we stay just two more minutes? Please?" I'd always say, in a voice made sleepy by the library's submarine languor. I'd been lulled by the moist crackle of book jackets, the light slap of the mules against the librarians' heels, the powdery light sifting through the stacks: All of it helped me forget, momentarily, the dread that my life was hurtling toward disaster in several weeks, when I would enter the junior high that resembled a minimum-security prison.

"No, listen—listen to me!" my mother would whisper fiercely, shifting her eyes to see if anyone noticed. "Please don't get me aggravated. We have to leave *now*."

I kept forgetting that my mother couldn't stay in public places for long that summer. In department stores she'd clutch my skinny forearm like a child terrified of getting separated from a parent ("Stick by me! Please!"). She avoided sandwich shops and movie theaters and beauty salons because, she said, they made her claustrophobic, she couldn't breathe there, she felt like something was starting to close in on her and suck her breath and she had to get out immediately. At the supermarket she had me wait on the checkout line for her, among housewives, until I gave her my signal and she lurched forward from the exit doors at the last minute, shoving bills into the cashier's palm.

We confused the housewives who surrounded us on those lines. They regarded us appraisingly—much the way their sons scowled and smirked at me in gym class, when I couldn't pass a football or sink a basket or throw a baseball more than ten yards. *Pussy*, those boys would mutter when I failed, with the stunning contemptuousness of someone spitting in my face. I'd fade toward the edges of the playing fields and pretend I didn't hear them. The memory stabbed me as I stood among their mothers, staring at the food-conveyor belt and wishing I could disappear.

I stuck out everywhere in my life now. I stuck out even in the library, where I knew I was welcome but strange: a thirteen-year-old boy among women and small children. The only mature male was a new employee who had recently emerged among the matrons in their floral skirts and wrap dresses, flustering them like a masher who'd wandered into a ladies' room and refused to get out.

This new employee's name was Mr. Isherwood. Aside from his incongruous maleness, he looked young enough to be one of the female librarians' obstreperous sons. He had a shag haircut. Maybe he was twenty-one, maybe twenty-five or twenty-seven. A callow restiveness quaked under his brown suits, and his sharp gestures pricked the haze of sedation his coworkers had conjured so carefully around themselves like pockets of perfume. Mr. Isherwood walked in a herky-jerky way, pivoting fast on the heels of his Frye boots like a cadet alert to attack, and he often cocked his head acutely like a listening dog, twisting his face into scowls and grimaces. When he spoke, which was rarely, he jabbed the air with gesticulations and he refused to make eye contact.

I could tell Mr. Isherwood didn't want to be bothered or noticed, but this was impossible. You couldn't take your eyes off him. He was very tall and skinny, with a shock of black hair and anemically pale skin, and when he barreled into a room the temperature dropped a few degrees from his cold glances. He kept himself mostly in the office behind the charge-out counter, typing index cards on an old Royal and speaking into a rotary phone as he smoked. The first time I spied him back there, his long fingers were pinching a Parliament and a white ascot of smoke unfurled around his head.

I decided he was handsome, or at least dashing. He was arguing with someone on the phone, and a few fragments of his conversation splintered out of the office: "idiotic," "ludicrous," "pretentious twaddle," "cretins." I backed away from his voice as if from buckshot.

We met a few weeks later, in July, when the library was short-staffed and he got summoned to the charge-out desk ("Russell? Could you assist us for a moment, please?"), where I was second on line. Mr. Isherwood stomped from his little office with an audible huff, rolling his eyes like an adolescent ordered to set the table.

"Yes? What?" he asked the head librarian.

"These nice people need to have their books checked, please."

He grunted. A woman in a tennis dress in front of me stepped forward and handed him Jacqueline Susann's *Delores*. He glanced at its cover and smirked. "Oh. Great. Summer camp," he said.

"Excuse me?" she said.

"Nothing. Nothing. Lost on you." He slid the book back at her with one long finger, as if it were contaminated, and said, "Next!"

The head librarian spoke up, drawing the tennis-dress woman to her section of the desk. "Did you enjoy *Jonathan Livingston Seagull*, Joyce?" she asked the woman.

"Oh, *yes*." The woman fingered her terrycloth wristband, grasping for the right words. "It was so . . . so *realistic*."

"Of course it seemed realistic," Mr. Ishwerwood said. "That book could've been written by a bird." He took my copy of *The Ballad of the Sad Café*, grinning at me, and then he twice patted my book lightly, his palm hovering over it as though he'd become distracted or he was about to bless it. I blushed and studied the grain of the counter between us.

"So, may I go now, or what?" I heard him say.

"Yes." The head librarian sighed deeply. "Thank you, Russell."

"Did you get a load of that strange little man?" my mother asked me in our Oldsmobile on the way home.

"What little man?" I said. "He was tall."

"You know what I mean," my mother said, shooting me a don't-be-dim look.

"I guess he's a librarian," I said.

"A librarian." My mother laughed inexplicably, then scrabbled with her free hand for something in her pocketbook, where her Valium prescriptions rattled. She swabbed her forehead with a tattered pink tissue. "A librarian. Imagine that." As an afterthought she said, "Keep your distance," and then turned on the radio to cushion the space left by her command. She reminded herself aloud that we needed to buy furniture polish for our cleaning woman.

From that point on, whenever she announced a trip to the library, fear tore the lining of my excitement. I worried I might somehow betray to Mr. Isherwood that I'd been contemplating him between visits—remembering him, the details of him, with a raw and absurd nostalgia, as if we had a real history together. Mr. Isherwood's bony wrists, Mr. Isherwood's big Adam's apple, the way Mr. Isherwood raked his hand through his hair in exasperation and released a scent of English Leather and cigarette smoke. My thoughts about him had a muggy thickness that made my breaths go short. I remembered the exact way Mr. Isherwood pronounced the word *cretin* (which I looked up) and how he glowered at unruly children till they stopped dead in their tracks and ran to their mothers' skirts.

I had never encountered power quite like that before. Not the power to be loved but the power to be unloved, to be despised even, and not to care. I tried to imagine what it would be like to shrug insouciantly at my classmates when they faulted my athleticism or to laugh when they mocked me for volunteering to answer a teacher's question (Ooh, he's so smart!). Maybe the power to be unloved came from ascending a ladder of intellect where everything else looked unimportant: gym class, my mother's demands, and the renegade attractions that sometimes disrupted my reading or made me wake in the middle of the night, sweating and jabbing the mattress.

But I couldn't imagine it. Instead I took to imitating Mr. Isherwood in my bedroom, saying *cretin* and *ludicrous* and glowering at the mirror, pretending I was looking at someone other than myself. I quoted an argument he'd had with the bossy children's librarian, after he'd lambasted one preschooler for yelling and another child for nearly walking absently out of the library with an uncharged book. ("When a child is undisciplined it's a matter for their parents," he'd said. "When he steals it's a matter for the police.")

My mother's initial impression of Mr. Isherwood hadn't improved. A few weeks earlier he had helped her charge out one of the self-help volumes she'd vainly taken to reading and he'd given her "the creeps."

"You should've seen the way he looked at me when I handed him this," she said, holding up *How to Be Your Own Best Friend.* "Like I was taking out a dirty book."

"He probably didn't mean it that way."

"Don't tell me what he meant. You don't know what the hell you're talking about."

I didn't let on that one day, while she was flipping through magazines, Mr. Isherwood had accosted me in the stacks. I was searching for a biography of Paul Newman, whom I'd recently seen in *The Long Hot Summer,* shirtless and exquisite as he held a white pillow against his sweaty chest. I wanted to research Paul Newman's improbable beauty the way other people studied UFO's. I was on my knees scanning a bottom shelf when Mr. Isherwood showed up and said, "What are you looking for?"

His reedy voice startled me; I rose to my feet so quickly all the blood rushed from my head. For a second I thought I might black out.

"Nothing," I said. "I'm not looking for anything. Thank you."

"Well, you could've fooled me," he said. "You're looking for nothing rather *intensely,* I'd say."

"Oh. I mean, not anything specific."

"Wouldn't you like to be?" His head shook a bit as he spoke, then he steadied his gaze on me. "Undoubtedly that would be preferable to scrabbling around on the floor like an infant." He pursed his lips. "Tell me your interests."

"Oh—I'm probably in the wrong place," I said. "I like novels. Sorry to bother you." I began to walk away.

He said, "Which novels?"

I turned around. I didn't know the correct answer. When I said I'd recently been reading *Siddhartha* and *Beneath the Wheel,* one side of his upper lip curled in a thwarted snarl.

"Right. Hesse," he said. "I suppose that's a start. But Hesse is . . . shall we say, second-rate. If you like Teutonic brooders I have just the thing for you. Stay." He raised his hand like a stop sign. "Stay right there." He scurried away and returned, handing me a copy of *The Magic Mountain.*

"It's purple prose, but it's *good* purple prose," he said. "*N'est-ce pas?*"

"Thank you," I said, though I didn't know what "purple prose" meant. Or *"n'est-ce pas"* for that matter. "Thank you," I said again.

"Mann is challenging for someone your age, but you seem atypical." He tilted his head upward. "You're a big reader, aren't you?"

"Yeah—Yes," I said. "I guess."

"I can always spot one." He relaxed into a semislouch and scanned me head to toe. Then his eyes darted and he seemed to be speaking to the shelf above my head. "I was exactly like that."

"Like what?"

"Like *you*. Before this job ruined it."

"Ruined—?"

"Please," he said. "You don't want me to go into it. Trust me—you don't." But when I fell silent he kept talking. He said the banality and bad taste of the library had all but turned him into "a pod person" and "a drooling imbecile." He was so exhausted by the provincialism of the town (where, he said, the chief cultural activity seemed to be clothes shopping) that he could barely summon the energy to watch television at the end of the day, much less read. He was actually a scholar, if I could believe it. He had gone to Cornell on a full scholarship and he was merely biding his time until he could save enough to enter graduate school. The only reason he found himself stuck in the library was that his uncle, a big-shot county administrator, had pulled strings and gotten him the job. His library *superiors* couldn't fire him without "petty political fallout" from his uncle, but they loathed him.

"O lucky me. To have job security in a recession." He rolled his eyes. He said the library was just his penance for some unknown transgression. Some unidentified circle of hell. Some limbo. He would last six months at the outside.

"My God." He raked his hair. "Listen to me! Maundering on like a lunatic. As if this is of the slightest interest to anyone."

"No. It's interesting," I said. And it was—it was fascinating—though I didn't comprehend half of what he said, like someone listening to a lush travel log of a place he's never been.

"Good of you to say that, but a lie. It's tiresome." He extended his long hand. "I didn't catch your name."

I told him my name.

"Alors." He squeezed my hand surprisingly hard and smiled broadly for the first time. The smile transformed his face. He had a large mouth, with even, white teeth, and before his smile faded and he looked haggard again a fugitive handsomeness flashed like some vivid life he hadn't had, or perhaps never would have, or perhaps would sustain only in flashes, and this filled me with a mysterious sadness. I started chattering to bridge over the feeling, saying things I thought he would like to hear: that I read e. e. cummings; that I rarely watched television; that I enjoyed subtitled foreign films and modern art.

He said "yes" and "umph" at regular intervals, until I wore myself out and the silent me returned. I stared dumbly at my new book.

"Thank you," I said again. "I appreciate this."

"What?" Mr. Isherwood said.

"Your help."

"My help." He laughed a laugh that was just a breath before walking away. "I assure you what you call *'my help'* is, exactly, nothing."

For the next month, Mr. Isherwood and I circled each other like wily house pets. I would arrive at the library and walk past the checkout desk until I noticed him noticing me from the back office, and then I'd let him find me in the stacks. He'd always start our conversations by saying, "Tell me what you're looking for," and then he'd notch up my tastes. He led me to Flannery O'Connor instead of Carson McCullers, claiming McCullers was "interesting but soggy." He told me to jettison Rex Reed's movie reviews and start reading someone named Pauline Kael. He nodded absently when I praised Kurt Vonnegut, whom I didn't really understand, and handed me a book called *The Loved One* by Evelyn Waugh—"Evelyn with a hard *E*"—who turned out to be a man instead of a woman. I forgot about finding the Paul Newman bio and instead concentrated on Mr. Isherwood's suggestions, which seemed like radio signals from an island with a native language only he knew how to decode.

Our conversations went uninterrupted because his coworkers avoided him, and also because I was spending more time alone in the library now. My mother had recently taken to dropping me off there and picking me up when she was done shopping by herself. In the past few weeks she'd been able to do that. She had gotten better, tentatively. A library book called *Peace from Nervous Suffering* had miraculously helped her through her change-of-life days. She was calmer now, coming into my room for medical checks infrequently. Between these episodes she read and reread *Peace from Nervous Suffering* the way fundamentalists study the Bible.

Her change astonished me, but I didn't dare remark on it. I was afraid the slightest self-consciousness might cause her to regress. Instead I crouched quietly on the stair landing and watched her reading at the kitchen table one level below. Her face slackened as she read, and like heat waves her relief radiated up toward me until I was loosed from my own tensions: my horror of junior high, my fear of other boys, my dread of my percolating hormones, and my dread of Mr. Isherwood, who compelled and frightened me like a brilliantly colored bird that had gotten trapped inside the house, careening against the false sky of ceiling and desperate to get out.

All that tension disappeared briefly. For a moment it was just me and my mother again, my mother and her child, and we were safe in an aloneness where our oddities wouldn't matter.

But then suddenly it ended.

One August afternoon, a female librarian informed my mother that she could no longer renew *Peace from Nervous Suffering*. She had reached the maximum limit by renewing it three times already. After the next ten-day loan period, she'd have to hand it over indefinitely.

My mother took the news like a death in the family. She was numb for a day, then she slipped into a maelstrom of panic and pulled me in with her. "What am I going to do?" she said the next morning, having barged into my bedroom for the first time in weeks. "Tell me what I am going to do."

"Don't worry, Mom," I said. I got the Yellow Pages and flipped to "Bookstores," sure that I could help her. But the situation turned out to be worse than I'd imagined. One by one I called every bookstore in the county while my mother hovered near, and one by one they reported that *Peace from Nervous Suffering* wasn't in stock and wasn't available for ordering either. There was a new edition coming out, so it was between printings.

"What are we going to do?" my mother said. Now she was shaking.

"It'll be okay," I said. "It will."

I called every library in the county system and discovered they didn't shelve the book or that it was already taken out; they had waiting lists for the book, with first preference given to local residents. Then I called the publisher, who confirmed that the book was between printings and totally unavailable for the next two or three months.

"Did you tell them it was an emergency?" my mother said.

"Yes. Something like that."

"Something like that," she said. "Give me that goddamned number."

When she got the same response she retreated to her bedroom and slammed the door. The radio played a Bee Gees song. When I knocked she yelled that she needed to be alone, which was fine with me, but I knew it wouldn't last. Within four days she had totally relapsed. Her hands shook at the dinner table in anticipation of losing the book. She reappeared in my bedroom to check the striations in our fingernails and the lumpish bones at the base of our necks. She ordered me to accompany her to Bloomingdale's. (Stick by me! Please!) I imagined that I would soon be on the supermarket line again between housewives, mothers of the football players and class clowns, and that my mother would boycott the library in protest—out of rage or spite or whatever emotion had yet to emerge—and refuse to let me go by myself.

We were desperate. So it did not surprise me that my mother proposed we steal the book from the library, and it did not surprise me that I quickly agreed.

She laid out our plan over dinner. She would return the book to the library, and once it was back on the shelves we would take it. Or, rather, I would take it and she would wait for me in the parking lot. She reasoned that if she wasn't present the day the book vanished, no one would make the connection. I would slip the book into my maroon nylon windbreaker and nobody would notice. Nobody would suspect a kid of taking out a book on nervous suffering, right? Nothing could go wrong.

We rehearsed every afternoon like actors in a community-theater production. We didn't go to the library in the meantime, and I missed it even though only five days had passed. I wore my cinch-waisted, maroon nylon windbreaker in my bedroom, and my mother planted *Peace from*

Nervous Suffering on the top shelf of my bookcase. It had an electric blue cover with black lettering. She watched from a corner as I circled my bed with mock nonchalance, sidling closer and closer to the bookcase until I snatched the book and made a run for it like a spy. She gave me directorial notes.

Slow down, she said. Tone it down. Unzip the windbreaker halfway, as casually as possible, and yawn or something to distract possible on-lookers. And don't stand directly under the book, but to the side of it. And pick up a few books beforehand, so *Peace from Nervous Suffering* could slip into the windbreaker while I pretended to examine one of the other books. And hold the stolen book under my arm, at my side, and the two decoy books against my torso to disguise it.

We kept going till I got it right. Gradually, with repetition, I went numb. I told myself that what we were doing was really nothing so out of the ordinary. The cool, popular boys often shoplifted and bragged about it in school, brandishing hocked magazines and blowing bubbles with stolen chewing gum. This might make me a little more like them: a normal outlaw. My mother and I didn't mention the possibility that I could be caught, and I didn't mention the potentially complicating pres-ence of Mr. Isherwood. Now was not the time to tell her I hadn't kept my distance.

The heist took place on a Friday in mid-August. It was ninety-one degrees, which made my windbreaker look ridiculous, and small children capered about everywhere because it was the library's weekly Story Hour. Their mothers plodded around in espadrilles, trying to shepherd their offspring before the children's librarian plopped down to read aloud.

I avoided the checkout counter when I entered, so Mr. Isherwood wouldn't see me, and I told myself all the potential witnesses around me were an advantage: It was unlikely Mr. Isherwood would come out dur-ing the hubbub of Story Hour. "Illiterate havoc," I almost heard him calling it. "An invasion of midget hoodlums."

It was agreed my mother would meet me in the parking lot exactly one hour after dropping me off; anything less than an hour might look suspicious. So I had time to kill. I paced the stacks away from Mr. Isherwood's office, sat down at a carrel, paced and sat again. I was

sweating in my windbreaker, but I didn't remove it for fear of drawing attention. Besides, removing it hadn't been part of our rehearsals
and I wanted to do everything as planned. When I finally cruised by
the shelf containing *Peace from Nervous Suffering*, the book seemed
thicker than the one my mother and I had practiced with, but I knew
it couldn't be.

I loitered in a daze for forty-five minutes, removing books from shelves
and pretending to read the first few pages. I held on to a few titles I
thought Mr. Isherwood would appreciate: *Madame Bovary* and *Goodbye,
Columbus.* Fingers of sweat trickled down my torso, and I grew a bit
woozy. I skimmed spines from every section except Sports and Children's, checking my wristwatch as intensely as someone measuring blood
pressure. Time had become more elastic and jerky—slower and faster
and then slower again. I was surprised how many or few minutes had
passed each time I checked. Fifteen. A minute and a half. Six. Near me
the children had settled down for a recitation of *Amelia Bedelia.*

With thirteen minutes left I wandered toward the self-help stacks that
bordered the children's section. I unzipped my windbreaker as practiced.
I looked both ways and saw no one. I quickly grabbed *Peace from
Nervous Suffering* and slipped it under the maroon nylon, hiding it beneath the Flaubert and the Roth. I zipped up again with my free hand
and checked my Timex. I had done it efficiently, but I didn't let myself
feel relief. Not yet. I still had eleven minutes to go, and I wasn't sure
how to occupy myself for the duration.

The children's librarian had gotten to the part where Amelia the maid
misunderstands her employer's command "Please draw the draperies"
and sketches a picture of the living room curtains instead. With nothing
to do, I moved toward the sound of her voice until I found myself in
the children's section. The children were sitting Indian-style on the floor
in a circular formation, listening and sending up explosions of laughter.
I loomed there behind them like a ghost, smiling wanly, until the librarian glanced up from the book and noticed me. She squinted for a
moment, then frowned; and then, catching herself, she remembered to
focus on the children and keep beaming at them. But her voice had
gotten lower and she gripped her book more rigidly. I could see my
presence had unnerved her—she was trying to ignore me and not ask

why I was hovering there—and I felt myself flush, as if I'd been caught fiddling with Play-Doh or stuffed animals.

When I turned to leave, Mr. Isherwood was standing right behind me, inches from my face. I nearly fainted from the shock.

"Oh. Hi. What are you doing here?" I whispered.

"I could ask you the same thing," he whispered back. "Unless you've decided to trade Dickens for Dr. Seuss."

"Oh—oh. No."

The children's librarian glowered at us warningly; we were distracting her charges. With a sweep of his arm, Mr. Isherwood motioned me away to another section, toward a big picture window facing the parking lot. I trailed him carefully and slowly, clutching the decoy books to my torso and clutching my mother's book against my waist, where it had settled while I was listening to *Amelia Bedelia*.

"So, what are your interests today?" Mr. Isherwood said.

"Nothing." I bit my lower lip. "Nothing really."

"Then what's that you've got there?" He glanced at the books I was carrying and I reflexively pivoted a few inches away.

"Oh, these? These are—I just picked them up here." I clutched the books tight to me.

"Clearly," he said.

"I was going to put them back right now. I'll be right back."

He raised his hand in the stop-sign gesture and said, "Wait. They might be worth holding on to. Let me see."

"No." I clutched them tighter. "I don't think so."

I turned my back on him for a second. I took a few steps forward before I felt his hand on my shoulder and I froze. For several weeks I had imagined how his hand would feel there, but it wasn't like this— cold and sweaty and capable of hurt, like any adult's hand—and yet it was, I now realized. It always was. I pivoted to face him again.

He was standing backlit before the big picture window, with an expression I'd never seen on him before. Perplexed or sad or something else. Behind him my mother's car glinted in the parking lot and I saw her, through the windshield, gripping the steering wheel with both hands as she waited for me. I wondered what she was thinking, but I couldn't tell. Maybe she would leave without me if I went way over the time limit. Or maybe she would look inside and discover me talking with Mr. Isherwood and understand I hadn't told her everything there was to know.

Mr. Isherwood was still standing there waiting for me to do something. So I stuck out my arms and gave him the two decoy books he had asked for. He examined them a moment, grinning before he spoke.

"Great—Flaubert," he said. "I was going to recommend this to you eventually, but you've beaten me to it." He tilted his head toward the ceiling as if addressing an imaginary lecture hall while I looked down at my sneakers. "Of course *Madame Bovary* is the definitive assault on nineteenth-century bourgeois manners. Which are, of course, not a whit different from twentieth-century bourgeois manners." He cocked an eyebrow and swept his arm in an encompassing gesture. "The evidence is all around us, no? *Plus ça change.* Yet Flaubert was sympathetic even as he skewered the fools surrounding him. He himself was bourgeois— only not petit bourgeois, which is a key distinction. He famously said, '*Madame Bovary, c'est moi!*' But of course no petit bourgeois could grasp the folly of—"

He stopped midsentence. It took a second or two before his silence registered as anything more than a pause to find the right words. When I looked up from the carpet he was staring at my torso, where *Peace from Nervous Suffering* was now bulging clearly under the nylon. When I'd handed him the decoy books under duress, I'd forgotten to scissor my arm back against my body.

"What is that?" he said, staring at the bulge.

"Nothing." I moved my arm against myself and turned away reflexively.

"Don't be absurd," he said. "I'm not given to optical illusions." He leaned forward and narrowed his eyes. "Of course that's something."

"No," I said, "it's not."

I examined the carpet again. We stood there for what seemed a long time, waiting for the other to do something. When I dared look up I saw his mouth had opened slightly. I clenched both arms against myself, but it was too late. He kept staring at the windbreaker.

Around us the children had started to dash and make noise again, for Story Hour had ended. But we didn't do anything until the children's librarian waddled up to Mr. Isherwood and started speaking to him breathlessly.

"Oh, Russell! *Good!*" she said. "I was trying to figure out where you hid the *typewriter* ribbons earlier, but you were in the"—she glanced my way and whispered in his ear—"the *little boys' room* at the time, and I didn't want to interrupt you!" She chuckled to herself.

Mr. Isherwood didn't answer her. He kept staring at me as she spoke to him. In response to his silence, the children's librarian turned toward me and trained her full gaze on my presence. She nodded.

"Yes. Hello," she said to me. "Aren't you a bit *warm* in that?" She eyed the windbreaker and my rigid arm, and her face began to light with interest. I was sure that in another moment she too would notice the bulge.

"Heavens," she said, "you're sweating all over yourself. Take that jacket off!"

I fingered the zipper of the windbreaker. Slowly, I started to lower it. I supposed that since Mr. Isherwood had already seen the book, there was no use trying to conceal it anymore. What would happen would happen now. I would be apprehended and punished and humiliation would cloak whatever came next, smothering it, like a blanket thrown over a weak flame. The sensation felt something like relief.

"No—don't do that," Mr. Isherwood said. "I'm a bit chilly here myself."

The children's librarian looked at him quizzically. His eyes darted from me to her and back again, and then he stabbed his fingers toward the distant charge-out desk.

"I know exactly where those typewriter ribbons are hiding, Miriam," he said. "So come along then." He charged ahead, beckoning her briskly, and he didn't stop walking until they were both several paces away from me. Then he cocked his head back in my direction and said: "As for you, you stay right there. Right there. We're not finished. There's something important I have to tell you."

I watched them disappear into the back office. I wiped my free hand on the front of my pants. For a moment I was my usual obedient self, freezing as he'd instructed. But of course I didn't stay there. I walked though the library's glass exit doors and through a vestibule toward a second set of doors, and when I got outside my mother's car rode up immediately like a carriage in a children's story I'd never gotten around to reading.

"Well?" she said when I got into the car.

"Here." I unzipped my windbreaker and dropped the book on the front seat. It thudded between us, halfway off the seat, but I didn't set it right again. We idled for a moment. When I glanced past her toward the picture window, I thought I saw Mr. Isherwood standing there, the large outline of him, coming closer and possibly squinting at the sun. I imagined he was frowning at my absence now, or that his expression was wide-eyed—the same queer mixture of sadness and anger and passion I had seen before, like a transitional feeling on its way to becoming something new and as yet unidentified. But I couldn't tell what he looked like for the glare on the window.

Mr. Isherwood stepped closer. I was sure that in a moment he'd visor one of his hands over his eyes and find my mother and I sitting there, and he'd finish figuring it all out.

"Let's go," I said. "Let's go already."

"Okay." My mother shifted gears, and the car lurched forward out of the parking lot, racing toward the first traffic light. I willed myself not to look back.

"Thank you," my mother said to me. "Thank you a lot." But I didn't answer her.

"Would you like to get a Baskin-Robbins on the way home?"

"No."

"Then how about we go to a bookstore or toy store. Anything you want?"

"No." I looked out the window away from her. I looked and I watched as the town slid by us, one street giving way to another, one avenue leading to the next.

"What's wrong with you?" my mother said. "Did something happen in there?"

I kept looking out the window. I shrugged and said nothing. But I repeated the question to myself many times: What was wrong with me? What was wrong? Nothing had happened in the library—nothing terrible involving screaming or the police, and now that I'd escaped there could be no proof anything was stolen. But I knew that I couldn't go back there, and that I'd refuse when my mother offered to take me in a day or a week or a month. I knew that my return to the library would be circuitous and long, and that when I hazarded a return Mr. Isherwood would be long gone, and gladly forgotten by everyone except me.

When I did return I had already completed my first year of junior high, and my mother had recovered on her own. Or if she didn't recover completely, I didn't want to know about it anymore. I wasn't hanging around in my bedroom by the time the spell of the stolen book dissipated for her. If she tried to waylay me for body checkups, I now said, "I'm doing homework" or "Please leave me alone" or "Go away, that's not normal." I took to hiding in other rooms when she went looking for me, and then I ventured out of the house by myself, reading my books in the backyard or in the trees or in the woods behind our house like a wild child.

My mother would sometimes call my name across the backyard, her voice glancing off the swimming pool and swelling through the maples, but I didn't answer. I made a point of wandering back in time for dinner. And when she asked where I'd been I wouldn't specify, and if she said "What is *wrong* with you lately?" I would only stare back at her with a look that startled and frightened us both, because it momentarily sliced through any desire I still had for her approval, or anyone's approval, and we both would fall silent. We went on like this for years.

When I finally went back to the library I was alone. I was researching an eighth-grade social studies project on the Spanish-American War. The female librarians nodded at me with a hazy sense of recognition, and I found the books I needed efficiently without their help. Within fifteen minutes I was done and ready to ride my bicycle home, hoping I wouldn't encounter anyone from school on the way back. But I didn't leave the library just then. I lingered a bit. I wandered through the stacks scanning the titles and not touching any of them, turning the corners warily as if I might run into Mr. Isherwood again, and wondering if he could tell I was thinking about him at that very moment, wherever he was. I wondered if perhaps he was thinking about me too, or if he ever thought about me, and what it was he thought.

I dreamed about him now and then. In these dreams we were older and met on a city street. Mr. Isherwood looked the same—jaggedly thin—but his hair had gray streaks, and he wore little wire-rim glasses and an English tweed suit. I was the one who spoke first because he didn't recognize me. But when I reminded him he remembered me immediately and he smiled his broad, fugitive smile. We told each other about our lives, glancingly summarizing the past twenty years, leaving out the boring parts and aggrandizing ourselves a bit. He said I should call him Russell now—he insisted—but I never felt comfortable doing that, and I never specified what he should call me.

The details of his life were always different. Once he'd become an architect, another time a curator of rare documents, another time a professor at a college I didn't know and another time a computer mogul.

He was always the one to walk away first. At the end of those dreams he walked away toward distant skyscrapers, toward the park or the subway or a school of speeding taxicabs. And there was always a wistfulness then, a hopeless, homesick feeling as his figure shrank away into nothingness. For years and years I stood there frustrated as he receded into the distance. I would awake still waiting to hear what he had to tell me.

Cool for You

Eileen Myles

For a long time we could wear any white shirt we wanted under our uniforms, but then they got over that. There were regulation shirts with Peter Pan collars. Not cool ones, though. These were utterly round, like girls in story books wore. Very ugly shirts. Nothing you could do about them. It was different in high school, but we're not there yet. I had twelve years of Catholic schools. In these uniforms I thought about breasts for the first time. And blood. And snot. Once I had an incredible sneeze that went flying all over my face. The nun, Sister Marisol, who taught math, thought I was laughing, so she ran over and slapped me across the face and then her hand was covered with snot. I went running out of the room, which was roaring. The boy I had a crush on that year, Chuckie Breslin, went up and took his handkerchief out of his pocket and stooped (because he was tall) and closed the door delicately. It was a riot, my friends said. I'm sure the doorknob was covered with snot. I mean, I was in a uniform when this happened. Something about the contrast between the uniformity of our look and all the feelings and body fluids flying around. I don't think they ever slugged you in public school. It was a known fact. We called the toilet the basement. I remember crying in there a lot. I never thought of myself as lonely when I was a kid, but I really was. I was always going to the bathroom because it was the only place you could be alone. It was so ugly. Big ochre-colored tiles. I mean dark, aged. The ceiling was dirty old cement. I had friends, and we would sneak in here during lunch and wet wads of toilet paper and fling them really hard against the ceiling and they would make these little piles of turds. It was really great for a while.

Then the voice would come. You'd do something for a while, it'd be fun, and then one day the principal would come over the loudspeaker and inform us all that someone was throwing toilet paper around in the lavatory. This must cease. And it did, because the next stage was the voice would want names and they would get names because someone would always turn you in. It was an opportunity to be good. It was not vague what good and bad were. There was a definiteness that went along with uniforms and everything else. Boys had a wider berth for creativity in garb. I remember those knitted ties in the fifties when mothers were dressing boys. And big corduroy pants, which really stank when they peed, and it seemed that boys peed a lot. Girls didn't do it so much. I wonder if this is known. Then boys got tighter pants and pointed shoes and thin ties. You would look at boys' asses. I guess we're in junior high now. And surprise! I would dream about being a boy, or else about getting one, and I would follow his haircut, him getting them, then growing out and looking good, because there was little else to do. If the boy I liked got hit by the nun and his hair was getting long, then it would swing around and he'd get all red and it'd be really great. When I would get hit I would never cry. And I was the only girl who ever got hit, but I'm more interested in talking about boys right now.

One boy, David Burns, was a total clown. He was always making incredible faces and doing things that would get us all in hysterics. Between each room was a door. This is about sixth, maybe seventh grade. A nun would go out, say, and leave the door open and ask the other nun to watch her room. It was like we were babies. So the nuns had struck the deal and the other nun was heading back to her board and we were all in that crucial moment of watching the nun go away, our heads lifted toward the doorway. David, as a clown, had incredible timing, so he took the moment to get up on his chair and do something incredibly goofy. It was very Jerry Lewis. He was wagging his tongue like a dog and he was humping and wiggling his hips, it was just a little gross moment of comedy. Really hysterical. Because the nun behind him had turned around at the last moment and right behind him salivating and dancing was her looking at him and us in horror. In some ways it was the funniest moment in my life. The utter silent horror of him getting caught doing the dog. It was parents coming down, the whole thing. It had to be, but it was so lovely.

Janet Lukas was a cool girl, having an older brother who was in the cool crowd, so she was second-generation cool and she lorded it over everyone. In about sixth grade her and I and her best friend, Susie Martel, who was kind of a smart femme, all took ballet lessons together at Fidelity House. Though I had spent my childhood crying for access to a musical instrument and lessons, or special art classes in Cambridge, what my mother deemed would be important for me to take part in was a ballet class. Now, this is because I was a tomboy, and there is nothing more threatening to a tomboy mother than a tomboy daughter. Same with the nuns. The whole world was a plot to turn me into a femme. Many years later when I had my first boyfriend in college, I inadvertently would confide in him that I was learning to ice-skate by watching the man in front of me at the rink, and he screamed in horror that I should not learn to skate from a boy. I would push the sleeves of my sweater up over my elbow and he would laugh and tell me to push them down. I looked like a man. I was obviously floating in a sea of desirable male images. I had learned to push the sleeves of my sweaters up from watching boys, and at the same time I was courting the approval of those who would demand I push them down. It's frightening to think of the excruciating balance in which I've lived my life. Is it simply masochism? I think it's even trickier than that. My mother wanted me to take the classes and I did. The teacher, Miss Temple, was a ridiculous-looking middle-aged woman with dyed blond banana curls. I mean, when I think of it, how would any dancer feel who was teaching beginning ballet to Catholic children in the suburbs for fifty cents a week? It was about 1960, so maybe it was cool. I remember her black Danskin tank top and tights. I remember a bag that she carried her street clothes in, but somehow she wound up in an outfit that was neither in nor out, which I thought of as dancer, or Bohemian. She wore red lipstick. She would encourage us to mime her movements. She broke into a kind of curtsey. One leg would slide forward, and she would say something like "part a shoo." She would repeat it quickly, pursing her lips, "part a shoo, part a shoo." She would go around touching us, adjust our bows. I can't remember if I liked being touched or not. I liked the ballet bar. I liked raising my leg as high as I could and feeling the muscle stretch. I liked anything that made me feel strong and showed me how unbreakable I was. It seemed to be about this strength, ballet, and I liked that a lot.

One day Janet and Susie told me they were going to quit. A lot of our friendship in the ballet class had developed through making faces behind Miss Temple's back. She was gross, we agreed. "Red lips," went Janet, miming a woman putting on lipstick, as if there were some other way to be. I remember the weird feeling of vertigo, knowing that Janet and Susie were quitting and now I would have to quit because I had no way to explain what I liked about the class. The best thing about the class (in my "real" life—which meant everything outside of my thoughts and feelings) was that it made Janet and Susie like me. The feelings in my legs were too invisible to stand up for. I remember one night watching teevee with my family. It was educational teevee and there was a man and a woman dancing and the man wore tights and had a big protrusion between his legs, which seemed too big to be his penis. It had to be something else. It was part of the costume. It seemed like his sword. I thought it helped him pick the woman up. The woman wore her hair pulled back and had a light, short dress on. He would look so cool, holding her, lifting her. They wanted me to be her, not him. So I quit.

When I was twelve it was the last day of school and I was lying in bed and something felt wet underneath me and I felt weirdly sick. I got up and there was blood underneath me and I faintly understood, and I pulled myself up, I remember cotton around me, pajamas, and my sheets, and I carried myself downstairs, my bare feet hitting the fake wool of the carpet, and I can hear those dull thuds as I wavered down. I went into the bathroom and sat on the toilet and there was more of it, blood, and there was this whirring feeling inside of me. I thought I was going to pass out, and I did. There were big huge clots of blood, it looked like liver, which I hate, pouring out of this thing I wouldn't yet call cunt or anything. I didn't know about the inside of me. I was afraid to break myself. I knew there was an up, but I didn't go there. I thought I would get hurt. It was almost like I was already broken, somehow. I got up from the toilet and opened the door not even after flushing, I think. And I fell down in the doorway. Completely blacked out and collapsed. My brother came running. Mom, Eileen fell down. Oh, are you alright? I guess she got a look at the toilet. C'mon. You'll be okay. She pulled me up. Later I got one one those huge cotton pads to put between my legs and one of those obscene stretchy bands that have little hooks with claws through which you attach the thinner, almost gauzy part of the giant pad. Now it's all closed up. Then you flood one and you change it. I really bleed a lot. Years of it. Being a woman. Bleeding through my uniform in school. Blood on my seat. Just blatantly announcing to the world I was female. Excessively so, and I had been a boy for so long. Somehow my periods would have to be the worst. I remember some girls referred to it as their friend. It seemed to suit the weird advertising Kotex had. Soft, medium-range colors. The white product filling the dull inside of the box. Later, Tampax with that typeface that seemed Japanese. Do they print the boxes in Japan? Nothing in America is ever printed in that strange, mechanical, slightly Asian typeface. Where did it come from? Now I could get pregnant.

"The White Album"

Joe Westmoreland

The summer I finished seventh grade my family moved into our first ranch-style house. My father's company promoted him, and we were transferred to a suburb of Kansas City. We moved there right after school was out. Before his promotion we'd always rented roomy old houses near the center of the small Missouri towns where we lived. I loved those houses—they had so much history. Almost always some previous tenant left behind boxes or suitcases filled with memories. Once I found a box of photos of the man who lived most of his life in our house. Until I saw the pictures I'd just thought of him as the old man who died. The photos were of a young man in a high-waisted black swimming suit by the side of a pool with a group of friends. It was from the twenties. They looked like stills from an old TV movie. I tried to imagine what it must have been like living in our house when it was new. Those old houses were a lot of work for my mother to keep clean, even with six kids to help her. My mother loved our new house. It was only one story; there were no stairs to climb when she was tired. The plumbing worked. There was good water pressure. The wind didn't whistle through the walls on cold winter nights.

That summer we started getting on one another's nerves. My brothers, sisters, and I argued all the time, but I didn't know anyone else to go hang out with. To fight the boredom, my parents found a small country club the next suburb over with a golf course for Dad and a pool for us. Mom took us swimming a few afternoons a week. Toward the end of summer some new neighbors moved in next door to us. They had two kids. A girl and a boy. Donnie was two years older but only a grade ahead of me because he'd been held back. That was the first time I'd heard the term "held back" instead of "flunked."

Dad wasn't home much. When he was there he was usually in a bad mood. One afternoon he came home early and paced around the house, bitching and bitching and bitching. No one could do anything right. I was pissed because he wouldn't shut up even though nothing was wrong. He picked on Mom, but the house was in order. Maybe he was mad because she let my oldest sister drive my brothers and one of my sisters to the pool. My younger sister, Diana, and I hadn't gone that day. I couldn't stand listening to his constant evil complaining, so I went to my room and shut the door. All of a sudden Mom started wailing and moaning. I opened my door to see what was going on. She came running down the hall toward me with her hands up near her shoulders, flapping. She ran into their bedroom and picked up the black lacquered ceramic Buddha I'd made for her and smashed it to the ground. Then she broke something else. Diana came to her bedroom door and opened it a crack to peek out. Dad followed Mom down the hall into their room. As soon as we heard him coming, Diana and I quickly shut our bedroom doors. Through the wall I could hear them.

"What the hell is the matter with you?" he yelled.

She said, "I just can't take it anymore. I can't take it!"

He said, "Take what? You don't know how good you've got it. Can't take what anymore?"

She sobbed. "Oh, everything. No matter how hard I try I can't make you happy." I peeked out my door again just long enough to see Dad shaking Mom by the shoulders. "Stop it right this minute." It was the one time I was glad he was so stern. I couldn't stand to see her like that. She was my mother. She was the only thing that kept me from falling apart myself. He seemed like the voice of reason and sanity when he told her to stop.

Dad left the bedroom and slammed the door behind him. I heard the mattress squeak as Mom lay down on the bed and sobbed even more. The front door slammed. I heard Dad back his copper-colored '65 T-bird out of the driveway and take off, gunning the engine. Diana and I both came out of our rooms and looked at each other, helpless. We went to Mom's door and knocked. "Please, go away," she said softly. "Not right now."

Diana and I went into the backyard. Sneezy, my little half-dachshund, ran back and forth between my feet trying to get me to throw a stick. We sat down on the back-porch steps. Diana said it all started because Mom found a woman's phone number in Dad's pocket. "I hate him," I said gritting my teeth.

"Joe, don't talk like that."

"Why not? I do."

Diana said, "You'll get cursed if you talk like that out loud."

"I don't care." My hands were shaking. "We already are cursed, just having him as a dad."

"Joe, we'd better not tell Jimmy about this," Diana said. "It'll make him too upset."

"Why not?" I asked. Jimmy was our little brother. Usually the three of us, the young ones, knew what was going on with each other all the time.

"It's just he's too young to understand." She picked at some paint that was chipping away on a porch step.

"Okay, I won't say anything." Diana looked at me like she didn't believe me. "Honest!" I made a motion like I was zipping my lips. Then I crossed my heart. "But I don't hope to die!" That made her laugh. After that we didn't talk much, just sat close to each other.

A few minutes later Donnie came wheeling into his driveway on his bike with a new record. Glad to have something to do, I ran over to see what he'd got. He pulled it out of the bag and said in awe, like he was holding the Mighty Grail or something, "Look, the new Beatles record. 'The White Album'!" There was no picture on the cover. It was just blank white. "You wanna come over and listen?" Donnie asked.

I said sure. Sneezy wanted to come too, but she couldn't go inside Donnie's house. I knew Diana didn't want to be alone just then, but I was also looking for any excuse to get away, to do something to forget about the scene at home we'd just witnessed.

Donnie's mom was smoking a cigarette at her kitchen table, drinking a big glass of orange soda, and playing one of those word games where the page is covered with rows of letters and you have to find words and draw a circle around them. She had bleached blond hair pulled back in a French twist, tight capri pants, and a raspy voice. She was the exact opposite of my mom, with her short-cropped brown hair and faded floral-print housedresses. Plus, my mom was always busy doing house-work. It seemed like Donnie's mom was always sitting at the kitchen table smoking cigarettes, half the time talking on the phone.

Donnie was lucky because his parents had built him a bedroom in the basement. Our basement was unfinished. He had lots of privacy, a foreign concept to me since I shared my bedroom with my two brothers. Donnie's room was paneled with dark wood, and the floor was covered with chocolate shag carpeting. There was only one small window, high up. It was a window well, made out of corrugated metal with gravel at the bottom. Donnie said if the window was open too wide, these little frogs would jump onto his bed.

I was envious because Donnie not only had a room to himself, he also had his very own stereo system. He had a record player, AM/FM radio, an 8-track tape deck, and small speakers that separated from the system so he could put them in opposite corners of the room. He also had a light box attached to his stereo. It looked like a speaker, but when music played, colored lights flickered on and off psychedelically to the beat. The louder the music, the brighter the lights got. Donnie had a record called *Switched-On Bach* that was someone playing Bach on a Moog synthesizer. I'd never heard of a synthesizer until that album came out. Donnie played a fast part of the music, turned up the volume, and switched the record speed from 33⅓ to 45 rpm's so it sounded like the Chipmunks. The lights in the box sparkled frantically, making us laugh louder than the music. His mom opened the basement door and yelled for us to turn the music down.

Once I asked my mom if I could get a stereo system like that. She said sure, when you get a job, then you can buy anything you want. She said if there weren't so many of us kids we could have more nice things like that, but she would rather have all of us. She gave me a hug. That wasn't what I wanted. I wanted a complete stereo system with a light box. My brothers, sisters, and I used to sit around and imagine what it would be like if not all of us had been born. We thought of all the things we'd be able to have, like a room to ourselves, our own TV, stereos, go-carts. But none of us could imagine not being born. We could imagine each other not being born, but no one was willing to give themselves up so everyone else could have all that stuff.

Donnie ripped the plastic shrink-wrap off the album and put it on the stereo. We sat on the floor listening. I wasn't quite sure about it because it didn't really sound like the Beatles to me. I mean, I recognized their voices, but I still thought of them as singing songs like "She Loves You" and "Roll Over Beethoven." Donnie got up off the floor and walked over to his dresser. He said, "Joe, wanna see the new *Playboy*? I stole it from my uncle this weekend." He pulled it out of his top drawer where he'd buried it beneath his underwear. He flipped it open to the centerfold and pushed it in my face, laughing. I grabbed the magazine from him and started flipping through it. I'm left-handed, so I always flip through magazines from the back to the front when I first get them. Also, I had seen *Playboy* enough to know that sometimes in the back half was a section called "Sex in Film." It almost always showed naked men. Usually just their butts. But that was a lot for me. It was the one chance that I could get turned on looking at a *Playboy* with friends around and they wouldn't catch on. I don't even know if I re-alized that's what I was doing, just getting turned on by the men. But it was the only part of the magazine, besides the cartoons, that really interested me.

Donnie saw me looking at that section and pointed to a picture of Elliott Gould. "Look, even his back is hairy! Gross!" I was fascinated. I'd seen men at the swimming-pool locker room with hairy backs, but they were usually fat and old, not young and attractive like Elliott Gould. Donnie said, "He's so hairy I bet you can't even see where his pubes start and his stomach hair begins. Man, I hope I never get that hairy, I'm happy with what I've got now." I kind of laughed. He said, "What's so funny?"

"Nothing," I said. "It's just that, um . . . never mind."

"What?"

"I mean . . . I'm still waiting."

Donnie looked at me surprised. "You mean you haven't got any pubes?"

"No, I mean, well, kind of. I mean I don't have very many." I picked up the *Playboy* again and flipped through it, not really looking at anything.

"How old are you, twelve? I had pubes when I was twelve," Donnie said in disbelief.

"I'm thirteen and I do have some pubes," I said. "Just not a lot."

Donnie moved toward me. "Let's see. I bet you've got more than you think." I started to unzip my fly to show him when his mom yelled again for us to turn the music down before she came down and did it herself. I nervously zipped my jeans back up.

Donnie said, "It's weird. I'm only two years older than you, but look at mine." He sat on the edge of his bed and slid his jeans down to his knees. He pulled on his pubes and showed me how thick his hair was. He wasn't self-conscious at all. It felt like he was showing me a science project or something. He let me examine his dick and pubes close up. I had never seen that much pubic hair that close before. I only had a few pubic hairs, but I kept a vigilant watch over them. I counted them and watched them grow. I knew whenever a new one appeared. Donnie's pubes looked so good, so exciting to me. Blood started rushing around me. I felt warm. I felt happy and hopeful at the thought that someday soon I would have that much, too. Donnie was proud of himself. That close, his pubic hair looked like a dense forest. There was a dark moist smell. Kind of familiar, but different from my own. More like a man smell than a boy smell. I was in awe not only of his pubes but because I wanted to have a dick the size of his, with all that hair. Compared to Donnie's mature dick with that thick bush at its base, mine was a naked pencil. I was surprised that his dick was big. He was kind of overweight, just a big kid really. I told him I thought fat guys had small dicks. He didn't get upset that I called him fat. He said matter-of-factly, "Some of 'em do."

He spread the *Playboy* open on the bed and showed me how he jacked off. I sat next to him and watched as he spit in his hand and rubbed it on the head of his dick. Then he wrapped his hand around his dick and moved it quickly up and down. He didn't get very hard. It was just a demonstration. I was too shy to tell him how I did it. When I masturbated I had to be quiet so I wouldn't wake up my brothers. I lay on my stomach and humped the mattress until I came. My sheets always had yellow crusty stains on them, but my mother never mentioned it even though she was the one who washed them.

I wanted to watch Donnie some more, but he lost interest. He was more excited about the new Beatles record. He zipped up his jeans, scooted off the bed back to the floor, and propped himself against the bed. He picked up the album jacket and started reading the lyrics along with the music. I sat on the bed reading over his shoulder for a little while, then my eyes started wandering around the room. I looked up at his window and saw a little gray frog about an inch long jumping up over and over trying to get out of the window well. The music was soothing in a weird way. I liked it, but if I listened to it too closely, it made me a little uneasy. Donnie kept saying, "Wow!"

"Hey, Joe, I've got something else you might be interested in," Donnie said as he put the *Playboy* back in his dresser drawer. "Can you keep a secret?" He pulled a little brown pill bottle out of the back of the drawer. He held it close to me and asked if I knew what it was. He shook the bottle a little bit in front of me. I reached out and held his hand still so I could get a closer look. It looked like what I'd imagined marijuana to look like, only I never thought of it being kept in a pill bottle.

"What?" I asked.

He leaned over close to me and whispered reverently, "It's pot!" I thought he was bullshitting me. He took the white cap off the bottle. It couldn't be pot, it looked just like he'd picked off the top of some weeds and crunched them into the bottle. He held it under my nose and told me to take a whiff. I didn't recognize the sweet odor. He sat down on the floor and opened up the double album, and then sprinkled some out on the inside. "Come here," he said. "I'll show you how to roll." I sat down on the floor next to him. I was nervous. What if his mom decided to check in on him? At my house someone was always walking in and out of my room. There was never a long time alone.

I was surprised when I saw how good Donnie was at rolling a joint. He'd obviously been doing it for a while. He pulled two small pieces of white cigarette paper out of a little matchbook-type packet. His wet tongue slid across the gummed edge of one them. A fine string of spit stretched between his lip and the paper. Then he put the wet edge against the other sheet of paper, doubling the size to make it easier to roll. Donnie used "The White Album" as a lap table. The fold in the middle of the double album was perfect for resting the rolling paper on and catching pot that slid away. As he concentrated on rolling the joint, I stared at his eyebrows. They were short, not too wide across his face. He was paying such close attention to what he was doing that his eyebrows furrowed and his forehead wrinkled, making him look grown-up. My eyes followed the line of his eyebrows down the bridge of his nose to his cheeks. He had a few freckles, or sunspots as my mom called them. His lips were full. They were brownish instead of red like mine. He put the doubled paper in the fold of the album jacket and gently poured some more pot next to the paper. At first I couldn't figure out why he didn't put it right on the paper. Then he picked up the pot between his thumb and forefinger and gently crumbled it onto the rolling paper, making the pot leaves even finer. He picked up the cigarette paper with pot in it with both hands and started rolling it in midair. I was sure he was going to lose everything or the cigarette would break before he finished, but nothing like that happened. He rolled like a pro. He ran his tongue across the edge once more and sealed the paper. It was a tight white cigarette. He held it out to me and said, "Wah-la!"

Donnie's perfect joint captivated me. He was the coolest person I'd ever met. I automatically reached up to take the joint from him but stopped halfway. He moved closer to me on the floor, leaned into my face, and asked softly if I wanted to smoke with him. I got scared. I wanted to. I'd wanted to get high for a long time, but all I could think about was that Sonny Bono drug-education film they'd shown us in school the previous year and how a girl thought the blue stove-top flame was a blue rose and burned her hands trying to pick it. She flipped out and had to be taken away in an ambulance. Besides, if my dad ever found out I'd be in big trouble.

Donnie stood up on his bed, opened his little window, lit the joint, and took a couple of deep drags, blowing the smoke out the window. I thought I was getting high from the smell alone. I sat on the floor and looked up at him. He seemed bigger than ever, like he was growing right before my eyes. He looked at me and started laughing, trying not to let out any smoke, but some sputtered out anyway. He held the joint out to me and said, "You sure?" I wasn't sure. But I didn't move. I just shrugged. He jumped down off the bed and sat down on the floor next to me. His left thigh touched my right thigh. He put his arm around me and blew a puff in my face. I tried not to inhale, but part of me really wanted to. He looked at me like, what's the matter? Why not? I felt retarded. I didn't want him to think I was a chicken. If I got high with him, then we'd get to hang out more. I definitely liked hanging out with him. I smiled a wimpy, nervous smile, like maybe I will. But I never said yes or no. I was afraid if I even opened my mouth to say anything, I'd take a puff and then it would be all over for me, just like that girl in the movie. He was sitting too close to me. I couldn't think. I was getting the jitters. I ran my fingers through the chocolate-brown shag carpeting. Donnie gave up and said, "Oh, well. Maybe some other time." He stood back up on the bed and blew a couple more clouds out the window. Then he put the joint out, folded up the album, and poured the leftover crumbs of pot back into the little pill bottle. He put the roach in the bottle, too. After that we lay around on his bedroom floor, propped up against his bed, and shut our eyes while we listened to the weird sounds of "The White Album." Donnie was stoned. I pretended like I was.

I was having a great time, but I knew if I stayed much longer I'd get in trouble. Dad would be back, wanting to know where I'd been and who gave me permission to go to Donnie's in the first place. I thought I heard my mother calling me home. I tried to block her voice out of my mind. Donnie flipped over the album. Side B, second record. I stayed for as long as I could.

When I finally went back home Mom was in the kitchen fixing dinner. She looked like she always did, the busy housewife. You couldn't tell by looking at her how upset she'd been that afternoon. Everyone else had come back from swimming. Dad was back, too. He was watching TV in the front room with my brothers. The girls were helping Mom set the table and finish up fixing dinner. Only Diana and I knew what had happened earlier. Our eyes met as she was putting plates around the table. She gave me a sad smile. Sneezy was on her mat in the corner of the kitchen by the back door. She sat up when I looked over at her and wagged her whole body in excitement. I went over and petted her and whispered "I love you" into her floppy ears. When I went in to see what was on TV, Dad looked at me with an evil, cold stare and then turned back to the TV. He knew that I knew. Even though I didn't know everything, I knew what had happened between him and Mom that afternoon. I was a witness.

Underwater

Paul Russell

After school I spent the hours of my childhood on the floor in my bedroom re-creating Civil War battles with toy soldiers. On flats of cardboard I drew roads, ponds, fields with colored chalk. Wadded-up Kleenex served as puffs of smoke from the cannons. Using battlefield diagrams from a history of the Civil War my parents had given me on my first day of school, I strove for accuracy. When I had deployed all my troops and memorized my lines, I'd invite my parents in to give them a dramatic presentation, complete with lights and music, of the course of battle. Their reaction, sadly, never quite seemed to live up to my expectations. To burn off the nervous energy left unexpended on those battlefields, I marched out to the backyard to swing for hours on the swingset beneath the vast elm trees. Once in motion, oblivious to everything else, I sang Civil War songs I'd learned from a Tennessee Ernie Ford recording. Feeling somehow safe and purposeful, I sang to shield myself from the impinging world. School frightened and unnerved me. I had few friends, though there were boys, even then, I admired in an inchoate way. There was Rick Shirey, the Yankee from Ohio, who always borrowed my glasses during lunchtime—an odd habit his mom had warned would damage his eyes, which guaranteed the budding young rebel in him just couldn't resist. What was there for me but to feel honored? I spent lunchtimes in a blur of happiness.

Then one summer my family left the South and moved west for the adventurous space of a sabbatical year during which my father, a mathematician at a small college called Southwestern at Memphis, would do research at Stanford University. We arrived in California in August of 1967, the end of the Summer of Love. Something was in the air, and it wasn't just pot smoke. But at age eleven I was alert to it, sniffing it out like a caged animal keenly sensing freedom. That year was an awakening for me. Puberty struck like violent spring weather. The boys of my new school, East Meadow Elementary in Palo Alto, were sexual boys, and I had never been cast among sexual boys before. It's not that they were having sex; rather, they radiated sex, its power and allure. We were a school of boys coming into sticky heat. We got hard in our pants, grabbed at one another's crotches, traded sex drawings we sketched covertly during class. We talked solemnly about the mysterious and exciting changes happening to our bodies, the public hair some of us were beginning to sprout, our nipples that felt strangely sensitive. Overnight we became achingly aware of our penises.

In the school library there was a supplies closet where some of the boys, it was rumored, went when the library wasn't in use. One spring afternoon, as Lex Bancroft and I, unsupervised, shelved books—an honor bestowed from time to time on A students—he confided to me that he and Brian Freeman had gone to the closet the week before. The window shades were down to indicate the library was closed, but still the afternoon light suffused the room with a tender glow. Lex hooked his thumbs through the belt loops of his jeans and splayed his fingers against his pelvis as if in triumph. Did I want to go? he wondered.

Those of us who had not been to the closet could only speculate about what, exactly, went on in there. I felt a bright spasm of longing—everything in the room seemed at once vague and luminous; we were on the verge, I sensed, of something truly amazing—when the door opened and our teacher, Mr. Bouchner, appeared to tell us the news that Martin Luther King had just been assassinated in that faraway city where I had grown up.

I remember he put his arm around me and said gently, "Don't worry, son. You're not to blame."

Nonetheless, on the playground the next day my progressive class-mates shunned me; I took it out on my favorite tetherball, pummeling the leather orb around and around the pole to which it was chained, as if it might be possible to punch into oblivion my Southern mix of shame and hurt and pride.

I never went to the closet with Lex Bancroft, though I eventually learned that boys showed themselves to one another in there, a gift whose profound generosity inflamed me, and of which I would be the grateful recipient with other comrades in other locations—the school bathroom, the swimming pool, Dirk Masten's bedroom—several times before the month was out. We were all in on it together, a commune of revolutionary goodwill. And the revolution, we were certain in those exciting days of change, was coming soon. Everyone would be under thirty. We would drive VW vans. "Puff, the Magic Dragon" would be our national anthem and Snoopy our national emblem. We would cavort naked and curious with one another like the kind, innocent, and serious animals we really were.

Dog-eared paperbacks circulated from boy to boy like love letters. Isaac Asimov, Arthur C. Clarke, and Ray Bradbury were our common currency. On the playground we were Kirk and Spock, Scotty and Mc-Coy. What science fiction did for me in those days, intellectually, was not unlike what happened when I lay in bed at night and thought my way through certain boys with a longing so powerful that it threatened—promised, rather—to levitate me right off the bed. I did not know what to do with that longing, any more than I knew what to do with the shivering knowledge that the universe is infinite, the stars uncountable, worlds upon worlds, each of which will alter our destiny forever, lie waiting to be discovered.

Somehow, in the midst of my sense of having wondrously discovered myself, I had neglected to consider that the sixth grade, unlike desire or the universe, was finite. The day after Robert Kennedy was shot, my family packed the car, hitched up the tent camper, and began the long trek back to Memphis. We meandered through Death Valley, the bleak vistas of Nevada, landscapes ever more scorched and barren. Wild with a loss that wasn't yet able to articulate itself as loss, somewhere in the Arizona desert, approaching the north rim of the Grand Canyon, I managed to put my finger, both metaphorically and literally, on what I was feeling. Sitting in the backseat of our Buick LeSabre, separated from my younger brother by a pile of boxes and thinking dreamily of my smart, sexy, fearless classmates Brian Freeman and Dirk Masten and Lex Bancroft, whom I would never see again, I discovered that by flexing my hips ever so slightly I could create a friction between my erection and the cloth of my underwear that sent me places both strange and astonishing, a journey that did not assuage my sense of loss or grief so much as express it on another, altogether transcendental plane.

It was a plane I tried to return to as often as possible during the long journey home. Back in Memphis another, less felicitous discovery awaited me. Either my old friends had changed profoundly, or I had. The spring of 1968 had been a difficult one for them: the garbage strike, the assassination, the riots that followed. I had watched all that from a distance; my classmates saw it up close. Even Rick Shirey's Southern accent was now stronger than mine. With a sickened fascination I listened as they snickered, *In Dallas they got them a president, and in L.A. they got them a senator, but in Memphis we got us a King*. That November, on election day, my seventh-grade class at Scenic Hills School cast mock ballots; the votes were evenly divided between Richard Nixon and George Wallace. A single vote for Hubert Humphrey—thank God for secret ballots—drew jeers from the other students.

I dove into the consolations of science fiction. Mr. Spock, that perpetual exile, half human, half Vulcan, the alien everywhere alienated, became my guide. I would live with stoic dignity. It even came to seem possible that I, too, was not entirely of this planet, that this meager place was not my home.

I discovered a fat, pale boy who, for his own reasons, was as much a misfit as I. Sitting in the back of the class, we began designing starships—powerful warp pods and luxurious crew quarters and hydroponic tanks that would grow food for the long journey to distant worlds. Inspired by the *Encyclopedia Galactica* from Isaac Asimov's *Foundation* series, we embarked on our own *Star Trek Encyclopedia,* a magnum opus in which we hoped to chronicle every bit of information about the galaxy in the twenty-third century that could be gleaned from the series. We took scrupulous notes, concocted entries on every planet the U.S.S. *Enterprise* visited, every gadget the show deployed, every character, no matter how minor, who showed up in an episode. We cross-referenced entries, sketched illustrations, formulated an index. Nevertheless, despite our avid attention, there was talk the show would be canceled due to lack of audience interest. It hardly seemed possible everyone else could fail to understand. From time to time, however, I would suspect the real truth. "All you care about," my mother complained, "is that silly *Star Trek.*" The adjective made me jump. I absorbed the insight warily. Though they quivered with the profoundest private significance, perhaps *all* the things I cared so passionately about—the accuracy of my Civil War reenactments, the boys of East Meadow, the mission of the U.S.S. *Enterprise* in the twenty-third century—were just silly.

Perhaps I had always been attracted to lost causes. When my friend changed schools the next year, we continued our increasingly quixotic venture by mail, sending each other new entries and plotting ways to pressure NBC into resuming the now-canceled series. Our brilliant solution: We devised little cards that said STAR TREK LIVES and, hoping against hope, inserted them into random books in the local library.

Every afternoon the summer I turned thirteen, my father insisted on taking me and my brothers swimming in the neighborhood pool. I resisted. I did not want my skinny legs and narrow chest to be seen there, though I craved seeing. There were boys like Paul Sessions, Brian Hogan, and Greg Smith I could not get enough of seeing. Every afternoon I put up a fight; every afternoon I was made to acquiesce. "Everybody likes to go swimming," my father told me reasonably. "Stop being so silly."

Then I discovered swimming goggles, an ingenious innovation, because all sorts of things happen underwater. Some boys my age are playing a game: They stand in a circle, chest deep in water; then one of them sets himself in motion, twisting like a top while the other boys feel for his crotch. No one else in the pool seems aware of what they are up to, but I with my goggles witness everything. After the game has broken off, two of them remain behind, their passionate underwater grappling giving way to more languid gropings. On another day, two boys have discovered that there is pleasure to be had from standing in front of the underwater jets and pulling out their bathing trunks so that the column of fresh water entering the pool bathes their genitals. Happily invisible, I submerge myself and watch. One of them has an erection he caresses with his hand.

On one long-awaited afternoon we came home early from swimming to watch the moon landing. The family gathered in the den, eager but hardly distraught with excitement like I was. As the lunar module descended, my heart was in my throat. I had never felt my heart in my throat like that before. For once, I felt oddly justified. What mattered most to me in the privacy of my soul—man's great adventure in space— was happening in public, for everyone to see. Landing on the moon: Did it not signal the august beginning of that new world I had glimpsed so briefly in California and then lost? In a matter of minutes we would know whether all that sublime future was possible, but for the moment, as the astronauts' voices calmly sent back information to Mission Control and touchdown loomed ever nearer, we did not yet know. And then the immense relief, the great exhalation of pent-up breath when Neil Armstrong radioed, "Tranquillity Base here. The Eagle has landed."

The world did not change. Out on the front lawn I gazed up at the moon, trying to comprehend that on its surface, at this very moment, stood two human beings invisible to my sight but nonetheless there. The next day I was back at the swimming pool, underwater, my goggles in place, trailing a dark-haired boy in a blue bathing suit, hoping against hope I might glimpse something memorable down there.

In photos of myself at thirteen I look blurred, not quite there, the kind of kid who's destined to grow up a pervert. Furtive, desperately unhappy, I felt at once superior to and terrified of everyone else. After my collaborator on the *Star Trek Encyclopedia* moved away, I kept to myself. After school, in the mindless escape that had replaced the backyard swingset for which I was now too old, I pedaled my bicycle anxiously, relentlessly, up and down the quiet street in front of our house. Because I was deathly afraid of dogs in those days, I never ventured any farther afield than that.

During class, I'd ravish boy after boy in my head while ancient Mrs. Pasley, standing under the framed picture of George Washington that got peppered with spitballs whenever her back was turned, droned on about prime numbers or, with more conviction, the benefits of carrot salad in improving her eyesight. The boys of Scenic Hills were not the sexual boys of East Meadow. Perhaps because we were Baptists and Pentecostals, the life of the flesh seldom surfaced, though I scrutinized my classmates ceaselessly for anything that would betray them to me. When such rare glimpses came—a boy would adjust himself in his pants, a fold of fabric would give evidence of the flesh concealed beneath— they were powerful and dizzying, food for starving thought.

One boy who always seemed to be adjusting himself was Eddie Wheaton, a sleepy-eyed charmer with a most attractive way of wearing tight beige jeans and brown penny loafers. Once I had to stop by his house after school; we were working on a science project together. He invited me to his room, a cluttered, wood-paneled cell in the basement. I sat on his desk chair while he reclined on his bed amid piles of comic books and dirty clothes, and as we talked he lazily scratched his crotch for minutes at a time. I gazed dry-mouthed, uncertain, secretly electrified at what might have been the stirrings of an erection beneath the denim of his jeans.

When I was thirteen there was nothing to do with myself but dream. I had perfected—or at least I fooled myself into thinking I had perfected—a nearly motionless, invisible classroom masturbation, a refinement of that technique I had accidentally happened upon in the backseat of the family car on the way to the Grand Canyon. Only if someone were to study me as attentively as I studied the oblivious objects of my longing could I be detected, and I did everything I could to insure that no one would ever bother to look my way. I flattened myself against the wall as life rumbled by, even going so far as to adopt an invariable and austere wardrobe of black trousers and white shirts so that no change in my attire from day to day might render me in any way conspicuous to the gaze of others. Beneath that puritanical surface, however, Dionysian revels regularly led to that honeyed climax during which I felt, if only for the fleeting moment, free of everything that hemmed me in.

For private sessions at home I had culled a small stash of treasures from whatever meager sources were at hand—the Sears, Roebuck catalog, certain issues of *National Geographic,* photos I occasionally clipped from the newspaper of boys so arrestingly beautiful that they were the real news, more than commensurate with a lunar landing in their power to awe.

Unexpected things aroused me. I had begun, of late, to get hard when I arranged Civil War battles with toy soldiers, or when I deployed those soldiers in my own scenarios. A small band of soldiers tries to fight off, against impossible odds, a vast opposing army. Their destruction is certain, but still they fight on. It was the certainty of their destruction that I found so inexplicably exciting, their valiant lost cause overwhelmed by insurmountable forces, helplessly swept away. Battles like the Alamo, Custer's Last Stand, the three hundred Spartans at Thermopylae stoked complicated fires within me.

Other scenes could only be enacted in words. I'd invent episodes involving various boys at school. Three of them meet in the woods. The two older ones tie the youngest to a tree and take the kind of advantage of him he's always secretly wanted them to take. Or four boys are in a treehouse, the bravest (and handsomest) starts daring the others to show themselves to him. One thing leads to another, which leads to another. I never visualized myself a participant in these imagined romps; rather, I watched underwater, through goggles. More than the physical exertions I put them through, what finally excited me was simply the possibility that boys could know one another intimately, that they might want to undertake with one another something so silly or shameful as kissing or touching or any of the other kind and innocent and serious things I imagined for them, alone in my room on dark winter afternoons after school.

A secret voluptuary, I chased with relentless concentration throughout my thirteenth year a single-minded goal: ecstasy, that fleeting and exquisitely painful moment in which I could stand outside myself, become more than merely myself. If masturbation was the first crude avenue I discovered, other, more refined substitutions followed. In the music of Wagner and Mussorgsky and Ravel I could detect monstrous exhilarations uncannily like my own. Certain lines of Shelley and Tennyson shivered down my spine. Though my family seldom went to the movies, my father took me to see *2001: A Space Odyssey*. Its opening music, that solo trumpet calling forth a cataclysm of orchestra and timpani, struck me with the force of revelation. My father explained to me that this was the prelude to a much larger symphonic work, *Also Sprach Zarathustra*, by a German composer named Richard Strauss, and that the music was inspired by a book by the philosopher Friedrich Nietzsche.

Parents beware: Knowledge is dangerous. I proceeded to the library, where the librarian strongly discouraged me from checking out *The Portable Nietzsche*. I persisted, however, and for nearly the whole of eighth grade I struggled to hear that book's prodigious, disconcerting music. Once deciphered, its crescendoes could leave me exhausted and panting. C. S. Lewis observed about literature that it doesn't really matter where you start, because everything leads to everything else in the end. In the next several months I moved on hungrily, hauntedly from Nietzsche to Hermann Hesse and Jean-Paul Sartre and thence, in my stumbling, half-comprehending way, to Jean Genet and Marcel Proust. Thus my initial, innocent devotion to science fiction led me promiscuously far afield, to places where I began to suspect there might roam, without shame, others like myself.

A curious thing happened to me from time to time. I'd be standing in the lunch line, or walking through the corridors on my way to class, or sitting at my desk watching the blackboard or some boy, and suddenly, without any whisper of warning, I'd feel in the pit of my stomach, around the region of my heart, an emptiness so profound that it seemed possible a person might die of it. For a few harrowing moments I no longer knew who I was. I could, in fact, have been dead. But then the horrible sensation faded, and I would be back inside myself again.

Mostly these devastations arrived in me for no apparent reason at all. But I remember one more dramatic incident. Eddie Wheaton had been leaving the school cafeteria when the metal edge of the closing door, as he stepped outside, caught his heel. He went down in a yelp of agony.

Blood drenched his white sock, his brown penny loafer. The pain in his handsome face was alarming, the way it clarified him like a fierce light able to shine right through the skin to the soul. I did not love him, though I wanted him terribly, in a parched and thirsty sort of way. How deeply I regretted that, in my flushed confusion, I had done nothing that afternoon he had extended—perhaps—some purposely ambiguous offer my way.

Our teacher, Mr. Stewart, whose beard shadow resembled Richard Nixon's, made his way through the little crowd that had gathered. He knelt beside Eddie's writhing figure and lifted him into his arms, cradling the hurt boy's suddenly slack weight the way Mary holds the crucified Christ in Michelangelo's *Pietá* (I had studied, avidly, certain of the master's creamy-white marbles). "Calm down," Mr. Stewart might have said to the rest of us as well—for we were not calm, I remember; we were hysterical, crowding close to see Eddie's marble-pale face, bending down to pick up, delicately, with something like awe, the bloody loafer that had dropped to the sidewalk. Grim-faced, Mr. Stewart spirited his charge away to the school infirmary. Later in the day we would learn that Eddie's tendon had been nearly severed, that he would be on crutches for months. Still later, after school was out, I stood in the bright winter sunlight, waiting for my mother to come pick me up, and looked up into the moonless blue of the sky. Without warning, that emptiness around my heart opened wide.

This was everything there was. The bare trees, the bleak red brick of Scenic Hills School, cars coming and going. My own slightly numb self. There was nothing more. I felt sick and hollow inside. Then, as suddenly as it had appeared, that spooky, precarious sensation passed and I was still standing in the parking lot waiting for my mother to arrive, wondering how, exactly, I would tell her the sensational story of what had happened to Eddie Wheaton at lunch.

First Passion

Etel Adnan

Why is it that when one has more past than future, life's earliest memories acquire a frightful acuity? More and more I realize that my childhood and early adolescence surge in front of me too often, as if they have become a person—a different person each time—who stops me in the street, begs for something I don't understand, and then disappears not behind some corner but into some fog, some oblivion.

This person could be the self itself, imbued with its own conscience, my childhood self resurrected (or rather returning periodically), asking questions, asking for accountability, demanding the attention it never got back then, yearning eternally for what it yearned for originally and never achieved. We are not only haunted by such ghostly figures but practically hunted, stalked by memories that we don't manage to shake off because something in us knows that their death will be our own death. That is, if they ever could die: They may have acquired a life of their own, and there we will never go.

It is true that I was a lonely child, had no brothers or sisters from my mother, my father having had three children from a previous marriage—whom he had abandoned in many ways, and who were living in a different country. There were no little cousins of my own age either. This situation did not make me an especially unhappy girl, but it pushed me, I am sure, to be always seeking friends with whom I could share toys, emotions, thoughts, and games. I was born and raised in Lebanon, amid kids who had extended families—families, it seemed, ad infinitum; I was forever the little outsider whose family appeared extremely meager compared with everyone else's. Even now, friendship always looks to me a bit miraculous and, above all, precarious, like everything else.

Beirut, in my childhood, was a garden city with small neighborhoods, quiet streets, uneventful lives. My school was just a small street away from home; it was run by French nuns who compounded their own Jansenistic brand of Catholicism with a colonial arrogance and gave us a strange kind of education—a bookish one, totally alien to our environment—creating an isolation from both our own traditions and our own inner need for a happy world. In such schools the view of the world was incredibly narrow, dominated by an invisible Father who distributed more punishment than reward to little girls who spoke of sins they couldn't commit and waited for recreation time like inmates in some of the milder prisons of this earth.

Home was a lonely, though lovable, place. I was aware that my mother was unusually beautiful and that my father was much older; she often made sure that this latter fact was known. My emotional life seemed clear: I loved both my parents and that was all.

But that was far from being all. My heart was full of emotions. Emotions about what? I don't think things were too clear, on any score, in my childhood. My heart was beating, yes, my mind was busy, swimming in the sea was such a happy experience, day after day in the summer, when nuns weren't around for a change.

Playing with classmates was the highest emotion: running in the school's courtyard, chatting endlessly on the way home around four o'clock, dragging my feet, chewing time, arriving thirty minutes later than expected. I was usually trying to be the focus of attraction, and most of the time I was. As children must select a best friend, I paired off mostly with a little classmate my age, Anissa Chaker. I remember her face, her appearance, with great clarity, as if I saw her only a few weeks ago. She had green-blue eyes, very curly black hair, rather pale skin, and high cheekbones. She lived a few blocks down the road, halfway between the seashore and my house. Her mother had died, and she lived with her father and three older brothers. My mother liked her; I think she liked that she came from a "good family," a place my mother could trust. So I was often—and I would say solemnly—"sent" to play with Anissa in her beautiful, traditional house, which was built of stone, with arches and a balcony. This started when I was, I think, seven and went on for a few years. (In fact, I remained a friend of Anissa's till late adolescence, until the youngest of her brothers fell in love with me and became an insistent boyfriend, taking me to horse races and to watch a stranger game called pigeon hunting, where he would bet on the guy who would bring down a pigeon with a single shot. Little by little I lost track of him, and then of her, after I went to finish college in Paris.)

In our classrooms the children were seated on benches, each with two desks that opened vertically and in which we could leave our books and copybooks. An ink pot was inserted on the right side of the case. We were assigned our seats by the teacher-nun. It happened—I must have been age nine—that I was seated next to a girl whose name was Helen. I liked Helen the very first day we sat next to each other. She was quiet, noticeably quiet. I was a restless child and rather outgoing, proud of stirring things up, admired by the teachers for my studies and dreaded by them for my lack of discipline.

I don't think it took me long before I realized that Helen was unlike all the other kids. Gradually I grew to feel that there was a difference in my eyes (or rather I should say my heart) between Anissa and Helen. Anissa remained my friend, with all the comfortable feelings that friendship produces, all the freedom of movement that it entails. I could run with her in the school yard, eat cake at her home, chat, laugh, spend hours in her garden among the flowers. But with Helen, for the first time in my life I felt shy, intimidated, awkward in front of another child, and I was aware of it and couldn't manage the situation. I was too serious with her, too attentive, exceedingly proud to walk with her until we reached her street, happy for the privilege of being invited into her home, where she had an older sister and an older brother. Anything concerning her sounded of the utmost importance and *glamour*. Why was her home big and rather sad, silent, formal? It was to impress me no end.

This went on for two years. I "loved" Helen differently from anybody else, almost like in the movies, not quite, though not unlike, either. Because of her I entered that zone that one experiences in youth, of half-denials, half-truths about oneself and one's affections, and I remained in that zone for quite a while—until my middle twenties, and through several other passions. It is a tragic situation, due to this sixth sense that we have for what is expected from us and what is not, what is allowed and what is considered shameful. Why and how we have it, I don't really know, but it happens early in life, and with some people it never gets resolved.

I discovered within my heart a kind of secret space that Helen inhabited, where I would mentally talk to her, and where I would notice her extreme beauty—which was real, not merely imagined. She had the most beautiful eyes I ever saw in my whole life, and later I realized that they looked like Garbo's—she always looked a bit sleepy when she looked at me (and at anything). Her eyes were not blue but the color of dark honey, and they looked clearer when the sun hit them; her eyelashes made huge shadows on them, practically down to her cheeks. I was speechless most of the time with her, thinking of her while she was present, exactly like I felt ten or twelve years later when I fell in love—I wouldn't say more deeply, but more explicitly and more violently—with a woman I met in Paris during my student years.

Beirut in the thirties was itself a preadolescent city: newly installed as a capital for a nation carved out by the Allies from Syria. It smelled of jasmine and orange blossoms, and you could look at the sea from almost any street. I already loved it as a child, sensed its beauty and enjoyed any contact with it, such as going to the market with my father or running down the street to the swimming places. The most mysterious of all experiences, back then, was seeing a movie. Oh, the movies, what a love affair, what a passion for the unreachable! There were few movie houses in the city and children didn't used to go to them, but my mother had (as I understood later) a boyfriend, and she would go with him to the cinema and take me along, usually in the evening and in the winter. I would fill my head with the black-and-white shimmering of the screen and see good-looking grown-ups come very close to each other to create a languorous atmosphere that I called love. Early on movies formed my sensibilities (for better or worse), and movie stars became my archetypes of desirability. Men or women were equally desirable, equally magical, with maybe Garbo having an edge on them all.

In the school yard I would tell the kids assembled around me of the things I saw. One day I was caught by a wretched nun in the middle of a dance performance—I think Garbo's mazurka—that I was giving as a means of explanation. I was deprived of recreation for two weeks, but all this just increased my fascination for the erotic quality of black-and-white moving images, to such a point that half a century later I still find something of that undying erotic quality in even such benign images as Ansel Adams's flowers or trees.

What made things even more magical to me was that a new cinema, with velvety red seats and huge red curtains had just opened, the most beautiful, the most prestigious in the city, and that cinema, the Roxy, belonged to little Helen's uncle! So going to the Roxy from the time I was not yet eleven until much later, even when I didn't see Helen any-more, was tied to her image. A visit to her was enhanced by the fact that that uncle was rumored to have lived in America (something only connected to movies) and had come back to add to the city its newest dream house. That was the place where through the years I watched *Blood and Sand, The Scarlet Empress, Anna Karenina,* and, later, *The Barefoot Contessa.* And on and on . . . Given the shyness (or the awe) Helen created in me, she was barely closer than the movie stars, all too present in my head and in my heart, and so little or not at all in my everyday world.

Something happened, I can't remember what, but I was mad at her for something—or nothing, that's the whole point—and stopped talking to her although we were still sitting on the same bench. I felt a mixture of sorrow and some other feeling I couldn't define, even then, and I retreated into myself when it came to her—I could not get out of that mood that had taken hold of me. My sadness must have been so evident that one of our teachers, a young lay teacher, who must have seen how much we were friends, came to me one afternoon just when class had ended and stopped Helen on her way out. She brought us together saying, "Come on, little ones, you have to make up," and looking at me she said, "I know how fond of her you are, so let's stop this nonsense."

I remember acutely that I had been desperately waiting for such a moment, but—and I wish I knew for sure why, because that situation renewed itself later with other people, and I always reacted the same way and lived to regret it—I *refused* to open up and admit that things weren't normal, that the little storm, certainly all of my own doing, had gone away. Thus I went on playing with all the children save the one I was desperately missing.

We must have been then in the second year of our relationship, somewhere between friendship and something else which we were too young to name, yet we were aware of its intensity, of the trouble, the stirrings it was creating in our souls. I attribute those feelings to Helen as well because by then she wasn't talking much to anybody but me, and with me she was quiet, aloof, dreamy, or just content. After the scene of the impossible reconciliation (which I still regret), she went her solitary way, but not for long. She became friends with an interesting schoolmate who I knew a bit, a red-haired and blue-eyed Russian girl who was, I learned later, the daughter of an exiled Azerbaijani prince who was living in Moscow when the Revolution erupted and who had sought refuge in Lebanon. Tania Nahidchevansky was her name. I was intrigued by both the person and the name, and when Helen and she became "best friends," I would look at them and think Tania was a lucky person and that I would never reestablish the exclusivity I had once had with Helen.

(I think that Tania and I did talk to each other, the more so because Tania was an outgoing child, aware of her influence on others, of her special presence and her exotic appeal in our little crowd.)

Around age eleven the children in that French system of education had to pass an exam, a "certificate" signaling the end of elementary school. The nuns built a lot of expectation around that end-of-the-year examination, especially because failure meant one could be prevented from going on to the next level of classes. We needed a card for that, with a picture glued on it, the equivalent of a passport photo. There were about twenty of us in that class, and we all went to the photographer, and I think I talked to Helen then. We were each given two or three more pictures than needed, and we began to exchange them with our friends, and Helen gave me her picture and I gave her mine.

In my house I didn't have much that was exclusively mine, but I had a little drawer where I kept my pencils, erasers, pencil sharpener, and maybe a few copybooks. I put Helen's picture in a corner, on top of the other things, and every time I would open the drawer I would look at it, bring it close to my face, and once in a while kiss it, barely, and put it away again. One day I put a little flower on it and it left some pollen, a tiny yellow spot, and I was so relieved to see that it didn't harm her face but was close to the corner of the picture.

My own wanderings, my nomadic university life, my incapacity to transfer many belongings from place to place, and ultimately the war in Lebanon, which followed my settling in California—all that forced me to discard a lot in my life, ending up with very few documents of the past. Even the most valuable ones were lost, but that little picture of Helen appears once in a while when I reshuffle some of my old papers.

Helen also told me that she was changing schools, that Tania was doing the same, and that they were going to the College Protestant Français, the only non-Catholic French school in the city. It was more expensive than the Catholic ones and had a prestige of its own, as it was run by Mademoiselle Weigman, a strong-headed woman who is now quite famous. Her students were some of the richest, most beautiful, and most intelligent girls. Something was unique about the college, and in Catholic circles it was always rumored that it wasn't religiously correct to go there. I came home and told my mother that I wanted to change schools too. Her reaction was immediate: "They don't believe in God there!" Although she was Greek, born in Smyrna and exiled in Beirut, she must have heard such slander and believed it. There was no chance that I would go to the college.

I knew that Helen's company was lost for me. I thought about it constantly, in that realm of our minds where some ideas, ideas that are also feelings, linger in a permanent though weightless way; it is a melancholic cloud, a thin veil, which becomes all too familiar and takes years to disappear, if it ever does.

A year or so later—I must have been twelve or thirteen—I was bicycling on the Corniche, the wonderful avenue that borders the sea, and which was walking distance from my home. Somehow my mother had allowed me to learn to ride a bicycle, and there was in the neighborhood a little store where one could rent for a few piastres one of those graceful little machines. Extremely few people rented them for pleasure, and they were mostly young boys. But one afternoon my path crossed Helen's and Tania's; they too were bicycling on the Corniche, and they waved at me. I was so surprised to see them that I was almost run over by a passing car; I swerved and fell. The car stopped, the driver made sure that I was all right, and when I stood and got back on the bike the two girls were already far away. I rode in the opposite direction, returned my bicycle, and went home.

Time passed, including World War II, my early university years, and studies in Paris, Berkeley, and Harvard. I settled in California, which I love and still call home, but sometime before the beginning of the Lebanese civil war I had returned briefly to Beirut (only to be forced by the fighting to come back to the United States). There was in Beirut a well-known little café called The Horseshoe, popular among the artists of the city and some journalists. Next to it I discovered that a store selling luxurious clothes had opened during my prolonged absence. It belonged to Helen's sister, Mary, and I was moved to have fallen upon traces of Helen. (Mary had an American name because the family had emigrated to the States and it was only after the children were born that they returned to Lebanon. That explained why there was something special about those two little girls who had gone to school with me.)

One day, seeing Helen through the front window, I entered the store and said hello to my old friend. She didn't show much surprise, but a faint smile and a passing light in her perpetually beautiful eyes encouraged me to say a few words. I learned that she was married and had two children. That was almost all she had to say. "What are you doing now?" I asked.

It was summertime, and she said that she was going to the beach. "Why don't you come with me?" she said, and I thought I would. But I didn't. I noticed that she was as pale as when she was little, as diffident, as dreamlike. If I had just met her for the first time, I would have found her lovable, appealing, the type of person that I would have liked to know more of, in a quiet, silent way. It was as if the separation never existed, as if we were the children we had been: shy, innocent, with a whole imprecise space ahead of us, with no worries, no knowledge of any kind, no past and no notion of future, two little beings happy to be together and not even aware of that happiness.

But I didn't go to the beach. I don't even want to know if I was right or wrong. In the course of my life I have thought about love over and over again, and I still do: Love is the most important matter we have to deal with, but it is always the hardest. It comes about like a wave of infinite strength and creates the fear of drowning; it inhibits our intelligence, paralyzes our will, looks hopeless from the start. At least this is how it appears to most people, and how I have always experienced it. It bypasses the channels of reason; it is foolish by essence and seems to spring from some inner region of the mind—or of the soul—where panic resides. It creates a desperate need, the need to arrest in space and time the person beloved; it has to do with the absolute. It usually ends in tragedy because it is in essence a fever, a flame, an energy that moves with no control and brings aberration to our behavior. This is why everyone kills his or her own love, out of desperation: We seem to lose the battle in fearing to lose it, we prefer to die than to doubt, we suffer in order not to suffer; we are doomed, and we are wrong.

The Wind in the Louvers

Andrew Holleran

I should have known when my sister was banished from our house while I was still in fifth grade, simply because she had been caught by my mother writing letters to a sailor in the U.S. Navy. But then how was I to recognize the change that puberty would bring to both of us when I did not even know what sex was? The length of time it takes to go from the fifth grade to the eighth is not very long—three summers, four falls— but looking back, the change that overtook both me and my sister seems not just astonishing but explicable by only one thing powerful enough to alter both our lives the way it did: sex. She went off to a boarding school run by nuns. I stayed home and had a social rise and fall: In sixth grade, I was so popular that when I arrived at parties other boys hissed; by seventh grade, I was home alone every Saturday night with a stack of peanut-butter-and-jelly sandwiches and a book.

We were living at the time on an island off the coast of Venezuela, where my father worked for an American company in a mostly American community whose customs (Little League, Boy Scouts, community church, Youth Canteen, summer-recreation program, Fourth of July) were all copied from their models back in the States. It was 1955. All I knew of sex was a strange, revolting sound that tinctured my sister's voice when she sang popular love ballads around the house—a sound that was about as appealing to me as fingernails being dragged across a blackboard. That sound, the sound of her sexual awakening, really, was what caused the trouble. Though our island was much too small to be on the list of usual ports for American naval vessels, that year one did stop and my sister—six years older than I, already a rebellious sophomore—went down with her girlfriends to the dock to meet some sailors. A few months later my mother discovered, among the blouses in her dresser drawer, letters she was getting from the man she had met that day. When my sister came home drunk from a date soon afterward, it was the last straw. My mother was not about to deal with my sister's coming of age, or the insubordination that went with it; so off she went to the nuns in Massachusetts. We would not speak to each other for another two years.

This left me clueless about sex—an only child, in effect, who would have to negotiate his own rite of passage from fifth to eighth grades unassisted by a confident, unafraid, and, most important, older sister. It was my sister who had taught me to roll up the sleeves of my T-shirts like the boys in her class who worked on jalopies; it was my sister who had brought her girlfriends over to the house, where one of them had provided a big breakthrough in my life by telling me that one could read and eat a sandwich at the same time (two activities I'd thought wholly separate till then), a discovery that would revolutionize my own puberty. But then the letters were found, she vanished, and I became, without her offsetting presence, an intensely religious boy who began reading *The Lives of the Saints,* built an altar in his bedroom, and continued to play with girls instead of boys.

I thought this was because there were more girls than boys in my neighborhood; but it wasn't just that—girls were more fun. Boys were boring; wandering in packs, throwing rocks at lizards, bullying other kids. (My sister had always been my protection against them.) After she left, however, what had been unremarkable for most of my childhood— save for the occasional father who wondered, out loud, why I was always playing with girls—now became an issue. In sixth grade, barely accustomed to my sister's absence, I became aware that all the women in my life were to be taken away when one day a father came home, found me playing with his daughter, and shouted, "Doesn't he *ever* play with boys?" in a tone of such fury, it froze both me and Russeen for a moment in midplay. I blushed. Then she laughed, and we resumed our activities. Even these were changing, however, in sixth grade; no longer tag, or pirates, or marathon prayers to induce an apparition of a saint. My class had suddenly turned social and I with it. Russeen was the most popular girl in sixth grade, and it was to her house I went as her consort after school every day to draw up the seating charts (boy-girl, boy-girl) for the entire row our classmates occupied at the movie theater on Saturday afternoons, and to practice our dance steps to the records popular at that time (the Everly Brothers).

Our new social life was in a way easier for me than for other boys because I'd played with girls most of my life. Girls now had crushes on boys, and I became a sort of intermediary between the two sexes, belonging to neither and both.

That year Russeen begged me, in fact, to call a very popular boy two grades ahead of ours, disguise my voice, and ask him what he thought about her. A week later he learned somehow that I had made the call, and tried to drown me at the beach.

At least, he held my head underwater so long, I thought I was going to drown—a panic that was my first initiation into the adult reality that now lay beneath this shift in the relations between boys and girls. Donnie Baylor, the eighth-grader, was muscular and blond, with a pug nose and large lower lip; he wore a silver identification bracelet, white T-shirts with the sleeves rolled up, and engineer boots. He was in our high school on the edge of town; we were still in sixth, at the elementary school, where that year, oblivious to my impending doom, I was the uncrowned king of our class. I wore paisley vests with a gold watch fob and penny loafers to our dances, and jitterbugged to "Hound Dog" so well I and Russeen always cleared the floor; I was expert at spinning girls in quick, tight circles that caused their hair and skirts to float for a few seconds. I was not so good at spin-the-bottle, however.

One night at a party in someone's bungalow I was asked to go into a dark room, where each girl took her turn ordering the boy she wanted to kiss her, and where I was supposed to neck with Betty Ward. I was so offended by the idea, I made a point to trip over the furniture, bang my shin, and completely dissipate the erotic atmosphere by a string of Jerry Lewis–like pratfalls. I didn't want to be left alone with girls; I would dance with them in public, but nothing else. When a boy in my class, Gary S., talked in a dreamy voice about having to stop every other step to kiss Dana P. when he walked her home from the movies, I couldn't understand his pleasure. When I walked Dana home one night, I made a point to keep talking—about the novel I was reading *(The Robe)* and the early persecution of the Christian martyrs—who, like me, would have thrown themselves off the rocky promontory our path bordered before they submitted to unchaste desires. No girl, not even Dana under a tropic moon, was going to get me to touch her.

One of the new facts about life, and one that did not seem in any way unpleasant, was that I wanted to touch boys instead—or rather, one in particular, the son of a minister who lived two houses down from mine, and whom, years earlier, I and the neighborhood kids used to watch, from the privacy of a hedge, while he and his sister slid naked on their stomachs over the patio floor his mother had wet with the garden hose. John was sort of a loner in sixth grade; handsome, with violet eyes as thickly lashed as Elizabeth Taylor's and a chipped front tooth, he wore a blue ribbed muscle shirt, a thick black belt, jeans, and the ever-popular engineer boots—an outfit a juvenile delinquent could be proud of. John was very nice, however. The summer of sixth grade we used to swim underwater and try to goose each other. We also went down to the tennis courts at night and, sitting on the bleachers by the coral caves, compared our genitals; our testicles were the same size, but his penis was longer than mine, a fact he courteously dismissed by saying, comfortingly, that mine would grow.

The caves by the tennis courts—where we also smoked our first Camels and then went home and confessed to our mothers—were only one of several interiors that had become forbidden and erotic; the most erotic was a Dempster Dumpster left in the school playground that year, where John and I would squat on heaps of paper, pretending to go through them to see if there was anything we wanted (Scotch tape, typewriter ribbons, books), while playing the genital game—grab, squeeze, let go.

All I had to do was climb into the Dumpster to be overwhelmed with the delicious gloom of sex.

Life was becoming increasingly divided into exteriors and interiors. The school and the beach were the chief exteriors. (The beach we attended every day in summer as faithfully as school was merely school without teachers or supervision, really, a school in which the children, unmediated, taught one another the crueller lessons of life.) Interiors were the coral caves, the Dumpster, and, for the first time, my own bathroom, which had never meant much to me before except as a place I was ordered to take a shower. Now I did not dislike showering at all. I spent considerable time staring at myself in the mirror. I even, one day, while the maid was ironing shirts in the room beyond the bathroom door, found myself with something I had no idea what to do with—an erection, which I thrust forward like a beak as I walked in circles around the tiny bathroom, offering this astonishing thing to the medicine cabinet, walls, door, shower curtain, till finally it went down, and I dried off, dressed, and went to school.

I suppose I must have masturbated because I remember John telling me that unless I peed immediately after ejaculation, I would never be able to urinate again for the rest of my life, but I don't remember any orgasms alone or with my friend. "Alone or with others" was the new, dreaded phrase I had to read in my missal when I examined my conscience before confession after such incidents—"obscene acts, alone or with others," to be precise. And now that interior (the confessional) entered my life, because of what the others (bathroom, cave, Dempster Dumpster) had become.

Being a minister's son, John had not the slightest interest in religion; his obsession was model airplanes. I was still so religious, however, that John looked to me sometimes like Robert Taylor in *The Robe,* a handsome Roman officer whose chest was as broad and well-shaped as any piece of embossed armor. Though a sense of sin, of shame, had now entered my life—exteriors versus interiors—I still fancied myself virtuous, however, and loved to linger, when I opened my book, on the maps drawn on the frontispiece tracing the journeys of our hero and heroine from Antioch to Jerusalem to Rome. The coral wastes of the dry desert island on which we lived were the Holy Land. One day at the beach I came upon a man who had just caught an enormous shark, suspended on a hook for everyone to admire as he talked excitedly in rough language about his catch—and I, little soldier of Christ, martyr and apprentice saint, stepped up and denounced him for taking the name of God in vain. What I was upset by I am not sure: the cruelty of his killing the magnificent shark, the profane language, or the rough masculine personality of the man. At any rate, he told me to shut up and go home, and I eventually did, thrilled and frightened by my standing up for God.

In fact, the summer I chastised the man who'd caught the shark, the summer Donnie Baylor held me underwater, everything seemed to have acquired a darker undertone. It was clear, for instance, that I could no longer play with girls—not simply because their fathers disapproved of it, but because the girls themselves had changed. Yes, they were still friendly, but they were preoccupied too; they seemed to regard the boys we'd talked about on the phone in a way that excluded me; their own asexual cheerfulness was gone. And boys made the beach dangerous. I stayed away from their games of tag played on the diving board with a knotted, wet T-shirt. I was no good at baseball either; when the ball was hit to my section of the outfield, I stood there with my flat glove raised like a tray as it descended from the sky, knowing full well I could not catch it. Nor did I like Boy Scouts. The night my father set out with me for the father-son banquet down at the Esso Club, I literally jumped out of the car as it was leaving the driveway rather than go through with it, and my father (what can he have thought?) kindly acceded to my reluctance and let me stay home. One day at Boy Scouts I had to get in the ring and box a friend; the minute I landed a blow on him, unless my memory is grossly exaggerating, I refused to continue. This seems incredible now, but the gloves that to other boys might have seemed attributes of their identity seemed cruel to me. That term of praise—"He's *all* boy!"—left me sick at heart, knowing it was a form of approval I would never merit. When my father took me to the barbershop I bridled. The barber, all smiles, could not have been nicer; but sitting there among the men of all ages, listening to them joke, I felt a fraud. (Sitting with my mother and her friends on the porch, however, I flourished.) When I got home with the talcum powder on my neck and my new haircut I went right to my room, and reopened my book—since I could no longer run next door and play with the girls who lived there.

The pain of this disjuncture—between what is expected of us and what we are—is very sad in retrospect. It's for this reason: We no longer fit. We can no longer assume we will evolve with our peers—we have become something else, something foreign, ill-fitting, unadmired. At the beach that summer I had no courage to stand up to the wiry athletes who seemed to have no fear of anything as they lined up to jump off the second story of the big dock on a knotted rope attached to the diving board, so they could swing out before dropping off into the ocean. I was afraid, even of the massive pilings underneath the dock (where we waited for our turn), which each time a wave receded I could see were covered with white crabs. Even the dark patches of water created by the seaweed growing on the bottom frightened me in a way they did not other people and I began to feel real fear for the first time in my life. Fear of violence, fear of other boys, fear of seaweed, just fear. Though I swam one day with my friend Duncan all the way to a little island on the reef, over much deeper water, the shadowy, echoing space beneath the dock, and the ocean we plunged into from the rope, all scared me; I knew something was changing, that life itself was now deep water and always would be.

I found escape that summer in clear, bright narratives—big, fat historical novels I could lose myself in. When I was through with *The Robe,* I read *The Silver Chalice,* and when I finished that, I read *Quo Vadis,* and then, *Ben Hur,* and then *The Egyptian,* and then *Pharaoh,* and then *Gone with the Wind,* and then *Desirée.* There were no parties to go to. The intense social whirl of our sixth-grade class had dried up. We were all preparing for our move to the seventh grade, at the high school on the edge of town; in some sense the class had already begun to disintegrate before it was absorbed by the larger organism. Still, it was a shock, when school started in the fall, to find ourselves at the large, modern, breeze-swept high school where upperclassmen actually had cars; where we went from being the eldest to the youngest in a single stroke. The slate was wiped entirely clean. Power belonged to one group alone: the upperclassmen. They were boys like Donnie Baylor, whom Russeen could pursue on her own now, as he slunk around the sunlit halls with other guys who brought motorcycles to school—boys who put their packs of cigarettes under the rolled-up sleeves of their T-shirts, boys who had rippling triceps muscles and faded jeans, boys my sister had tried to dress me like years before. The only notice they took of us was to kidnap one of my classmates, Ted W., take him to the pet cemetery, and inspect his penis to see if it was as large as people said. Otherwise we were ignored.

One afternoon while I was leaving school an upperclassman from Tennessee yelled at me, "Do you have hair on your balls yet?" in a voice that was friendly but with an accent so thick I had to make him repeat it three times before I understood the question; but that was the only time I was singled out. The intense sexual pressure of sixth grade— those games of spin-the-bottle, of long walks home from the movies— was now curiously dissipated; the high school was so much bigger, we were all free to go our separate ways.

One of the girls I'd played with as a child, a girl who lived just down the street, sat in front of me in homeroom; one day when I whispered a question behind her during study hall, she seemed not to have heard— then she turned, all of a sudden, so that her hair swung dramatically around her head in a golden cloud that looked like something in a shampoo commercial before it fell back to her shoulders, and I thought: *She did that for me—to look attractive.* I ignored the effort; I was having none of that. Instead I took trombone lessons, studied hard, walked home after school with two nerds as serious as I was about studies. There was no way to pursue a social career; that belonged to the upperclassmen who had automobiles in the high school parking lot, who hung around the bowling alley I passed on my way home. When I went to the beach on weekday afternoons I swam alone. On Saturday night I was called into my mother's bedroom to attach the necklace she had chosen to wear that night or give my opinion of her outfit; then she and my father went to some party, while I stayed home, reading *Quo Vadis.*

Outside, in the street, the occasional roar of a jalopy, an engine being gunned, told me my classmates were out, at the Youth Canteen dance, or the pet cemetery, or someone's patio, smoking, drinking, necking, flirting, while I was as chaste and solitary as a secretly Christian slave in the house of Petronius Arbiter. I was certain I had no place in whatever people were doing out there. When I went out onto the porch, I could see the forlorn lampposts, set in concrete foundations whose whitewash came off on our hands when we used them as our lookouts playing pirates; now they stretched down the hillside like sentinels on the edge of the Roman Empire, into the darkness, where everything was a mystery.

There was one boy my age who befriended me in seventh grade—a big, tall, handsome, effeminate guy whose nickname among our classmates was Daisy Mae. I went to his house a few times after school that fall until a classmate gave me a girl's name, too, one day in the hallway. (How strict and alert were these guardians of heterosexuality! The father who blew up at finding me yet again playing with his daughter, the classmate quick to christen me with a girl's name.) I had never even heard the word *homosexual,* but I knew what *sissy* meant when a boy called me that in front of my mother one day. I told her she had misheard; he'd called me Missy, a nickname I'd been given—I was so panicked I couldn't think.

So I withdrew further into books and studies—unable to choose either of the paths my life had split into, bereft of my big sister's guidance (though even she might have been stumped by this problem). My marks in seventh grade were good, and by year's end I had rehabilitated myself in my classmates' eyes. Nobody hissed; I was elected to the Student Council. But I had little social life. Social life, after all, is based on sex. I walked home with Donna Sue and Suzanne past the bowling alley to our separate bungalows, no longer a boy who played with girls—or boys—after school. Only John remained, two houses down. Now we played our game of grab-the-genitals at his house, in his own bedroom—imitating heterosexual coitus with our clothes on—though I realized I wanted to play this game, and initiated it, much more than he. Finally even this game stopped, and with it, John's friendship. After that I spent my afternoons sitting out back on the steps with the maid as she straightened her hair with a heating iron, plaited it, and sighed with homesickness for her native island of Sint Maarten—a twelve-year-old boy and a forty-seven-year-old woman, waiting for someone or something to come down the street. I was being schooled in loneliness.

*   *   *

The summer of seventh grade there appeared at the beach two seventeen-year-old brothers visiting relatives for a few months from some town in Pennsylvania; both were very handsome. One day one climbed up the steps of the big dock after finishing a dive the girls on the beach had all admired; his brother suggested he adjust his bathing suit, which the ocean had molded to his genitals, and he said, "Why? Let them see what I've got." It was a remark that made no real sense to me at the time, though years later it would become the mantra of cruising. At the time I heard it, I did not consciously desire the brothers with their dark brown eyes, hairy chests, blue-and-white striped bathing suits, standing on the dock after their dives, streaming with seawater. I spent evenings at home with a book, listening to the sound of the wind trying to get through the louvers—as tightly shut against the breeze as I was against sexual maturation. The world was still safe in my comfortable room; outside, the palms still shook in the constant trade wind, the moon still glittered on the indigo sea; my grades were good, my parents were happy. I had my books and peanut-butter sandwiches, piano lessons, church; but the altar I'd made in my old bedroom was now dark, covered with dust, devoid of magic when I went in, and all the elements, the patterns of my adult life, I see now, were already set—the feeling that I was not the person I was supposed to be, that I had secrets, that I was alone, that books were my refuge, that with them I was safe. So safe I would pause to relish this fact as I read—and put the book down every now and then to just listen to what was outside: the moan, the whisper, the shriek of the wind in the louvers, a wind that had blown for many miles over the dark, chafed sea before it met the resistance of our house— a wind as steady, as unstoppable as the self-recognition I would delay for fourteen years, merely because this truth was so painful, so unthinkable at the time, so not-what-was-wanted, it felt like a kind of exile from everyone I loved. Puberty isn't easy when you don't fit. When I next heard my sister's voice (at the start of our furlough back to America, two years after she went away to the nuns), the minute she spoke my name on the phone from Massachusetts to our hotel room in Miami, I surprised everyone—my sister, my parents, myself—by bursting into tears.

Thirteen

Jacqueline Woodson

That summer, my uncle's girlfriend came to live with us. Barbara was seventeen, Donna Summer beautiful, and pregnant but not yet showing. I knew of the pregnancy only from the overheard whispers of adults and Barbara in the late-summer afternoon retching in our bathroom. Many days, as I left the house to join my friends, I passed the bathroom, where the door, slightly ajar, revealed Barbara on her knees, holding her dark, curling hair with one hand while the other gripped the toilet seat. Outside, my friends and I sat in a line along the curb, watching the boys play skelly and tops and whispering among ourselves about Barbara's baby. We were scared of Barbara and of the thing she had done. Some nights, as we curled into one another at slumber parties, we played family and vied for positions of father.

Some mornings, against a backdrop of bacon frying and slamming pots and pans, my grandmother would complain about guests who didn't know when to go home and the mud tracks my younger brother and I were prone to leave across her kitchen floor. Yes, at thirteen I was still a girl—building forts with my brother in the backyard, twisting the hair of my dolls into braids, giggling with friends over stolen glances of the naked bodies in our fathers' magazines. I was tall and thin that summer, with knobby, ashen knees and only the barest beginnings of breasts. My friends' bodies had outgrown mine, and in the dark forest of our back-yards, we counted pubic hairs and stared in wonder at one another's newly forming breasts—first a nipple, then a small knot behind the nip-ple, then, by fall, the eventual swelling that would continue long after we had stopped meeting, long after we had grown silent and secretive around each other. One morning, I pressed small squares of toilet tissue between my T-shirt and breasts only to discover that it showed through—tiny white swatches against the dark background of my skin. I wanted more than my own tiny breasts. But there was something deeper to my longing. I wanted to remain in our backyards, whispering about our bodies. I wanted my friends to pull their shirts above their breasts and let me stare.

The autumn before, my older brother had landed a role in his high school's production of *Those Damn Yankees*. On opening night, as every-one in my family readied themselves to go, I stood in the doorway of my mother's bedroom pleading with her to allow my best friend, Maria, to come along. I was afraid of my mother. She was tall and heavy-handed, given to fits of yelling from which I found myself shrinking away. But that evening, I wanted to be sitting in that dark theater beside Maria, and I let the tears run freely as I pleaded with my mother. My mother, sensing my desire, turned slowly away from the closet where she had been standing in the midst of a small clothing crisis and yelled, "What are you—a lesbian?" And weakly, quickly, I said no.

Alma was a lesbian. She was Barbara's age and wore her hair in an Afro that floated in a soft black circle around her head. Some afternoons, she sat showing Maria and I how to clean our Pro Keds with a tooth-brush and bleach until the soles gleamed as white as the canvas. She promised us there would come a day when we'd be able to make our own decisions and wear Pumas like hers, but we didn't believe this. Our mothers rejected Pumas, calling them "mannish." They had a list of mannish things including Kangol hats, tailor-made, no-side-seam, and carpenter pants (both half carpenters and overalls), hands in the pockets, any sport that didn't require two ropes or a song about Miss Lucy, most styles of platform shoes, strutting, and three-piece suits. Through borrowing, buying, and trading, Maria and I managed to acquire an assortment of the banned items of clothing, which we often stored at another friend's house and changed into on our way to school.

That summer, Maria and I found other girls to surround us, salves against the sting of my mother's questions. Up and down our block, there were groups of girls—the Halsey Junior High cheerleaders practicing routines on a stoop; Lisa and Patricia's a capella group singing "Wishing on a Star" in three-part harmony; Trina, Gayle, and Neesie's church group sitting along the curb with their heads pressed together over *Tiger Beat* and *Jet* magazine. Our parents understood and encouraged girls in groups together—safe from boys, safe from two girls alone.

Because Alma was Maria's aunt, we were allowed to sit on the stoop with her and once in a while visit her at Maria's grandmother's house, where we spent hours going through her closet, trying on her wide-collar floral shirts and leisure suits. That summer, Alma had a girlfriend named Miriam, a pale, green-eyed girl with hair feathered back like Farrah Fawcett's. We loved her instantly and fought over who got to show her the latest Hustle and Click-Clack steps, who got to play with her hair, and who got to sit next to her on the stoop. They never kissed in public, but one evening, Maria and I hid in Alma's closet and peeked from behind Alma's lime-green curtains to watch them.

"She was tonguing her down," we gossiped later. And our friends, who hadn't been there, giggled with us and imagined the many other things they must have planned to do had we not giggled so hard that they discovered us.

I didn't know then that the idea of growing up like Alma frightened me. I knew there was an edge to her I was afraid of. Once, when a neighborhood girl-gang stole our pizza money, Alma pulled her Afro back into two cornrows, slicked her face with Vaseline, sought them out, and fought the leader. After that, my friends and I walked through our neighborhood without being afraid. And although we bragged about the fight for months afterward, I didn't want to be a fighter, and something about Alma's edge told me that fighting was something she had always needed to do.

"Don't let anybody mess with you," she warned us. "And if somebody hits you and you stay hit, then *I'm* gonna kick your ass."

We believed Alma. But we also knew that we were her girls and would always be her girls and that no one would ever mess with us and get away with it.

That summer, we bought halter-cut T-shirts and pressed scripted letters onto them—our names, our nicknames, our Zodiac signs, where we fell in the order of our group—Jackie as Cookie, Aquarius, #2. Maria as Candy, Leo (You Know!),#1, Diana as Dimples, Sagittarius, and so on, until we had formed a knot so tight, so impenetrable, we thought nothing could or ever would separate us. We slit our fingers and mixed our blood, we took the tunes of popular songs and changed them to words about our friendship. We bought pizza and split the slices down the middle so that we could share them and have room left over for Italian ices. And every Saturday we shopped for matching outfits until our wardrobes were so alike, we no longer needed to borrow one another's clothes. Boys followed us; we flirted with them, ignored them, then flirted with them some more. At night we kissed them in the park, then went home with each other. At slumber parties we paired off and practiced kissing, then switched partners and practiced some more. While Bread's "Make It with You" played on our stereos, we imagined ourselves falling slowly into the arms of delicate, faceless lovers.

One morning, I woke at dawn to ambulance flashers outside my window and a man in white strapping Barbara into a chair.

That summer "Oooh Child" poured from everyone's radio and we sat in a row along the sidewalk with a transistor turned up as loud as it would go, singing along. We knew something was going to get easier, but we didn't know what. We knew a "someday" was coming, but we didn't know when.

It was the last any of us would see of Barbara. As I hung out the window watching the ambulance make its way down the block, I didn't know this. I knew she'd be eighteen in a month, that her favorite flowers were tulips, that once she had seen a whole field of pink ones when she was little and driving west with her mother. I didn't know her mother's name or where she had lived before our house. "I don't think I love your uncle," she said once. And maybe I had shrugged, not letting this confession sink in. I was thirteen with no idea what love was.

Barbara left behind, among other things, a bra—a thirty-two double-A that puckered with air in the places where breasts should have been.

That summer, the summer I was thirteen, I sometimes returned to my little brother and the solitude of our backyard. And together we built forts, swam, ate bologna-and-cheese sandwiches cut into quarters on paper plates, dressed and undressed our Barbies and G.I. Joes.

And some evenings, I snuck the bra and my Kangol hat into the bathroom. Standing in the mirror, with the hat on backward and Barbara's bra against my breasts, I'd turn slowly from side to side, feeling scared.

And maybe, yes maybe, just the tiniest bit, free.

Contributors

Etel Adnan is an Arab-American poet and writer from California. Her poetry has been translated into many languages, and she is the author of *Sitt Marie Rose,* a novel on the civil war in Lebanon. She has taught in thirty American universities and colleges.

Michael Albo is a writer and performer living in New York City. He has written for *Details, Paper, Out,* and the web sites *STIM* and *Word,* and he performs these blurty, funny monologues, too. "MACOS" is from his upcoming first novel, *Hornito, My Lie Life.*

David Bergman's latest work is *Heroic Measures,* a book of poems. He edits *Men On Men,* a biennial collection of recent gay fiction, and teaches as Towson University.

Rebecca Brown is the author of numerous books, including *The Terrible Girls, The Gifts of the Body, Annie Oakley's Girl,* and *The Dogs: A Modern Bestiary.* She lives in Seattle.

Clifford Chase is the author of *The Hurry-Up Song: A Memoir of Losing My Brother.* His writing has appeared in *Newsweek, The Village*

Voice, and *Poz,* as well as in *Threepenny Review, Boulevard, Nerve,* and other magazines and journals. He lives in Brooklyn, where he is at work on a novel.

Justin Chin is a writer and performance artist. He is the author of *Bite Hard* and the forthcoming *Mongrel: Essays, Diatribes & Pranks.*

Lisa Cohen's nonfiction and fiction have appeared in *Ploughshares, The Voice Literary Supplement,* and *XXXFruit,* among other publications. She is currently at work on a novel.

Regina Gillis grew up in Acton, Massachusetts. She lives and works in New York City.

Jim Gladstone, a Philadelphian, is the author of a forthcoming novel, *The Big Book of Understanding.* His wide-ranging cultural criticism has appeared in many publications including *The New York Times Book Review.*

Gabrielle Glancy's poems have appeared in such publications as *The New Yorker, The Paris Review,* and *New American Writing.* A recipient of a 1990 New York Foundation for the Arts Fellowship, she currently lives in London, where she is at work on a novel set in Cairo.

Robert Glück is the author of eight books, most recently *Jack the Modernist,* a reprint, and *Marjery Kempe.* In 1994, the *Dictionary of Literary Biography* named Glück one of the ten best postmodern writers in North America. He lives "high on a hill" in San Francisco with artist Chris Komater.

Andrew Holleran is the author of three novels, *Dancer from the Dance, Nights in Aruba,* and *The Beauty of Men,* and a book of essays, *Ground Zero.*

Doug Jones graduated from Columbia College in New York, where he works as an interior designer. He has written and produced for off-off-Broadway, including *Halston at the Laundromat,* which he also performed. He lives in Brooklyn without pets.

Wayne Koestenbaum is the author of *The Queen's Throat* and *Jackie Under My Skin,* as well as two volumes of poetry, *Ode to Anna Moffo and Other Poems* and *Rhapsodies of a Repeat Offender.* Persea will be publishing his third book of poems in winter 1999. He is a professor of English at CUNY's Graduate School.

Bia Lowe is the author of *Wild Ride,* a collection of essays. "Waiting for Blastoff" is included in her forthcoming collection, *Splendored Thing.*

Michael Lowenthal is the author of a novel, *The Same Embrace,* and the editor of *Gay Men at the Millennium* and *Flesh and the Word 4.* His writing has appeared in *The Kenyon Review, The New York Times Magazine, Best American Gay Fiction,* and *Men on Men 5.* He lives in Boston.

Marcus Mabry's first book, *White Bucks and Black-Eyes Peas,* a memoir on race and class, was published in 1995. He is working on a second memoir about coming out in Paris while a correspondent for *Newsweek.* He lives in Johannesburg, where he is *Newsweek*'s Africa bureau chief.

Robert Marshall is a visual artist whose work has been exhibited throughout the United States and Europe. He lives in New York City, where he is completing his first novel, *Ixtlan.*

Eileen Myles is a poet who lives in New York and Provincetown, Massachusetts. Her recent books are *School of Fish* (poems, 1997) and *Chelsea Girls* (stories, 1994). She coedited (with Liz Kotz) *The New Fuck You: Adventures in Lesbian Reading.* "Cool for You" is from her forthcoming novel by the same title.

Mariana Romo-Carmona, an immigrant from Chile, is the author of *Living at Night,* a lesbian novel set in the late seventies. She was coeditor of *Colorlife!, Queer City, Cuentos: Stories by Latinas,* and *Conditions.* She teaches at Goddard College's MFA program.

Paul Russell, a professor of English at Vassar College, is the author of the novels *Sea of Tranquility, Boys of Life,* and *The Salt Point.* He recently completed his fourth, *The Pederast.*

Ralph Sassone is a graduate of Brown University and a former editor of *The Village Voice Literary Supplement*. He lives in Manhattan and teaches at Vassar College.

Joe Westmoreland has been published in the anthologies *Discontents, The New Fuck You,* and *Best American Gay Fiction,* and in journals and queerzines such as *XXXFruit, My Comrade, Straight to Hell,* and his own *joezine*. He lives in New York City and is currently finishing his first novel.

Jacqueline Woodson is the author of a number of novels for adults, young adults, and children, including *Autobiography of a Family Photo* and *If You Come Softly*.

Rebecca Zinovic teaches at the University of California. She is currently working on a series of essays.

Acknowledgments

I'm indebted to Edmund White and Bernard Cooper for their generous advice and encouragement; my agent, Maria Massie, and my editor, David Szanto, for their close attention and care, as well as Joshua Greenhut, Gideon Weil, and the rest at Witherspoon Associates; Michael Lowenthal for recommending this project to David Szanto; Gabrielle Glancy for her inspired editorial suggestions, including the book's title; Robert Glück, Jeff McMahon, Patrick Merla, and Sarah Schulman for putting me in touch with many wonderful writers; the corporation of Yaddo, where I began writing about seventh grade; John Kureck, Erin Hayes, Maggie Meehan, and Noelle Hannon for invaluable guidance and support; and all the contributors for braving painful memories and turning them into art.

Copyright Notices